SIGNS & WONDERS 101

101 DAYS OF MIRACLES

Jena Rawley Taylor

Copyright © 2019 by Jena Rawley Taylor

All rights reserved. This book or any portion thereof may not be reproduced or used in any manner whatsoever without the express written permission of the publisher.

Printed and self-published through Kindle Direct Publishing by Jena Rawley Taylor in the United States of America

A portion of the proceeds of the sale of this book will be donated to Faith City Mission to feed the homeless, clothe the naked, and preach the Gospel to the poor.

First Printing, 2019

Inquiries directed to Jena Taylor, 3812 Fleetwood, Amarillo, TX 79109

Please note that many of the names in this book have been changed when permission has not been granted.

www.signsandwonders101.com

ISBN: 978-0-9882480-2-1

DEDICATION

This work is dedicated to the homeless, needy, and poor. The lost, least, and littlest who taught me the most about the Kingdom of God

CONTENTS

	Title	Page
	Acknowledgments	i
	Forewords	1
	Introduction	5
1	Mysteries	11
2	The Paul Experience	15
3	Teleios	19
4	Encounter	23
5	Intimacy	27
6	Truth	33
7	The Word	39
8	The Seed	43
9	Kingdom in Healing	47
10	The Testimony	51
11	Kingdom in Prophecy	57
12	Spoken Words	63
13	Seeing	67
14	The Mailman	71
15	Action vs. Reaction	75
16	Joy	79
17	Obedience	83
18	Courage	87
19	Power	91
20	Charity	95
21	Boldness	99
22	The Desperate	105
23	The Books	109
24	Deliverance	113
25	That Which Was Lost	117
26	Identity	121
27	Go	127
28	Compassion	131
29	Needy	135
30	Physics	139
31	Transformed	143
32	Changed	149
33	Touch	153
34	One Body	157
35	Lay Down Your Life	161
36	The Glory	165
37	The Tent	169
38	The Mountain	173
39	Gentle Touch	177
40	Pool of Bethesda	181
41	Fear	185
42	Deliverance	189
43	Oppression	193
44	Forgiveness	197
45	Gratitude	203
46	Abiding	209
47	Religious Spirit	213
48	Prior Prayer	217
49	Trauma	221
50	A Sweet Touch	225
51	The Painting	229
52	The Box	233
53	The Words	237
54	Broken Hearts	241
55	Consequences	245
56	Faith	249
57	Works	253
58	Stand	257
59	Hope	261
60	Identity	265
61	Distance	269
62	Investigation	273
63	Protection	277
64	Besieged	281
65	The Plan	285
66	Raised from Dead	289
67	Fruit	295
68	Woman at the Well	299
69	Presence	303
70	I Heard	307
71	The Power of Prayer	311
72	Whoever Says	315
73	Confidence	319
74	Set Free	323
75	Breakthrough	327
76	Territory	333
77	Instructions	337
78	Mercy	341
79	The Limp	345
80	Provision	349
81	Amazed	355
82	Oppression	359
83	The Impossible	363
84	Tormented	369
85	Just Believe	373
86	Giving it Away	377
87	Lost and Found	381
88	The Christmas Story	385
89	Rhema	391
90	Fasting	395
91	The Orphan	399
92	Generational Curse	403
93	Intervention	407
94	Hearing His Voice	411
95	His Will	415
96	The Library	421
97	The Lame	427
98	Paralyzed	433
99	Kindness	437
100	Gifts	441
101	Learning Curve	445
...	Author's Note	449
...	Hindrances	451
...	Entry Points	453
...	About the Author	455

ACKNOWLEDGMENTS

To my extraordinary husband who literally raised me from the dead on the bathroom floor. Thank you for advising and supporting, editing, and encouraging me through the whole process. Thank you for your patience and forbearance.

To Dorsey Wilmarth who taught me so much about publishing and editing, who was willing to have those lively discussions with me about theology and doctrine and yes, politics. Thank you for making me a better writer.

To Dr. Vicki Keathley, you are the most intelligent woman I know, and your insight was invaluable. Thank you for walking me through the perceptions and nuances of my words, tearing down the barriers between denominations.

There are some people who crash over one's life like a tsunami and bring new life and light and enthusiasm. That tsunami for me is Julie. Her extraordinary enthusiasm is catching. Thank you, Julie Ballard, for unselfishly dedicating your time and energy, expertise, and enthusiasm to this project.

To my assistant, Danita Morrow, who kept me from leaping off the ledge on several occasions and proofing the manuscript. Thank you for guarding my time.

I am so grateful for my mentor, Pam Eubanks, whose gentle and wise words reeled me back in from the dark side. To David Aduddell, a brilliant graphic designer, whose calling is secretly to the Mission.

Thank you to the staff and students whose stories are nothing short of a miracle.

Thank you to my Board President, Paula O'Neal, whose passion for the poor and lost is ferocious. Thank you for your grace toward me and for being my cheerleader. Thank you, Randy O'Neal, friend and encourager, who saw the gift first.

Thank you, Madison Coston for having the faith to believe when I did not.

My special thanks to Don and Paula Avirett for introducing me to the miraculous in the first place. I thank you all.

FOREWORDS

The book you are holding is no ordinary piece of literature. It is a collection of stories about our amazing Heavenly Father, and his demonstrated love for his children. Kim and I have known Jena, and her husband Jay, for 20+ years. Passionate pursuers of Jesus, their lives are dedicated to seeing His kingdom advanced. These stories of miraculous healing and restoration will strengthen your faith and challenge you to put it into action. Jesus cares! He cares for the hurting, the lost, the forgotten, and the found. He cares for you. As you read these pages, let your faith grow. And be sure to listen for His voice, because the next miracle may be one prayer away.

Jimmy Witcher
Senior Pastor, Trinity Fellowship Church

I was blessed to meet Mrs. Jena Taylor in December of 2013 when I joined the Hope for Women recovery program at Faith City Mission where she presides as Executive Director. My life was instantly changed by God's love and grace. Miracles overflowed. Today, I am 5 ½ years sober from methamphetamines and my relationship with my grandson is fully restored after being out of his life for 3 years. At present, my children are 4 years sober and I have an additional 3 grandchildren. I have seen so many financial and health miracles in my life, all because I chose to be obedient to God. A passage I would love to share to those facing trials and feeling hopeless is Romans 5:3. It states, "We rejoice in trials, knowing that our trials produce perseverance, and perseverance produces character, and character produces hope, and hope does not fail." Mrs. Jena, thank you for joining my journey in life and giving me a place to fall apart so God could build me back up!

~ Former Faith City Mission Student Michelle Russell

I came to Faith City Mission by way of a trick. I was incredibly lost in the bottle. Vodka was my closest friend. My dear aunt came to pick me to take me to get a coke, and instead she brought me to Faith City Mission. I was determined not to stay; I was furious! I reluctantly agreed to stay, seemingly against my own will. I was miraculously healed while at the Mission and my life has forever changed. I am now the Men's Manager for our Hope for Men Program, the same program I graduated from six years ago. Faith City, to me, means hope. I was drifting off course and adrift at sea until I found this beautiful place I now call home. I am found. They showed me the way to salvation and granted me mercy at every turn. There is hope out there for everyone, the addicted, the homeless, the helpless, and the needy. There is always hope at Faith City Mission, and this book of miracles will give people just that...HOPE! Jena Taylor has had so much trust and faith in me when I didn't even have it for myself. She is the one that put the seed in me to see me through my journey here at Faith City Mission. She is a great coach, always teaching me new things. When she was at M.D. Anderson in the hospital for her own afflictions, she was incredibly joyous for me when my liver was healed. She never thinks of herself and is always ready to celebrate the miracles of God!

~Former Faith City Mission Student Alex Romero

Being homeless and hopelessly addicted to meth was what brought me to Faith City Mission. It was a safe place, a place where I could find myself and find my spiritual man again. Faith City is a scene in the movie of my life where I am now giving back what was so freely given to me. It is my greatest desire to love people that are unlovable, for I was once unlovable. I believe with all my heart that this book will open the eyes of the blind. By that, I mean the people whose eyes are closed off to the truth as it is written, that God can and is still performing miracles on this earth today, just as he did before in biblical times. Nothing has changed. God has not changed. Jena Taylor has taught me how to believe in myself. There are times when I have been discouraged and downtrodden, but her words to me always are, "I am your biggest fan." It means more to me than gold to know that someone is on my side and cares for me. I am now the Head of Security at Faith City Mission and my wife is the Director of Food Service. This wonderful establishment has given me so much confidence in all areas of my life.

~Former Homeless and Faith City Mission Student Bill Shaw

I lost my whole life as I knew it in my forties to alcohol. I once had a high paying job, a wonderful husband, and a beautiful family. I had been to three different rehabilitation facilities and nothing worked. My family said their peace and sent me packing. They were done with me. My sister suggested Faith City Mission in Amarillo and I reluctantly decided to go. It was the best decision I have ever made. I graduated, went back to the same high paying job as before, and relapsed in no time. I came back to Faith City Mission and was given a second chance by the woman who wrote this book. She emulates Christ, because He is a God of second chances. I am now living in freedom and working at Faith City Mission, grateful to give back what was given to me. I now help others in their journey toward faith and freedom from a lifestyle that kills. This book is going to change lives, for it shows that God sees and knows us in such an intimate way that He leaves the 99 to come chase the one, and that is you and me.

~Former Faith City Mission Student Sydney Woolard

This book will open the eyes of the blind.
Miracles still happen.

INTRODUCTION

If one ruminates for very long on the sheer scope and convolution of the Father's intention concerning the human race, the subject becomes complicated pretty quickly.

His creation - the sun, planets, moon and stars - this island home we live upon are all so astonishingly brilliant. One could spend a lifetime studying one tiny aspect of it, say, butterfly wings, and never come to the end of all its glory and beauty. The human race, however, is capable of less honorable displays of naughtiness. Oh, we have our moments of beauty and brilliance, but left to our own devices we can become quite hateful.

There is documentation that, on more than one occasion, God threatened to wipe us off the planet, and one could hardly blame Him. In many ways, it could be said that we are the Father's crowning achievement, but also His greatest failure. It all seems to do with this one little characteristic of His design when he created the human race. It is free will. Unlike the rest of creation, we are free to choose.

Those are frightening words, because choices have consequences. As it has been said, "You are free to choose, but you are not free from the consequences of your choice." Over the course of human history, we have made quite a disastrous muddle of it.

And yet, from the beginning, God had a plan for that as well, a whipping boy to stand in for us and all our shenanigans, to wipe away our failures and give us the unmerited right to step into a different realm. While we live in a very physical world, God has provided access to another existence, should we choose to accept it. It is called the Kingdom of Heaven, where nothing seemingly is like our world.

In that domain we are given the rank of royalty, no matter what our lineage is. We each have the privilege of "best friend status" and fireside chats with the Father any time we wish it. Everything else in that Kingdom is a head scratcher as well. For example, we must give in order to receive. In order to be honored, we must be a servant. To be forgiven, we must forgive. In addition, not eating causes powerful things to happen, and evidently, being persecuted is a good thing, as is martyrdom.

The Kingdom's laws are quite different from ours and can actually override our natural laws; hence, those anomalies called miracles, signs and wonders, as well as supernatural healings. Gaining access is so simple a child can do it, yet so difficult that many miss it altogether.

Growing up in the church, I learned a great deal about this domain, but like the butterfly wings, it all seemed terribly complex and obscure. I knew a lot about theology and doctrine, heaven and hell, and behaving myself, but very little about God as Papa, our own dear Father extending His open arms to us in such an intimate way that He might give us the Kingdom.

I was classically trained in fine arts from the age of seven and later received a degree in studio arts with a minor in art history, as well as a second degree in Art Education.

My parents then apprenticed me under well-known and highly successful painters and sculptors. My parents were determined to make me a professional portrait painter.

I acquired artists representatives in the major cities in Texas and developed a wonderful career in portrait painting. I met the most delightful people and painted many beautiful children. It was a lucrative business.

I painted thousands of portraits over the years including Neil Patrick Harris, Kika de la Garza as Chairman of the Agriculture Committee in the House of Representatives in Washington D.C., best known for starting the Food Bank, even George W. and Laura Bush's twin girls, Jenna and Barbara, which hung in the White House. I felt fortunate to have such a wonderful career. I adored my work.

Windom Books approached me to illustrate a children's book called "Fairy Tea" in 1991. There were 115 watercolor illustrations painted in 6 months. It was published in 1992 with a second edition. It was an extraordinary experience I hope never to duplicate.

As a portrait painter, I often listened to "books on tape," as they were called back in the day in my studio while painting commissioned work. One day, a new friend offered to let me listen to her tape collection as well. The first set was a motivational speaker named Zig Ziglar. It was entertaining until I heard him say these words, "I am so grateful that I know, and I know that I know that Jesus is my Savior."

I stopped painting, with my brush in mid-air, and pondered the statement. How do you know that you know? I have recited the Nicene Creed every Sunday of my life since I was 6. "I believe in One Lord, Jesus Christ, the only begotten of His Father before all worlds. God of God, light of light, very God of very God, begotten not made, who for us men and for our salvation came down from heaven…"

Paint brush still in mid-air, I pondered on. I believe? Is that like knowing? That must be what he meant about knowing. He meant believe. But the whole concept worried me like a "what if I don't get asked to the prom" worry.

It continued to nip at my thoughts over the weeks. I did not know of anyone who might be wise enough and unbiased enough to give me a straight answer without spouting doctrine. I KNEW doctrine. This felt altogether different.

One morning as I sat in my bedroom chair, coffee in hand, I presented my laundry list of requests to the Lord. As I prayed, something subtle changed in the room. I felt the shift, as if someone dear to me had just walked in. I paused and cocked my head listening to the quiet of the house. And then, for the first time in my life, I heard words in my head that were not mine.

"Jena, why don't you ask Me into your heart?"

"What does that even mean?" I did not know.

"Just open your heart to Me and let Me come in."

"But I teach Sunday school, and arrange the flowers on the altar!"

"I know. So, will you let me come in and be your Lord?"

"For heaven's sake! I am an Episcopalian for crying out loud!"

"That's okay, just invite Me into your life."

I suddenly found myself on my knees on the floor which I had never done, and raised my hands, which I had never, EVER done, and I asked Him in. There were no bells, no choirs of angels, no brilliant flashes of light or thundering voices. All I heard was the birds singing in the trees outside the window, and someone mowing a lawn somewhere.

I got up and went to wash the dishes. As I washed and looked out the window above the sink, I became conscious of the fact that I "knew."

I knew in my knower that Jesus is my Savior. It was nothing at all like believing. Peace settled over me and a joy I had never known before. God had extended His arms wide to me and given me the key to the Kingdom. Like a child, I took the key and experienced a miracle, my own salvation. I became a citizen of another country, and I did not even know what that was, except for this incandescent sense of wellbeing.

It felt similar to the feeling one gets when it has snowed the night before and bundled in every conceivable garment, one explores the neighborhood. It was the same neighborhood, but very different now and every new view was a delight. It was the familiar clothed in beauty, as was the feeling of excitement and anticipation of what lay around the corner.

I turned from being a good soldier to being a daughter. He had utterly burned my wires, fried my bacon, and thrown my breakers. I wanted to know everything at once about my Father and His Son.

I did not own a Bible of my own and my Book of Common Prayer was not forthcoming in answers to all my questions. I did not really know where to turn. Oddly enough, several of my girlfriends were experiencing the same thing I had. We began to gather and compare notes. We stumbled onto an older woman, probably in her forties, who was clearly miles up the road from us spiritually. She agreed to become our Bible teacher.

At our first study, the woman asked us to turn in our Bibles. Not one of us had one. Oops.

Sadly, I could not afford a new Bible, but when I returned from the grocery store one day, I noticed something on the front steps. When I picked it up, I realized it was a spanking new leather-bound Bible. What good fortune. I had no idea who had put it there, but "yah" for me! I began reading it like a murder mystery that just can't be put down. It created more questions, but the stories were astounding.

Slowly, the Kingdom opened to us. It was like a wild and extraordinary treasure hunt revealing astounding mysteries such as the power of the fast, the power of the tithe, the laying on of hands for healing, and the miracles.

As the years progressed, I studied the finer points of healings and miracles, multiplication of food, and the softening of a hardened heart. People were healed. I saw so many wonderful miracles of provision, prayers inexplicably answered, even a plague of grasshoppers fall dead as we marched through our garden commanding that they do so.

I began to volunteer at a homeless shelter where I was astonished to see miracles and healings happen on a regular basis. Blind eyes were opened, HIV healed, cancer eradicated, bones mended, and the paralyzed walked. It was all so astonishing and marvelous. We were like children reveling in the Father's kindness to let us see the Kingdom of God open before us.

It occurred to me that we might need to document these wonderful stories but was unsure how to go about it. Was it a sacrilege to expose the stories on social media? I wanted to think it through, and I did not want to misstep or displease the Lord. I did not want to touch the sacred.

While attending a conference later that year, a woman named Patricia King, head of a major ministry, stopped in the middle of her talk. She walked down to the second row where I sat near the aisle. She pointed her finger at me and asked me if my name were Jen.

"It's Jena."

"Jena, I have a Word for you. The Lord says to write the stories down and put them on the internet. They are going to galvanize the church into action."

She turned and walked back to the front and continued her talk.

I sat there completely stunned. How did she know about the stories and my hesitation to write them?

This woman did not know me at all, so this had to be another sign and wonder. God spoke to me through her. I collected the stories and made videos for Facebook, telling of the incredible things God was doing.

One morning in my prayer time, I heard the Lord tell me to write a daily devotional format with a workbook assignment on the principles of the Kingdom and the accompanying stories.

After a resounding "YES!" to the Father, I did nothing for exactly one year to the day.

On the same date of the next year, the Lord visited the subject again and simply told me that He could always get someone else to do it. I begged for a second chance. I would get up a couple of hours earlier and write. He agreed.

I began writing a devotional book of 101 principles of the Kingdom and the accounts of our own experiences with these principles. My hope was to encourage the sick to believe for a miracle and spur the Church into action, but mostly to please the Father.

I hope this devotional encourages anyone who is desperate for healing or a miracle to build their faith each day by the principles and the real-life stories. Each day requires an action on the reader's part and space to write down what happened due to their action.

It is my heartfelt prayer that lives change, miracles happen, and believers are galvanized into action. I pray that His will be done, and the Kingdom come to earth as it is in Heaven through each of us.

~Jena Taylor

DAY 1 – MYSTERIES – TOM

It has been my observation that Jesus made many astonishing statements to his disciples as well as to the multitudes when He walked on the earth. The words were incomprehensible to those around him.

Jesus referred a great deal to something called the Kingdom of Heaven or the Kingdom of God, a place that was not a place. He compared it to such strange things as a mustard seed, a pearl of great price, keys, and violence. I am sure there were some sideways glances between the disciples. Jesus went on to speak of people who are "not far from the Kingdom," and of people who will be thrown out "where there is weeping and gnashing of teeth."

Out of nowhere Jesus then said, "Do not be afraid, little flock, for your Father has chosen gladly to give you the Kingdom." What is this mysterious Kingdom? Where is it? What are its laws? And do I want it?

The Word of God tells countless stories of this astonishing Kingdom. Each one gives us a glimpse into a world altogether contrary to ours, and yet somehow familiar.

There is a splendid story in the book of Acts telling us of a man who hated this Kingdom and its ruler, Jesus Christ, with every fiber of his being. He was a Jew, revered among other Jews having every title and pedigree. His loathing was so great he dragged Christians from their homes to have them imprisoned or executed.

One day while traveling the road to Damascus, a light from Heaven flashed all around him, knocking him to the ground and striking him blind. Jesus, in His grace, wanted to use Paul in the Kingdom in extraordinary ways. On that road in the dust, Paul literally saw the light. Paul went on to encounter the Kingdom and went to the ends of the earth to share its power with others.

There was a man who came to the Mission to get clean and sober. He was ex-military as was his father before him. He was used to living his life under verbal abuse and control. The man was filled with a rage toward everyone and everything.

One day at the beginning of Staff and Student Chapel, I saw him clutch his heart and run out the door. Alarmed, I ran after him with a security guard close on my heels.

"Tom! What's wrong?" I yelled as we caught up to him.

"I think I am having a heart attack!" he cried, pain clearly written on his face.

I led him to my office to check his blood pressure, which was sky high.

"Justin, take him to the ER and stay with him." I waited anxiously for a report but heard nothing. Finally, after 24 hours, Tom called me with test results.

"The doc says I have an 89% blockage in my right calf. Part of the clot broke off and traveled to my heart, which is the pain I was experiencing in Chapel. It miraculously passed through the heart and is now lodged in the carotid artery in my neck. If it dislodges, it will go to the brain and I will die instantly. I am a walking time bomb. The doc is giving me medication to dissolve the clot, but it is a slow process and I must be checked every week."

After a few days, Tom was out of the hospital and back in the program. His anger seemed to have dissipated some, replaced now by fear and concern.

The following week it was my turn to preach. I felt like God wanted to focus on bi-polar disorder. We had seen many mental illnesses healed at the Mission. We know firsthand how cruel it can be and the impact it has on people's lives. But we have also seen many cases of God's healing mercies toward the mentally ill.

"I feel like God wants to heal bi-polar disorder today. If that's you, would you stand up?"

Nine people rose to their feet, including Tom. I prayed asking God to heal His little ones with this disorder, but in this case, no one felt anything.

No one, that is, except Tom.

Although he was too frightened to say anything at the time, he later told me that he suddenly felt red hot heat on his right calf and neck when I prayed. It began to burn unbearably. He wondered at the time if God were healing his blood clots.

A week later, he went back to the doctor for another scan. After a long wait, the doctor came into the examination room and just stared at Tom. Finally, he asked, "Tom, what have you been doing?"

"I am living at Faith City Mission getting clean and sober," he replied.

"No, really, what have you done?"

"Nothing! I am trying to get sober and turn my life around," he insisted.

"Tom, I have seen your scans. I have seen the clots. Today they are both gone. And it appears that you never had them. That is not medically possible!"

"Doc, let me ask you a question," said Tom. "Do you believe in God?"

"I believe in Allah," the doctor replied.

"Well," said Tom, "it was Jesus Christ who healed me."

What an extraordinary story. God, in His grace and mercy, reached down and touched an angry drunk who did not care one dot about Jesus. Nevertheless, God's healing power had coursed through his veins and dissolved the clots.

Tom was never the same after that. He was on fire for Jesus, who healed him. All the anger drained away and he was a new man, a new husband, and a new father with a new body.

The Kingdom of God is freely given if we turn our hearts to it. To participate, we need only be available and alert to what He wants to accomplish on the earth. In essence we become much like the mailman who delivers the mail to an unsuspecting world.

Luke 9:1,2

Matthew 6:10

Acts 9:1-31

Kingdom Principle: The mysteries of the Kingdom are made available to all, believer and unbeliever alike. It knocks some to the ground and raises others out of their rage. It knows what is needed.

Prayer: "Lord, I want to know this Kingdom You have invited me into. Teach me its ways and its laws. Most of all, teach me my part to play in it. Amen."

Activation: Find three scriptures in the Word that talk about the Kingdom of God. Write down all of the characteristics of the Kingdom that you find.

What did you learn?

_____

_____

_____

_____

_____

_____

_____

_____

DAY 2 – THE PAUL EXPERIENCE – ELIZABETH'S TEETH

When I was a little girl in the early fifties, my family went to church every Sunday morning. On our way, we passed a church of a different denomination.

One Sunday morning as we drove by, I saw grown men dressed in devil costumes shooing cars away from the parking lot. I was alarmed.

There was a large banner on the lawn announcing something called a "revival" the next week. I did not know what a revival was, but it could not be good. "Daddy, what are those men doing, and why are they doing it?" I asked from the backseat of the family station wagon.

"Well, Honey, some denominations use base emotionalism to attract membership to their churches. In our church, we rely on Holy Writ and the traditions set down hundreds of years ago, and the sacraments."

Secretly, I thought I would like to see some of that base emotionalism because frankly, our church was pretty boring. As a little girl, I would pass the time trying to sit perfectly still on those wooden pews by marveling at the ladies' beautiful dresses and glorious hats.

Years later when I had my own little girl, we followed our parents' Sunday morning traditions. I had grown to love the sacred beauty of the Eucharist, and its reverence of the communion.

One day, however, a friend asked us to one of those revivals that I had heard of. My daughter and I went, not knowing what to expect.

The "lively music" quieted down and the preacher issued an "altar call." He invited anyone who wanted to ask Jesus into their heart to come forward. I had never heard the term "ask Jesus into your heart" so I was unclear what that was exactly. My ten-year-old daughter tugged on my dress. With tears in her eyes she asked if she should go down. I smiled and nodded. She and another little girl went forward and prayed the prayer with the visiting evangelist.

After the fiery sermon about Elijah calling fire down on Mount Carmel, he invited anyone who needed healing to come forward. Again, my little girl tugged on my dress and asked if I thought Jesus would heal her teeth. Her mouth was an orthodontic nightmare that was going to take years of braces (as well as thousands of dollars we did not have).

I had not one drop of faith that Jesus would heal her teeth, but I took her forward and stood behind her as we lined up across the front of the sanctuary. I could hear the evangelist coming closer as he prayed down the line. I sensed a light growing brighter and brighter as well as a presence I had never felt before. I was beginning to feel a little wobbly. When the man reached us, he wiped the sweat from his eyes and pointed to my daughter.

"I don't know who this little girl is. I have never seen her before, but I am telling you she will be a mighty warrior in the last days in the Kingdom of God." Then he pointed to me and said, "And you, ma'am, will be responsible to raise her up in the admonition of the Lord!"

Bam! Down we went. Our bodies had become noodles, and we both found ourselves on the floor. It was a bit of a shock and I had no idea how we were knocked back in such a ferocious manner. Nevertheless, I knew that no one had touched us. We simply collapsed to the floor. Years later I read the book of Joshua and found that it happened to him as well when he saw the Lord of Hosts, just as it did centuries later with Saul on the road to Damascus.

Elizabeth never received prayer for her teeth, but the next morning we realized that they were perfectly straight. It was the first miracle I had ever seen. God reached down and, in His grace, healed a ten-year-old of her embarrassing teeth. The Kingdom of God had come upon us.

I recalled several Sunday school stories of parents bringing their children to Jesus for healing or restoration. He healed them all. Not really knowing what I was doing at the time, I had brought my child to Jesus, and He healed her.

We both encountered the Living God that night. The Kingdom came into our midst, and its power did impossible things. Quite frankly, I have never been the same. Like Joshua and like Paul, I was knocked down and my life changed forever.

In the church I grew up in we prayed for the sick, but never expected anything to actually happen. Prayer was just a courtesy. But that night at the revival, I discovered that prayer can unleash the power and might of God's Kingdom.

Joshua 5:13,14

John 18:4-6

Mark 5:21-42

Kingdom Principle: Childlike faith can release the power of the Kingdom in healing.

Prayer: "Papa, I want to see Your Kingdom as a child. Will You give me childlike faith so that I might know Your ways? Will You show me the Kingdom?"

Meditation: Think back on your own walk with the Lord and describe a moment when you had an encounter like Joshua or Paul.

What happened?

DAY 3 – TELEIOS – HOBBY LOBBY

There is an extraordinary Greek word used in Scripture several times that beautifully sums up the full overarching purpose of God's Kingdom here on the earth. The Greek word is "*teleios*" (pronounced tel-aye-os). It is used in the story of a rich young ruler and his encounter with Jesus. The young man had a rudimentary grasp of trying to inherit eternal life but knew there was more to it. He approached Jesus to clarify the issue. "What must I do?" he asked. Jesus spun through the Commandments, but the young man had kept them all. Then Jesus got to the heart of the matter.

"If you wish to be complete, go and sell your possessions and give to the poor, and you shall have treasure in Heaven. Oh, and by the way, come and follow Me."

The word "complete" carries with it a wonderful concept of destiny. *Teleios* is the Greek word here which basically means to arrive at the intended purpose of one's life. In other words, "If you wish to arrive at the intended purpose of your life, go sell your possessions and give to the poor."

I have heard it said that for this particular young man, the issue was his love for money that kept him from completely entering in; everyone's addiction is different. Nevertheless, the point here is the young ruler arrived at the intended purpose of his life.

Jesus said, "Follow Me," only to those who were destined to be His disciples. Grieved, the young man went away for he was very wealthy. He walked away from his destiny, to be a disciple of Jesus, because it was just too uncomfortable to change. He could not give up his obsession.

In the book of Hebrews, the intended purpose for Jesus's life is spelled out: "Behold, I have come to do Thy will, O God." I am thankful every day that Jesus chose to walk out His purpose, to wipe away 100 billion failures in an instant. In reality that statement, "to do Thy will, O God" applies to every creature, rock, and star that exists. It is the summing up of all things. Every one of us is required to discover what His will is for our own lives. It is our North Star.

The summing up of all things is achieved one day at a time, one act at a time. How do we know what that is? We do what the rich young ruler did. We ask Jesus, "What must I do today?" I have learned to walk out any given day with intentionality, I watch for the nudge, the tell from Holy Spirit that directs me to act.

One day as I was pulling into the Hobby Lobby parking lot, a middle-aged woman walked toward me. It is a very common occurrence in my life to be approached in parking lots. I love it because I know God is up to something. At any rate, the woman said sheepishly, "Excuse me, can you help me? My car just broke down."

Now most people become wary at this point trying to figure out the con. Personally, I don't care if it is a con, because God plans to "con" them right into the Kingdom.

I asked her where her car was. She indicated several rows over. As we began to walk over, she explained that she was driving in from another town close by to see a friend in the hospital. Suddenly, her car just quit. She was able to at least guide it into the parking lot. As we walked to the sedan, I noticed her struggling to walk. She was very awkward in her gait.

"I notice that you are having trouble walking. Is there something wrong with your legs?"

"Actually, it is my back," she said, "I broke it several years ago and I have never been able to walk normally since." Aha, the nudge from God; I knew now why He put her in my path. He wanted to heal her. I knew in my knower that He had selected me to be the conduit of this healing.

"Do you mind if I pray for you?"

"I would love it if you would pray for me!"

I laid my hands in the small of her back and began to pray for God's healing power to come and touch her back. Suddenly, she started to move around.

"The pain is gone. It's just gone!" She started to walk up and down beside her car. "Look at me! I'm walking!" We began to praise God and suddenly we were both hit with the presence of the Holy Spirit. Right there in the parking lot we had our own revival, jumping up and down, waving our arms, and shouting thank you to the Lord. She hugged me and thanked me and acted as if she was about to leave.

"Wait a minute, what about your car?"

"Oh! I forgot," she said. She unlocked the car and slid into the driver's seat. "Oh my gosh! Did you see that? I just slid into the seat. I have not been able to do that in years. Thank you, Jesus!"

She tried to start the car. It would not turn over. I scanned her instrument panel looking for the problem. Her gas gauge was on empty. I pointed it out to her.

"But I put twenty dollars' worth of gas in the car before I started out. That should have been plenty."

"Well, whatever the reason, we need to put gas in your car."

"But I don't have any cash."

"God knows you don't have any cash, but He has provided a way to get gas into your tank. If He can heal your back, don't you think He can put gas in your car? He sent me here to help you."

We walked across the street to the gas station and bought a plastic gas can, filled it up, and walked back to the car. After we poured the gas into the tank, it started up perfectly. I directed her to the station to fill up the rest of the tank. I followed in my car. As we pumped the gas, I looked for leaks or dribbles.

"I think you are good now," I said. "Take this twenty so that you won't be stranded again. And go see your friend."

God apprehended one of His own that day. She was made new. Likewise, I was able to walk out my own destiny through her. I accomplished my *teleios* that day. Thank you, Papa for a glorious day!

Mark 10:17-22

Hebrews 10:7

Ephesians 1:9,10

Kingdom Principle: Everyone is born with an intended plan for their lives. When we walk into that plan, we are made perfect or complete.

Prayer: "Lord, today, I want to walk into my *teleios*, my purpose. Please nudge me when the moment comes, and the opportunity presents itself to do Thy will. Amen."

Try this: Look for your *teleios* moment today and boldly walk into it.

What happened?

_____

_____

_____

_____

_____

_____

DAY 4 – ENCOUNTER – JACKIE

There is a magnificent Psalm that I read and reread often. It is written in the first person, and it speaks of God's intimate knowledge of each of us - our thoughts, our ways, and our words. Despite all our shortcomings and failures, He still lays His hand upon us.

The writer speaks directly to his God. In conversational fashion, he goes on to speak of how God knit him together in his mother's womb, and that he is fearfully and wonderfully made.

"My frame was not hidden from Thee

When I was made in secret,

And skillfully wrought in the depths of the earth.

Thine eyes have seen my unformed substance

And in Thy book, they were all written

The days that were ordained for me,

When as yet there was not one of them."

~ *Psalm 139:15-16*

Every human in the history of civilization was watched over and knit together in this marvelous fashion. And every single one has a book written about their days on the earth. It would behoove us to remember that.

At the Mission, we work hard to keep that in mind. How we treat those that are in our care is crucial. The people who come to us are desperate and their circumstances are dire. Most are homeless; many are addicted to alcohol, meth, or cocaine. Some have been violated in every way possible. Abused, brutalized or neglected as children, many carry serious wounds and scars. Our job is to love them. Are they a mess? Absolutely. Rude, angry, rebellious, hateful, lost, and confused, they come needing the most basic things, like food, shelter and clothing. We provide all of those things, but what they really need is a supernatural healing of their souls.

One such little one came to our doors from prison. She brought with her a prison mentality. She was angry, hateful, belligerent, and by God would not do anything that we asked of her. Her eyes were slits of fury. I sensed more than a couple of demons in her soul. In classes, she proved to be disruptive without the most basic modicum of normal behavior, all the while spouting off vile practices of prison that should not be spoken of in the darkest corner. She was truly a mess. The staff all knew that the brutality from her young life had caused all this hostility. She was like a wounded animal in the woods that would lash out if you tried to help it.

One day we had a guest speaker in Staff and Student Chapel. This Chapel service is not only open to our long-term students, but to guests off the street as well as many visitors from the community who have heard of the miracles that occur on a regular basis. They come for their own healing.

Rodney is a regular speaker. Head of his own ministry, he is a heat-seeking missile and a wild man in the pulpit. On this particular day he was on a roll, when suddenly he stopped in the middle of his sermon and looked into the women's section of the Chapel. He pointed to one of the women and demanded that she stand up. I turned in my seat to see who he was pointing to.

"Oh my Gosh! It's Jackie (our prison rebel)," I thought to myself, "She is not going to stand up. She is going to cross her arms and stick her little chin out" (referred to around the Mission as "lock and load").

I watched those angry slits of her eyes and thought, "We're in for it now." Gradually, before my very eyes, I watched her features soften and her eyes grow wide. She stood up. In that instance, I saw a miracle rivaling the Red Sea parting.

Rodney then pointed to the aisle and told her to come out to him. You could feel everyone holding their breath. Suddenly, she moved to the aisle. We were hoping that she would not take a swing at Rodney. In truth, Rodney came from the street gangs of the worst part of town. He was a recovering addict as well, so I wasn't really worried.

As she stood before him, he began to reveal her destiny to her and what God had planned for her life. In good old Pentecostal style, he shouted the heavens down upon the girl. Suddenly she broke. She doubled over and began to sob uncontrollably. Rodney put his hand on her shoulder and comforted the child within. Still, she sobbed as every wicked and evil thing within her simply melted away.

When the service came to an end, she was still crying. The Word says that the Lord captures every tear in a bottle. Rivers of tears were captured in His bottle of tears that day. God bent down and encountered this girl in such a powerful way that she has not been the same since. She is quick to offer a beautiful smile and a word of encouragement. The oddest thing to me is her sense of decorum. Her manners and politeness would make even the queen proud.

Somewhere along the way, she must have been taught how to treat others with kindness. I would never have thought kindness was in the girl. Prison had obliterated it. Pure animal instinct to survive had replaced it, but our God cut through all of it. The book of Hebrews says that "the Word of God is living and active and sharper than any two-edged sword piercing as far as the division of soul and spirit." God used that two-edged sword as cleanly as a surgical scalpel on Jackie, carving away with precision the cancer that was eating her from within.

Jackie has reunited with her children; even her oldest son has been able to forgive her and tell her those miraculous words that every mother wants to hear, "I love you, Mom." It never ceases to amaze me what God can do in an instant of time, that which could not be done in a lifetime of self-improvement. II Corinthians speaks of a new creation. Jackie is that new creation. "The old things passed away and behold the new things have come."

Psalm 139:1-15

Psalm 56:8

II Corinthians 5:17

Hebrews 4:12

Kingdom Principle: The Word of God applied gently and with great love is able to surgically cut away the anger and bitterness of an anguished heart and heal the wounds, all in a moment's time.

Prayer: "Lord, Your kind intent toward me is extraordinary. You wrote a book about me and all that You have planned for me. Help me to know deep in my being Your love for me and Your intentions for me here on the earth. Amen."

Assignment: Ask the Father to show you some of the things that He wrote in your book before you were born. Write down what He reveals to you. Be intentional about how to carry out what is written in your book.

What did you discover? What do you plan to do about it?

_____

_____

_____

_____

_____

_____

DAY 5 – INTIMACY – ON THE FLOOR

There are some days when, we as Christians, perform well, don't get into a lot of trouble, and are marginally successful with our temper while driving. At the end of the day, we pat ourselves on the back for our good behavior.

The trouble is, that while behavior does matter, it is not really the standard of measurement used in the Kingdom (I think I just heard a few gasps).

Take the first man and woman for instance. Adam and Eve enjoyed their time in the garden with the Lord, walking in the cool of the evening with Him, visiting, sharing, and experiencing companionship with Him. In the beginning, it was not a matter of behavior. It was a matter of intimacy with one another. It was the original standard. It was fresh, it was new, and all things were good.

That all changed with the bite of a single apple, the fruit from the one tree they were not allowed to eat. What was the significance of that tree? Why could they not eat from it? But eat they did and, in turn, performed the first conscious and deliberate act of violation of the Father's command.

When they ate that fruit, everything changed. For the first time in human history, short as that history may have been, the dawn of disobedience came. Still today, that disobedient act breaks faith with the Father. It brings fear and shame; hence, the fig leaves.

Their disobedience damaged their relationship with the Father. Instead of hope and glory, they fell into a life of fear and doubt. Now, instead of intimacy with the Father, they suffered a separation from God and sought reconciliation through their good behavior. To them, that required performance - something like, "I don't drink, and I don't dance, and I don't take a second glance."

Trouble is, it did not work. It just made things worse. Adam and Eve, like all those who have followed them, had deluded themselves that they could actually behave. We have a pretty good record of how that turned out over the ages.

There is one thing that an addict has the privilege of knowing that most believers do not. Addicts know they cannot behave their way into sobriety, or anything else for that matter. If they could, they would have already accomplished it.

They are fully aware of the fact that they simply cannot refrain from taking another drink, another hit, or needle. They are fully aware that it is not possible. They know that unless God utterly wrecks them, they have no hope.

Sadly, the addict is further along in the Kingdom than the average church-going Christian who is under the delusion that he can control himself and is able to achieve some modicum of goodness (oh, don't look so holy; deep down you know). Addicts know they are desperate. The average church-going Christian does not.

God has ways of getting our attention in order to alter this illusion in our walk with Him. He is so kind that He will use circumstances to clear our vision, our hearing, and our belief system. If we are not catching on, He sometimes raises the volume. If we stubbornly refuse to listen, He may employ other methods.

One may be "put on the shelf" indefinitely. I have seen believers who have been in church every Sunday and Wednesday of their lives for 40 years. These are good people, but not terribly effective in impacting the Kingdom. I was one of those.

Another alternative is the "time out chair." In my own experience, this is a very uncomfortable place to be, knowing that nothing is wrong, but something is just not right. It feels like being an insect stuck to a board with a pin, able to wiggle ones little legs a little, but going nowhere.

Then there is the "wrecking ball." I have found this to be a cataclysmic tool of epic proportion which, in a moment, changes the very core of a person. I have seen God use the wrecking ball to free a misguided lamb, addicted or not.

My parents molded my theology. I loved Jesus and did all the prescribed duties of a good churchgoer. I had even been introduced to Holy Spirit. My husband was an elder in a church of 10,000 members and we led a small couple's group weekly. In addition, I led a ladies' Bible study luncheon (with seasonal dishes). We were, as they say, "fat and sassy."

One day, I was painting in my studio. I received a monthly teaching tape from a Christian ministry in the mail. I put it on to listen while I painted. Only it was not the dear old gentleman I had spiritually grown up with, but some crazy lady who was talking nonsense and shouting indiscernible words like a mad woman.

I could not fathom who she was, or why anyone would make a tape of her babblings. As she progressed, it became clearer. She was a missionary to Mozambique and was telling of the extraordinary miracles she had seen there. Blind eyes were opened, the lame walked, and food multiplied. I was shocked. As I listened, I became even more mystified. Machetes had been pressed to her throat. What in the world?? What is she prattling on about? AK-47's were held to her head. The dead raised? Dear heavens! This was so outside the scope of my organized little life.

And then it came. The wrecking ball hit me right in the chest. I became self-aware. I saw my life from 10,000 feet; I saw her life. I saw my fat sassy sin. The next thing I knew I was on the floor weeping, wailing, and repenting for my pathetic Christian life and my illusion that my good behavior had saved me. With tears shed and snot in the carpet, grief and shame racked me beyond anything I had known. If I had some fig leaves, I would have used them. I wanted to smash all those seasonal dishes to the floor. Eventually, I was able to find words to express what I was feeling inside.

"Lord, I see now that my life was about behavior, not intimacy with You. I repent. I cannot change myself, but You can change me. I want to be your friend again. I will go anywhere. I will do anything. But please don't leave me here in my pathetic life."

As clearly as anything I had ever heard, the Lord said, "Go to Faith City Mission."

I did not know what that was exactly, possibly a soup kitchen or something to do with the poor. I had heard of it but had never been there. I was unclear how I was going to help. Nevertheless, I was a woman on fire. I contacted the Mission and asked to volunteer. The next week at our luncheon (I think we were using the Easter bunny dishes at that point), I told the ladies what we were going to do. We were going to this place downtown and we were going to sort donated clothes (I did not actually want to have anything to do with "those people," so sorting clothes seemed safe). Needless to say, the ladies did not "see the light" and the whole group disbanded quickly. My close friend and I continued to go to the Mission every week.

Everything in my being was offended by the place. It stunk, it was dirty, and the furniture was stained and ripped. The Chapel and the dining room were the worst. They were dark and dingy and smelled of unwashed hair and urine. The people were frightening with their blank stares and filthy clothes.

"I would do drugs, too, if I had to eat here," I thought. Over the coming months, I came to know and understand these precious people and why they were in the mess they were in. The stories of abuse, neglect, and violence done to them were beyond imagination. My heart broke for them and decimated my smug sense of nobility and sassiness. In each face, I saw the face of Jesus, and through them, I found Him again.

One day as I prayed in that hideous Chapel the Lord wrecked me again. I was crying for these dear people and their constant self-inflicted wounds when the Lord said these words, "Do you see? I have shed My love for the homeless, the addicted, and the wounded abroad in your heart. When you do these things for these brothers of Mine, even the least of these, you do it for Me. It is your greatest treasure and your deepest hurt."

I was undone again. I could once again walk in the cool of the garden with my Father. Over the years here on this mission field, I have been humbled and grateful for this extraordinary experience of the Kingdom of God.

Proverbs 28:11

Matthew 20:25-28

Romans 5:5

Matthew 25:31-40

Kingdom Principle: The standard of measure in the Kingdom is not behaving oneself. The standard of measure is intimacy with the Father.

Prayer: "Jesus, do not leave me in my mess. Teach me the joy of knowing You through loving the least and the littlest. Thank You for being my friend. Amen."

Assignment: Today, kneel before the Lord. Pray the prayer above. Stay there listening to His voice.

Write down what you heard Him say to you.

_____

_____

_____

_____

_____

_____

_____

_____

The standard of measure in the Kingdom is not behaving oneself. The standard of measure is intimacy with the Father.

DAY 6 — TRUTH — PANCREATIC TUMOR

There are a great many people who enjoy watching science fiction movies. In the early days of television, there were series to watch such as Star Trek, with spaceships racing about the galaxies and parallel universes getting mixed up with each other. There were vastly different beings who stepped in and out of these parallel realities conquering, capturing, and causing all manner of chaos.

In truth, our world and the Kingdom of God are similar to these fantasy universes. There are two realities at play. One reality is fact. It is the physical world around us, what we see and experience. The other is the supernatural world - the Kingdom - the unseen world of angels, demons, miracles, signs, wonders, and truth.

We believe the physical world around us is real, and it is. The Kingdom, however, is more real. It actually takes precedence over the physical world. The physical world is the fact, but the spiritual world is the truth. Jesus said, "You will know the truth, and the truth will set you free." He showed us the truth by healing the sick, raising the dead, multiplying the food, casting out demons, and calming the storm. His Kingdom reality supersedes our physical reality.

There is truth in the Kingdom of God. There is also fact. These are two very different things. For example, let's say that you have been diagnosed with a terrible disease that will result in death. That's a fact. Tests have been run and the diagnosis made. But in the Kingdom of God, the truth is that, "by His stripes, we are healed."

The truth is, "If the same Spirit that raised Jesus Christ from the dead lives on the inside of you, He will quicken your mortal body unto life." Truth trumps fact every time. The question is, which reality will you pursue? The fact? Or the truth?

Jesus said, "Take care what you listen to. By your standard of measure, it will be measured to you, and more will be given to you besides." The question is, what is your standard of measure? The doctor's diagnosis? Then that is what you will receive. Or is your standard of measure the truth of the Word of God? Consider this Scripture, "These signs will follow those who believe. They will lay hands on the sick and they will recover." That quote is from Jesus's farewell talk just before He ascended to Heaven. It is His last bit of instruction to His disciples.

When I was diagnosed with a pancreatic tumor, I was experiencing the exact symptoms and diagnosis that my mother had; she died within a month of her diagnosis. The doctors certainly weren't helping matters with descriptions of "a tumor the size of a large lemon having already crushed the bile duct." It was all so very bleak.

That night in the hospital, I lay alone in the dark and cried. I knew enough about the truth vs. fact premise to know I must change my standard of measure, or I was going to die.

I turned my face to the wall and cried out to God as King Hezekiah did in the Bible. He was told he was going to die from his illness. On his deathbed, he turned his face to the wall and asked the Lord to let him live. God heard his prayers, and he lived another 15 years longer. I turned my face to the wall and asked the Lord for 15 more years. Exhausted, I fell asleep.

In the night, I awoke suddenly. My eyes were closed, but I could see a blue light through my lids shining down on me as from above. I opened my eyes to see what it was, but there was nothing but darkness. I closed my eyes, and the blue light appeared again.

How odd. I opened my eyes again to find the source of the light so I could turn it off. There was no blue light. After several attempts I gave up. All night long, the blue light shone down on me. I hoped it was a light from Heaven.

Although I tried, I could not mentally make the leap from fact to truth, from one reality to the other. I did not have the faith to believe. I cried out to the Lord. He gathered me up and held me under His wing, the safest place in the universe.

Every time I would begin to panic, I forced myself to climb up under His wing and rest. It became a daily thing, sometimes many times a day. I began to feel the warmth of His skin and hear His heartbeat. I felt safe again.

We flew to M.D. Anderson, a huge cancer hospital in Houston, and had a surgical procedure called the "Wipple "to remove the tumor. Later, the doctor waltzed into my hospital room and delivered the pathology report. The tumor was benign! No one was more surprised than him. It was a miracle.

My recovery in the hospital was long and arduous but progressing, until one day I felt quite ill. The doctor ordered blood work. There was internal bleeding that had to be stopped.

Back to surgery we went. I imagine it is somewhat like trying to find the leak in a flat tire. They found it in my stomach. The doctors stopped the bleeding, then took me to the critical care unit to recover. The CCU is a very dark and foreboding place. There are lots of bugaboos down there.

However, one night three angels came and sat by my bed. We talked about Jesus and how much we loved Him. My room was dark, but the light that emanated from their forms glowed all around us. It was a happy time. We just enjoyed the glory of the Lord together. The sense of peace came over me.

I returned to my room with strict instructions not to get up alone. I was quite weak and needed help to do everything. Late one night, I called for help. Two very large male nurses came. I asked for assistance in being placed on the portable privy chair beside the bed. One nurse, Ellis, picked me up like a rag doll and set me down, then turned to the other nurse to say something. I suddenly felt quite ill again.

"Ellis, I think I am going to faint." That was the end of that. I fell forward onto the bed and died. I suddenly found myself in another universe, a beautiful place with forests and pink air, huge oak leaves, glorious vistas, and strange blue and yellow birds with 16 wings each who sang in unison while roosting in the trees. It was the most beautiful thing I had ever heard or seen. I heard children running and laughing in a beautiful park. I felt perfect peace. "This must be paradise," I thought.

Suddenly, I opened my eyes and looked down. Evidently, I was lying on the floor and Ellis was kneeling over me, pounding me over and over on the chest. "Eight, Nine, Ten!" I closed my eyes and floated away.

I awoke later in the hospital bed and saw Ellis sitting next to me. He was quite pale. He told me what happened.

"When you fell down face first on the bed, I reached down to turn you over. You had a fixed stare with no pulse and no breath. You coded on me! We got you back, but your hemoglobin was 4. It is supposed to be at 13. Your body simply did not have enough blood to sustain life. We gave you several bags of blood. You rest now. I will keep checking on you through the night."

He came back several times, which was fine with me. I could not sleep. I only wanted to remember every detail of the glorious place I visited during my brief departure from my body.

The next morning, a team of doctors came in to discuss next steps, which included another surgery. I flatly refused. I was done and so tired of this world. I did not have the strength to endure any more. They argued and cajoled, but I refused. My husband was very concerned and stood by helplessly while I crossed my arms and shook my head. I was "locked and loaded" and being quite obstinate.

"What if this happens again?" I demanded.

"Then we take you back to surgery again."

"Absolutely not!"

The doctors were at the end of their rope.

There came a knock on the door. My husband opened it, spoke to someone for a minute, then came back into the room.

"Jena, do you know a guy named Warren Wright from school?"

"Warren Wright? Yes, he sat behind me in second grade, but I have not seen him in 30 years. Why?"

"Well, he is here with his wife. They were on their way to the airport when the Lord told him to come to M.D. Anderson and find you to pray for you."

As Jay led them into the room, I thought to myself, "Great! Now I have to play nice." It was awkward, since I barely remembered the fellow. He and his wife bent over me and prayed a short prayer and left. It felt like all the oxygen in the room got sucked out. We all sort of froze. No one uttered a word. Then I heard these words come out of my mouth, "OK, I can do it now. I will go to surgery." It was as if that short prayer changed everything. The Holy Spirit came over me and strengthened me in my soul in order to face what I could not face before.

Everyone galvanized into action. Doctors ran this way; nurses ran that way. Someone magically appeared with a shot and off we went to the operating room again. The surgery was a success. I do not know how Warren knew I was at M.D. Anderson, or how he found me in a 16-acre maze of buildings. I do not know how a 30 second prayer from a near stranger changed the atmosphere and changed me, but it miraculously did.

I am so thankful that God saved my life that day. I often recount all of the miracles, healings, and salvations I have participated in since then, not to mention the milestones in my children's lives and the grandchildren I have gotten to hold. Thank you, Jesus, for your unmerited kindness toward me, even when I was being a brat.

Psalm 91:1-4

Romans 8:11

Mark 4:24

Ephesians 3:16

Kingdom Principle: What you believe to be true is true for you. It is your standard of measure. If you believe the facts, you will receive the facts as your reality. If, however, you choose to believe the truth, then you will receive the truth. Truth trumps fact every time.

Prayer: "Papa, today I choose to believe Your truth in the matter, not the facts. I will embrace Your Word today concerning the matter. Amen"

Meditation: Think on an area of your life where you desperately need a miracle. Now, climb up under His wing and rest in Him. When you start to panic over the situation, climb back up to His arms.

What happened?

_____

_____

_____

_____

_____

_____

_____

_____

_____

_____

DAY 7 – THE WORD – PROSTATE CANCER

In the years that I have been an ardent student of signs and wonders, I have learned that aside from my relationship with the God of the universe, the most vital component to this parallel universe we call the Kingdom of God is the Word of God. In the book of Hebrews, the Word is called "living and active." Here is another head scratcher for the believer. How can something inanimate be living and active? I have come to "live by faith" on this one. When I lay hands on the sick and speak the Word of God, reminding Him of what He said, people are healed. Why? Is this some magic incantation?

In the book of John 1, it says, "In the beginning was the Word, and the Word was with God, and the Word was God…and the Word became flesh and dwelt among us, and we beheld His glory." Honestly, I could spend eternity meditating on these verses, their beauty, and their reality.

The passage is, of course, referring to Jesus. He is the Incarnate Word as well as the God of all. The use of "Word" here translates from the Greek as the spoken Word. Interestingly, the passage goes on to tell us that it was He by whom all things came into being, and apart from Him nothing came into being. The spoken Word said, "Let there be," and bam! Whatever He named came into being.

It is astonishing that the book of Genesis documents in detail just what the spoken Word accomplished. "And God said, 'Let there be light.' And there was light." I was once given a T-shirt that read, "And God said," followed by the mathematical equation for light, "and there was Light." My small mind is not able to grasp the physics that took place when God spoke those Words. All I know is that when it was all said and done, there was a living breathing magnificent universe that was not there before.

Jesus is God in the flesh, and He is the spoken Word. When He says something, all manner of things break loose. Blind eyes are open, the demons flee, and the dead are raised.

Jesus commanded believers to "heal the sick, raise the dead, cleanse the leper, and cast out demons." When believers speak His Word (living and breathing and active), things happen. A diseased liver is made perfectly new. The food is multiplied. The electricity is turned back on inexplicably. Funding miraculously arrives from a random source. Why? Because He IS the Word. I am just the UPS guy delivering it.

A perfect example is Steve. Steve was diagnosed with prostate cancer. He was devastated. He had bravely battled so many debilitating diseases already, and now he faced an even bigger battle. His discouragement was immense.

Steve was told to start chemotherapy right away to shrink the tumor before surgery. His new insurance had not become active, so he felt he needed to wait until the coverage would pay for treatment. I thought that was a really bad idea. I have seen firsthand what happens when one waits for the insurance to kick in. The tumor grows and spreads. Then it is too late.

I asked if I could lay hands on him and pray for supernatural healing. He reluctantly agreed. I laid my hands on his head and began to remind Jesus of what He said, "For you who fear My name, the sun of righteousness will rise with healing in its wings and you shall go forth and skip about like calves from the stall."

Several weeks later, Steve arrived for his first chemotherapy session. A tumor marker test was done. The doctor walked into the room and shook his head in wonder. There were no tumor markers. There was no tumor at all. God healed Steve all because Jesus commanded a little person to lay hands on him and pray a simple prayer. In His perfect Word, God healed Steve and gave him back his life, his family, and his profession.

When I read my Bible and study the translations, I am in awe of what it commands believers to do, which generates a supernatural result far beyond our human capabilities. And yet, when we put our faith in the Word, it is possible to see miraculous results. One does not have to be a spiritual giant to bring about those results. It just takes a willing participant. After all, as the saying goes, "Any old burning bush will do."

John 1:1

Genesis 1:3

Hebrews 4:12

Malachi 4:2

Matthew 10:8

Kingdom Principle: Any believer is able to access the Kingdom and its power by the Word of God.

Prayer: "Jesus, You are the Word made complete. Show me Your power in this Word and teach me the mysteries of it. Amen"

Activation: Find three Scriptures about healing, miracles, or signs and wonders that you are not familiar with. Meditate on the power of these Words. Now, speak these words over your situation. In addition, find someone who is ill and lay your hands on them and pray the Word over them.

What happened?

_____

_____

_____

DAY 8 – THE SEED – PARALYZED

A seed is an extraordinary thing. Within its tiny self is all the blueprint information causing it to sprout, grow and produce fruit. In the depths of the earth, with sunshine and water, miraculous transformations take place.

A farmer trusts the soil, rain, and sun to work their miraculous dance together to help the seed along in its pursuit. He knows not to dig up the seed and check on it. He knows to trust the seed to do what it does best.

In much the same way, the Word of God does what it does best when implanted in our spirit. In fact, Jesus said the seed is the Word. When we receive the Word "with an honest, good heart and hold fast to it, we would bear fruit with perseverance." In other words, we do not give up and dig up the Word to see how it's doing. Like the farmer trusts the seed to do what it was made to do, we as believers must trust the Word to do what it was intended to do.

A passage of assurance for me comes in Isaiah. "For as the rain and snow come down from Heaven and do not return there without watering the earth, and making it bear and sprout, and furnishing seed to the sower and bread to the eater, so shall My word which goes forth from My mouth; it shall not return to Me empty without accomplishing what I desire, and without succeeding in the matter for which I sent it." When I choose to trust that one verse, I can remain confident of His promise to me.

I came face to face with this concept in Guest Chapel one day. Guest Chapel caters to the spiritual needs of those who live on the streets. After the message, I told the congregation if they needed prayer for anything at all, we were available. We prayed for several people and off to lunch they went.

Finally, a man on a motorized scooter wheeled up. He was a bit slouched in his seat and his left wrist was held up to his chest by a shoestring tied around his neck. His left hand was clenched in a fist. His left leg was somewhat twisted and limp. His name was Mark. He had a massive stroke, and his entire left side was paralyzed.

Madison, a staff member, laid her hands on his leg. I laid my hands on his arm and hand. We prayed for God's healing power to renew this broken body. Quite frankly, we saw nothing, no improvement. Mark finally motored off to lunch.

Several weeks later, our Head of Security, Bill, popped his head in my office and said, "Got a minute? You are going to want to see this."

In stepped a gentleman whom I did not recognize. He looked familiar, but I could not place him, until I saw the shoestring holding his wrist up to his chest.

"You're the fellow with the scooter!"

"Yep, that's me."

"Where is your scooter?"

"I don't need it anymore. I can walk now."

"My Gosh! What happened?"

"The night you all prayed for me, I was sitting there watching TV, when it felt like a hot firebrand was stabbed into my chest. I thought I was having a heart attack. The pain was so intense. I really thought I was going to die. The heat eased off, and I was worried about the whole thing. I was trying to recover from the pain, when I suddenly felt the need to go to the bathroom. Without thinking, I jumped up and walked to the bathroom. I was doing my thing when I realized that I was standing without help and that I walked to the bathroom by myself! I thought, 'What have I done?!' I carefully walked back to my chair and realized I could walk! Really Walk!"

We all celebrated together at this astounding marvel. A miracle had truly taken place. God's affection for His people is up close and personal. He showed Himself faithful to Mark that night. The seed of the prayers sprouted and began to grow. It bore much fruit for Mark.

As we celebrated, the Holy Spirit nudged me to pray for his arm again.

"Mark, if God healed your leg, He will heal your arm and hand. Let's pray again."

Mark told us he had since broken his shoulder and it was not set. Indeed, there was a bone protruding as a large bulge under his skin and his shoulder sagged. He was a mess.

Bill and I laid our hands upon Mark's arm and shoulder where the bone was evidently out of place and prayed again. Again, we saw no immediate results.

"Well, that didn't work," Mark remarked.

"Wait a minute, Mister! You did not begin to walk immediately either. Don't throw your seed away! Let it germinate and grow. You reap what you sow if you do not throw the seed away."

Mark agreed with that and walked away.

That night, I felt such a burden for Mark and asked Jesus to heal his arm and shoulder. All night, I felt the need to keep praying for him.

The following morning, I was in Madison's office telling her about Mark's miracle and how the lame really did walk. We both noticed movement at her door. Mark was standing there grinning.

"Watch this!" he exclaimed.

He proceeded to move his paralyzed arm and shoulder all around. We literally leapt for joy for him. The seed had sprouted again, grown, and produced another miracle. What a story of the power of the seed being the Word of God.

The Word did not come back empty without accomplishing what He desired and without succeeding in the matter for which He sent it. God's tender mercy toward His least and littlest is extraordinary.

Mark 4:14-20

Matthew 15:29-31

Isaiah 55:10-13

Kingdom Principle: The Word of God is a seed. Given the proper decree and trust, it will germinate and grow into the supernatural miracle that it was sent out to accomplish.

Prayer: "Holy Spirit, today I choose to plant the seed of healing in my body. I will not dig up the seed or throw the seed away. I will water it and protect it. Will You brood over the seed and cause it to sprout and grow? Amen."

Try this: Plant a packet of seeds in a small pot. Water it and place it in a sunny window. Speak the Scriptures listed above over it and yourself every day. This is a prophetic act. You nurture the earthly seed and let it do what it knows to do. In the same way, nurture your spiritual seed and let it do what it knows to do.

Document your experience in this exercise:

_____

_____

_____

_____

_____

_____

_____

DAY 9 — THE KINGDOM IN HEALING — WALMART GREETER

One of the phenomena in the Kingdom that is available to us is supernatural healing of the physical body. There are numerous accounts in the New Testament of men, women, and children being healed - rich and poor, righteous and sinner alike made whole from every disease and malady. The Old Testament carries accounts of kings, orphans, and generals being miraculously healed.

When Jesus walked on the earth, he healed the sick and impaired. Then shockingly, he commanded His disciples to heal the sick, raise the dead, cast out demons, and cleanse the leper. These were all things they were not humanly capable of doing.

Through the ages, He has continued to command this of the Church. We are called to do things we are not capable of doing. We are told to lay hands on the sick, so people are healed of their diseases.

This is a frightening instruction. It is terrifying enough to approach a stranger and ask such delicate question about their person, but then to ask if one might touch them and pray for them is uncomfortable to say the least. What if they are offended, or refuse your efforts? What if they allow you to pray for them and nothing happens? The "what if's" of praying for the sick will prevent their miracle. Yet, all of that is beside the point if Holy Spirit whispers in one's ear and instructs one to pray. It comes down to obedience, pure and simple.

Some believe that healing passed away with the disciples and that we are no longer supposed to do that. I do not believe that. I am just a little person who wishes to see people relieved of their suffering; what have I or they got to lose?

In many cases there is no medical cure, so they will not get well if someone doesn't pray for them. Disputing the validity of miraculous physical healing is way above my pay grade and educational prowess. I press on to pray. I have been confronted by those who hold to the "healing is not for today" argument. I do not engage. It takes two to argue, and I leave that to the God of the universe.

One Saturday, my husband and I were checking out at Walmart. As we pushed our cart to the exit, we saw a young man, a greeter, sitting on a stool with a cane. He looked like his world had just caved in. I recognized him as a sacker at an upscale market in town. He once had such a vivacious personality, joking with the customers and always happy. Today he was miserable.

"Hey, buddy, you look so sad. Is everything okay?"

The young man looked up at us with such grief that my heart broke for him.

"No, I have lost my ability to stand or walk. My muscles have withered and there is nothing to be done. I was perfectly fine, then my legs became weak and my ankles gave way. I went to see my doctor. He told me that the antibiotic I had taken had a side effect causing withering of the muscles, especially in the legs and ankles. I cannot walk anymore without my cane and I am told it is only going to get worse. I am involved with a class action lawsuit against a pharmaceutical company who manufactured the drug. My life is ruined. All I wanted to do was go to seminary and stand behind a pulpit and preach the Gospel. Here I am, a greeter at Walmart."

"Well, let me ask you this. Would you rather receive a settlement in a lawsuit? Or would you rather just be healed?"

The young man flung his arms around me in a bear hug and exclaimed, "I would rather be healed!" He was crying now.

As Saturday shoppers milled all around us, my husband and I laid our hands on this young man and began to speak the Word of God over him. We decreed a complete healing for him. He sobbed and sobbed. We saw no change.

My husband questioned our doctor about the young man's claim of losing his muscle mass due to a particular antibiotic. The doctor confirmed that it was true and there was, in fact, a huge lawsuit going on because of it.

The following week I went back to Walmart for more groceries. As I exited the opposite door from the previous week's visit, I saw the young man whom we had prayed for the week prior. He was standing at the door, and his cane was gone. His arms were flung open wide and there was a huge grin on his face as he shouted, "Welcome to Walmart!" He was once again the young man I had seen and known as a sacker at the other supermarket, full of energy and smiles.

"Hey, buddy! Where is your cane?" He turned and recognized me, then gave me another bear hug.

"I went to my neurologist last week, and he ran tests. All the damage is gone! My muscles and ligaments are normal. God healed me! No more lawsuit. Now I can go to seminary."

Astonishing! It is still a wonder to me that Jesus lets me participate in the Kingdom in such a manner. He urges me to do something that I cannot do in and of myself. If I obey, extraordinary things happen. It has absolutely nothing to do with me or my abilities. All it takes is a willingness to be brave and step out and try.

Several weeks later, I saw the young man again. He proudly told me of his classes at Wayland Baptist University in pursuit of his dream to become a pastor. He was a changed man. God supernaturally reversed his damaged human form and made him whole so that he could answer the call on his life.

It is the way of the Kingdom of God.

Luke 7:22

Isaiah 53:5

Matthew 10:8

Kingdom Principle: Obedience opens the door to signs and wonders.

Prayer: "Jesus, open my eyes to this Kingdom of God, and give me courage to step up and do what You commanded me to do, even if I am incapable of doing it. Amen."

Try this: This week look for opportunities to pray for someone who is ill or injured in their body. Ask to lay hands on them and pray for them.

How did it go?

_____

_____

_____

_____

_____

_____

_____

_____

_____

_____

DAY 10 – THE TESTIMONY – JAMES

There is a very interesting pattern that forms in the Scripture about the testimony of God's people. God commanded the children of Israel to tell of His signs and wonders to their children and their children's children "so they will put their confidence in Me."

In other words, tell the kids what wonderful things I have done for you so that when they get into a bind, they will remember that I will do it for them as well.

In the same way, when we see God's miraculous power at the Mission, we give the testimony of what happened over and over so that when others hear it, their faith is built to believe that "if He did it for them He will do it for me." The word *testimony* in the original Greek means "a legal precedent in a court of law."

You have heard that when an attorney wants to prove his argument on a point of the law, he will review previous court cases to determine the precedent that should be followed. Once a ruling by the court is made, that ruling can become the legal precedent for future cases. The same is true in the courts of Heaven.

The book of Revelation speaks of the war in Heaven between the saints and the dragon yet to come. The prophecy declares that the brethren "will overcome him because of the blood of the Lamb, and the word of their testimony, for they did not love their life even unto death."

Again, the original Greek meaning of this word, *testimony* is a legal term in a court of law before the judge. Therefore, my testimony of the miracles and signs that I have participated in are legally binding in the court of Heaven.

There was a point at which I debated about putting these wonderful stories about God's signs and wonders on the internet, reaching out to a broader audience in cyberspace. It somehow felt sacrilegious. I told of them verbally in my speaking engagements, but I was dubious about the internet. I was actually at a conference to hear an international leader in this revival movement named Patricia King. She was speaking when, in mid-sentence she stopped, walked down to the second row where I sat, and pointed to me.

"Is your name Jen?"

"My name is Jena," I replied.

"Well, Jena, I have a word for you. Write the stories down and put them on the internet so that the church will be mobilized into action." I nearly fell out of my chair.

That is all it took for me. I began to post stories, photos, and videos on Facebook to give testimony to the revival happening in west Texas and God's mighty works. I was amazed at the response. Desperate people longed to believe in modern day miracles.

One day, I received a Facebook message from someone who had read the stories online. She told me about a friend who was lying in the hospital in a diabetic coma. In CCU, his organs were shutting down and he had pneumonia. He had been intubated in the ambulance and was not responding to any stimuli.

The doctors believed that his brain was also shutting down. She had been seeing the stories on Facebook, the "testimonies" of crazy medically impossible healings taking place at the Mission that were certified by doctors. She begged me to send the "prayer team" at the Mission to pray for her young friend. We don't have a prayer team, but we have a lot of individuals on staff who have prayed for people who were cured, made whole, and changed forever.

The woman who had contacted me had seen the testimonies of God's great deeds and believed it could happen for her friend. She did not stop there. She bravely took action on his behalf and called the Mission for help.

Her faith reminded me of the story in the Bible of the paralytic and his friends. The friends of the paralytic believed that if they could just get his bed down through the roof to Jesus's feet, their friend would be healed. They had heard the testimonies of all that Jesus had done for the blind, lame, leprous, and demonized. They were willing to offend others as they ripped a homeowner's roof apart in order to lower their friend to the feet of Jesus to see him healed. And he was.

Several of us gathered and went to the hospital to pray for this young man named James. As we arrived in the tiny CCU room and the family made way for us, I noticed a disturbing gloom in the atmosphere. I have sensed this at many deathbed situations.

It was as if the spirit of death had already arrived and had taken up his post to claim the individual. We laid hands on the patient and thanked God for His faithfulness, His Goodness, and His will to heal. We cited testimony after testimony of His miraculous works by Holy Spirit, as well as his countless promises to "heal our diseases."

The young man became agitated and flailed in the bed. We recited the Word to him, and he settled down. I have seen this phenomenon happen often for patients who are "on their deathbed"; they seem to be wrestling with something.

In each case when the Word was read to them of God's love and protection, they would become still, as if listening to the tender words as they washed over the room.

The Lord spoke to me and told me to have the fellow perform a task. James' sister was holding his hand, which had been unresponsive. I was frightened that the family might become offended at my forwardness. Holy Spirit was relentless, so I took a chance.

"James, if you can hear me, squeeze your sister's hand. We watched as he raised her hand and squeezed it. The family was shocked! We were encouraged that his brain was still functioning. The atmosphere changed in the room. The Holy Spirit's presence came in, and we were overwhelmed. One of the prayer team members was hit so hard she had to go to her knees. We rejoiced loudly.

The atmosphere in the room utterly changed. The gloom was gone. Joy and hope had replaced it. The family cried and hugged us at this miraculous sign that James could hear them and respond. Their hope soared.

Two days later, James walked out of the hospital. He came to visit us at the Mission and thanked us for praying for him. He later came to join the program. He was bright and witty and always had a grin. James had not only been healed in his body, but God had healed his heart. Thank you, Papa.

Holy Spirit had quickened James' body unto life at our request. That alone has taught me the power of a faithful and determined friend.

Oh, God! Sometimes Your goodness brings me to my knees. I am again undone by Your desire for us to participate in this glorious Kingdom with You.

Deuteronomy 6:17

Psalm 78:4-7

Revelation 12:11

Mark 2:3-5

Kingdom Principle: Citing the testimonies of the miraculous in the past can be used as a legal precedent for the miraculous today.

Prayer: "Father, I believe the testimonies of Your goodness and Your power through the ages. I cite them as legal precedent in Your courts. I remind You of them now. If You healed others, you will heal me today. Amen."

Activation: Find and read three stories of God's healing power today. Take hold of them as your own. Remind yourself throughout the day that if He did it for another, He will do it for you. Apply these stories to your own troubles.

Write down the changes in your outlook and your belief system.

Citing the testimonies of the miraculous in the past can be used as a legal precedent for the miraculous today.

DAY 11 — THE KINGDOM IN PROPHECY — COLTON

In the Old and New Testaments, the prophets played a large role in the kingdom of Israel. There are a lot of very strange stories in the Holy Writ about prophets. In one, God commands the prophet Ezekiel to "prophesy" over a valley of dry bones.

Ezekiel did so, and the bones began to reassemble. Ligament and muscle formed, and flesh covered the bodies. God breathed life into those bones and the dead came back to life.

Theologians believe this was a prophetic message to Israel that the Jews would one day come back together as a nation after being dispersed throughout the world with no land to call their own for 2,000 years. In 1948, the world watched as this tiny race returned to its homeland and reestablished a nation of Israel once again. It rocked the entire planet.

In other Bible stories, prophets demonstrated God's power or brought messages of both warning and hope. Elijah was a fiery prophet in the Old Testament who called down fire on the altar of God on the Mount of Carmel burning up the ox, the wood, the stones, and everything in sight, killing the prophets of the idol god, Baal.

Isaiah prophesied the coming of the Messiah, and Malachi foretold of Messiah being born in Bethlehem.

God told Samuel to go to Jesse's house to anoint the new king from among Jesse's sons. As the handsome and strapping sons lined up, Samuel passed before each one waiting to hear from

God as to which He would choose. As he reached the end of the line, God had chosen none of them.

Samuel asked Jesse if he had any more sons. Jesse's reply was that "the youngest" was out with the sheep. A perplexing side note to this story is that Jesse would not even say the boy's name, and servants usually shepherded the sheep, not the sons. Why did Jesse not send for his youngest son, David? Some theologians propose that David, the youngest, was possibly illegitimate; hence, the poor treatment.

Nevertheless, David, just a young boy, was brought to Samuel. God told Samuel to anoint him as King of Israel. It would be many years and a lot of heartache for the young man before he would become known as king, but he is known to the Jews and Christians today as King David, a mighty man of valor and a man after God's own heart. Jesus was David's descendant from the house of Judah.

Prophets played a large role in the New Testament as well. John, Jesus's cousin, prophesied the coming of Jesus and the new regime, a new Kingdom. At the time, no one realized that it was to be a universal Kingdom throughout the world.

In much the same way, God uses His people today to prophesy over nations, politics, elections, and people in order to alter the course of human history.

For instance, a man named Lance Wallnau who is a well-known Christian speaker prophesied many months before the candidates even announced they were running that Donald Trump would be the next President.

Needless to say, everyone scoffed at the man and called him a lunatic, including me. He even wrote a book prior to the election citing why he prophesied such an outlandish notion. Did God speak to Mr. Wallnau? The Bible says a prophet is known by the outcome of his prophecy.

Regardless of our preferences for President of the United States, at 2:00 am the night of the election the entire nation reeled in shock. Donald Trump did indeed win that race.

Similarly, in some cases God speaks to another type of prophet to deliver a prophetic message to an individual. Often times this prophecy is given in support of God's previous work in that person's life. He wishes to bless or encourage in a certain way. God never speaks to his children through another in negative or harsh ways. If He reveals a doubtful character trait or sin, the prophet is to turn it to a positive prayer.

For years, I considered the prophetic in the church nothing more than parlor games, until the day a stranger spoke to me about everything I had ever done. My mind was changed. I decided to train for the prophetic. Our church had a large team of highly trained prophets, and I turned to them to learn more about the gift of the Spirit.

When Jesus spoke to the woman at the well, He told her of her past which legitimized what else He said that day, causing her to go gather the town to hear. His prophetic words gave credence to His other words to the town. I felt that I must have a better understanding of this gift mentioned by Paul in his first letter to the Corinthians, as well as in the books of Romans and Ephesians. After several years of classes and ministry, I had a rudimentary understanding of the gift.

One day, I was preparing for our annual Easter service and dinner at the Mission. I made it a point to ask God if He had a Word that He wanted to share. I got still before Him.

Oddly, He usually shows me a shirt, specifically its color and cut. The Word for the man or woman or child with that color on comes to me. It may be a healing or a miracle, or something about that person that I could not possibly know. This particular day, I saw a pink button-down collared shirt on a man. Our guests do not wear preppy pink shirts, so I was dubious. Nonetheless, I received the Word from the Lord.

At the beginning of the service I got up and said, "If you have on a pink shirt, raise your hand. Two hands went up. One hand belonged to one of our new students who had come to stay with us to get clean and sober. The other was a guest off the street (so much for my theory about guests and pink shirts). I did not know either of their stories but told both men what the Lord wanted to say to them specifically.

"The Lord says, 'Son, I love you with an everlasting love. I am your Father, and you are My son. You have doubted this often. I am about to prove it to you once and for all. By the end of this Easter weekend, I will send you a love letter in the form of a miracle. Then you will know that I am your Father and you are My son."

I then prayed for the men and went on with the service.

The following Monday morning as I arrived at work, Colton, the student with the pink shirt, came to me literally glowing.

"Mrs. Taylor, you are not going to believe it, but I got my miracle on Saturday!"

"Colton, buddy, what happened?"

"I was minding the front desk on Saturday when the mail arrived. I sorted it for staff and students when I saw an official-looking envelope addressed to me from the state. I was so frightened to open it because I have a felony charge pending for possession of a controlled substance. It is my third felony charge. This time it means prison for me. I finally opened it and read it."

He handed me the envelope. I pulled out the letter on official government stationery and read. In a nutshell it said that all felony charges against Colton were being dropped "for the following reason." Below it, there was a list of reasons which could cause the charges to be dropped. From the five options listed, Colton's correspondence stated that letter "E" was the state's reason for the action.

"E) In the pursuit of justice."

"What kind of reason is that?" I asked.

"I don't know, and I don't care! I'm free!" Colton said. We hugged and cried. God had been true to His Word to Colton, to prove his sonship. What a great miracle.

God used me like a Western Union Telegram to deliver a message about something of which I had no knowledge, because He wanted to show His love to Colton. What about the other man who had a pink shirt on? I do not know. I have never seen him since that day. Maybe I will hear his story in Heaven. I thank God every day that He allows me to participate in this phenomenal Kingdom that we have access to.

Ezekiel 37:3-10

I Kings 18:1-40

I Samuel 16:1-13

I Corinthians 12:4-10

Romans 12:6–8

Kingdom Principle: God disperses His supernatural gifts to the Church for the purpose of encouraging believer and unbeliever alike. If we actively pursue our giftings, they will grow in strength and accuracy.

Prayer: "Father, thank you for Your immense love for us, Your children. Thank You for speaking directly to us through Your prophets in encouragement. Amen."

Launch: Start a journal dedicated to the prophecies that you receive, both large and small. Transcribe the words into your journal and pray over what God has said to you through prophecy.

Note: If you have never received a prophecy, seek out a church in your town that operates in the gifts of the Holy Spirit. Usually these churches have regularly scheduled times that people can receive a Word.

What did you discover?

_____

_____

_____

_____

_____

God disperses His supernatural gifts to the Church for the purpose of encouraging believer and unbeliever alike.

DAY 12 — SPOKEN WORDS — THANKSGIVING

We have seen how important it is to be careful of what we listen to, for by that standard of measure it will be measured to us. In much the same way, we must be careful of what we say. Scripture says that death and life are in the power of the tongue.

In the miraculous Christmas story in the Gospel of Luke, the angel Gabriel visited two people with a stunning message.

To the young maiden, Mary, he announced that she would become pregnant by the Holy Spirit and bear the Messiah. Although unclear on the finer points of this miracle, she accepted the prophecy.

However, when Gabriel appeared to Zacharias in the tabernacle and told him that in his old age, he would have a son, a prophet that would herald the coming of Messiah, Zacharias was ambivalent at best and challenged Gabriel. For his misgivings, he was struck dumb. It has been speculated that Zacharias was made speechless so that his words could not nullify the angel's decree.

When we are hoping for a miracle, sign, or healing, it is crucial that we guard what we say. What we say influences the Kingdom's outcome.

This is irrational to me. I don't understand the logic of it, but I have learned the hard way that if I challenge the truth of God's Word with my words or complain to anyone who will listen, I will be sent to the mountain to take another lap, just as the children of Israel did. This is not for punishment. It is so that I will learn this very important lesson.

Looking back, I can cite a 15-year period when I foolishly shook my fist at the heavens and literally asked the Lord, "What are You smoking up there?!?" I don't recommend that. I could have avoided so much difficulty and saved years of pain if I had just kept my mouth shut and had a teachable attitude. It truly is a conscious choice.

The level of regret for that stubborn attitude and the ridiculous things that I said is gargantuan. Yet, I am so very grateful that Jesus patiently let me squirm like a bug stuck to a Styrofoam display with a straight pin, wiggling my legs to get free but going nowhere, in order to give me the revelation of my words' impact.

Refraining from saying negative things about any situation or any individual is a wonderful start, but it is only half of the process. The Bible says in Job, "Decree a thing and it will come to pass." Ask yourself this question: What you are longing for in your life? Is it physical healing? Is it a new job, or a new friend? Is it for a wayward child to come home or a miracle? Speak life over that need and do not give up.

Several Thanksgivings ago, we were preparing our huge turkey dinner for about 300 guests at the Mission. The meal consisted of turkey, sweet potatoes, dressing, and pumpkin pie, along with so many wonderful extras. The tables were all decorated with an autumn theme. The mood was festive.

The guests showed up in droves. We fed wave after wave of people, and still more came. This went on for hours with no end in sight. We came to the terrible conclusion that we were not going to have enough food.

The watchman at the front door held up his clicker and showed me the present count. We had passed the 300 mark. I ran to the kitchen to see how we were doing on food. We were almost out, and there was still a full Chapel waiting their turn to eat. The chef was already thawing hotdogs. We simply did not have enough food. And who wants to eat hotdogs at a Thanksgiving celebration?

Jesus's first recorded miracle was to turn water into wine. While at a wedding feast, the wine ran out. He instructed the servants to bring large pots filled with water and miraculously converted the water into wine.

On at least two occasions, Jesus multiplied tiny portions of food to feed thousands of people. On one of those occasions, the disciples told the Master there was not enough food for the people and that He must send them away to the villages nearby to purchase something to eat. He commanded them, "You feed them." There He goes again commanding us to do something we are not capable of doing.

As we struggled to figure out how to feed our remaining guests, one of our younger staff members, Madison, said casually, "We don't have to serve hot dogs, let's just pray that God will multiply the food."

"Fine, you pray, while I cook hotdogs!" I threw back.

She prayed the simplest loaves and fishes prayer, and we kept serving. She thanked God that there was enough food for the guests.

Did we see mountains of supernatural food appear? No, but the little food that was left kept filling plates. It was so mystifying, so outrageous. Finally, the last guest was served and had just as much on his plate as the first guest. I ran to the front door to see what the clicker had counted for our total number of guests; it was more than 400! God had multiplied the food by 100 plates. I thanked Madison who chose to decree a thing rather than thaw hotdogs.

Thank you, Papa.

Luke 1:26-38

Luke 1:5-25

Job 22:28

Mark 6:33-44

Kingdom Principle: In the Kingdom, there is always enough. The Father is more than willing to provide everything we need or ask if we just say the word.

Prayer: "Jesus, today I commit to You that I will speak words of life over every situation, no matter how bleak. When I fail to remember to do that, will You whisper in my ear and remind me that death and life are in the power of my tongue? Amen."

Launch: Write down each difficulty you are facing in your life and in the lives of your loved ones. Be as honest as you can be. Now, craft a sentence of life over that situation. Repeat that sentence every day.

What changed?

_____

_____

_____

_____

_____

_____

_____

_____

_____

_____

DAY 13 – SEEING – BROWN GOLF SHIRT

The book of John gives a wonderful example in the Kingdom of God when Jesus selected His disciples. Philip was one of His selections. He was from Bethsaida. Philip then sought out and found his friend, Nathanael.

"We have found Him of whom Moses and the prophets wrote. Come and see."

When Nathanael came to meet Jesus, Jesus made an odd remark.

"Behold an Israelite in whom there is no guile."

Nathanael was confused.

"How do you know me?"

"Before Philip called you, when you were under the fig tree, I saw you." Jesus prophetically saw Nathanael in the Spirit first, received the information about the young man next, then spoke it. The encounter was shocking enough for the young man that he instantly proclaimed Jesus the Son of God.

In the book of Acts, a certain Roman centurion who had converted to Judaism had become a devout man and prayed continually. According to the story, at the ninth hour he saw a vision. An angel of God came to him and told him that his prayers had been heard. The angel commanded the centurion to send soldiers to Joppa to a certain house by the sea to retrieve a man by the name of Simon Peter.

While the soldiers made their way to the house, Simon Peter went up to the roof and fell into a trance. He saw a great sheet lowered from the sky by the four corners. In it, Peter saw all kinds of animals and birds. A voice cried out, "Arise, Peter, kill and eat!"

Alarmed, Peter protested, "By no means, Lord, for I have never eaten anything unholy and unclean."

The voice came to him again, "What God has cleansed, no longer consider unholy." This perplexed Peter and he wondered what this vision and voice might mean. At that moment, the soldiers sent to retrieve him stood at the gate. Peter heard the voice of the Spirit say to him, "Three men are looking for you. Arise and go with them, for I have sent them myself."

Peter did go to the centurion and preached the Good News to the man and his entire household. The Spirit of the Lord fell upon them all and they began to speak in tongues. Peter understood the meaning of the vision - that salvation was for all - and he baptized them into the faith.

The entire ordeal was the divine opening of the door of salvation to the Gentiles.

What an astonishing story. Two men had visions of what was to happen. They were obedient to the vision even though they were unclear of the outcome. Their obedience changed the course of history.

In like manner, we as believers have been given the gift to "see" in the Spirit and receive information about an individual. It has been my experience that when God shows me a person and a piece of information about them that I could not know, He is setting up a dramatic encounter with that individual.

I speak the knowledge that I have no way of knowing and, like Nathanael, the person is shocked and becomes open to receiving the message from God. I have seen some extraordinary things happen.

One such occurrence was in our Staff and Student Chapel. "Students" are those who are enrolled in one of the long-term programs at the Mission to get back on their feet and start a new life. The programs are free of charge and the "student" lives with us for 8 to 12 months. One of these long-term programs is for those who suffer from addiction. The homeless do not have the means to pay for a rehab facility. Their only hope to get clean is here with us.

Early that morning, I asked the Lord if He wanted to touch someone that day. I immediately saw a brown golf shirt. Again, that is an odd garment to be seen at the Mission, so I was dubious. Nevertheless, I got the impression of massive anger, the result of childhood exploitation, that had governed the individual's entire adulthood. His anger was a very old friend and demonic in nature. God wanted to heal the rage. The Father went on to tell me that this was a matter of life and death.

I wrote out God's message to whoever this was, about healing the deep hurts so that God could deliver the individual from the anger that had destroyed his life. As I entered the Chapel, I saw several brown shirts, but only one was a golf shirt belonging to a student sitting near the aisle.

I stood up and read the Word of knowledge to him. He immediately burst into tears and sobbed and sobbed. I went to him and spoke to him as a mama and prayed for the encounter.

God hovered over him and gloriously healed his old wounds and delivered him from the fury in his heart. The storm of tears finally passed, and he looked up at me, face glowing, and smiled. Complete peace rested on the young man.

Later he told me that very morning he had begged God to stop the torture of these uncontrollable emotions of anger or he would end his own life. That man is a new person now. He is happy, pleasant to be around, and has graduated the 12-month program to get clean and sober. Jesus came to set the captives free and that is just what he did that morning for John. He has since been reconciled with his family and is able to see his children again.

Jesus restored in one moment everything the enemy had stolen from John. He chose to use a little member of His flock who asked to see and to know. In the Kingdom, any little lamb who is willing will do.

John 1:43-51

Acts 10:1-48

I Corinthians 12:8–11

Kingdom Principle: If we ask, God opens the door to the Kingdom so that we as believers are able to see things that we cannot see in the physical realm, and we are able to know things we are not capable of knowing. In many cases, this gift is used by God to initiate an encounter between Himself and a wounded soul.

Prayer: "Jesus, teach me how to 'see' in the Kingdom of God. Enlarge the gifts of the Holy Spirit in me, that I might use them for Your purposes in the lives of those around me, just as You did when you walked upon the earth. Amen."

Initiation: In your quiet time, ask God to show you something about an acquaintance, not a good friend. You will "see" an image. Study the image and every detail. Ask God to show you the purpose of the image. Write it out. This takes diligence, so practice this technique several times. Then go to the acquaintance and ask if what you saw was significant.

Write down what happened:

_____

_____

_____

_____

_____

_____

_____

DAY 14 – THE MAILMAN – BILLY'S DIABETES

God is so kind to us. In His communications to His people, He uses different tools to get our attention so that we may serve those around us. For instance, many times the Father will whisper in our ear to give us a message that we can pass along to someone with whom He wishes to communicate. It is much like being a mailman. One small caveat is required of the mailman, that he make himself upright before the Lord by keeping a fearless moral inventory; when made aware of a wrongdoing, he promptly admits it to God.

Isaiah was one of God's mailmen. God showed Isaiah a beautiful vision. Isaiah witnessed God sitting on His throne high and lifted up. His train filled the temple. Isaiah was immediately made aware of his own sinfulness saying, "Woe is me for I am ruined because I am a man of unclean lips and I live among people with unclean lips; for my eyes have seen the King, the Lord of hosts."

A seraph touched Isaiah's lips with a burning coal. Instantly his iniquity was taken away, and his sins were forgiven.

Then Isaiah heard the Lord, say, 'Whom shall I send; and who will go for Us?" Then Isaiah said, "Here am I. Send me."

God sent Isaiah to the people of Judah with a message warning them of coming disaster if they did not turn from their sin, and wonderful things if they changed their ways. God tried over and over again to warn them through the prophet. One significant promise was of the coming

Messiah to save them. This promise included His miraculous birth as well as His suffering and death on our behalf.

Like Isaiah, I am painfully aware of my propensity to transgress. Many times, in my secret place, God will make me aware of a misdeed on my part. I have learned to promptly admit it and make amends with the offended party. I have had to make amends to my husband, my children, my friends, and to my superiors at one time or another. And I have had to make amends to my subordinates, which I found the most difficult.

There was an occasion when I spoke in anger to my assistant for overstepping her authority. Although justified, my words were harsh and unprofessional. Later that day, the Lord spoke to my heart about it. In that moment, I was not a worthy bearer of His name. I repented to Him but knew what I must do next. I went to my assistant's office and closed the door. I repented to her for my temper and asked for forgiveness. She readily forgave me, and all was made right. That afternoon she came to my office.

"Thank you for apologizing to me. I have never had a boss who apologized before," she said.

The words struck me hard; I knew they were significant. In the Kingdom, making amends to someone, regardless of one's relationship with them, is imperative. But even more significant is the supernatural power it wields. This was the coal to my lips, and I was forgiven…again. When the Lord speaks and says, "Whom shall I send, and who will go for Us?" I can say, "Here am I. Send me."

Shortly after that, the Father spoke to me that He wanted to heal diabetes. I spoke to the congregation in Chapel.

"Someone here has diabetes, and God wants to heal you today. If you have this and want to be healed, stand up." Three or so people stood up, including Billy who is on staff as Ranch Foreman at the Mission Ranch. He has Type 2 diabetes and must give himself insulin shots. Even with his shots, the blood sugar levels fluctuated dangerously up and down.

I asked those around the standing diabetics to place their hands on the pancreas of each individual. Billy's wife, also on staff, laid her hand on his pancreas. Our Board President laid her hand on the wife's. We began to pray.

At lunch, Billy checked his insulin levels. They were normal. He checked again at dinner; still normal. All week his levels were normal. He even ate a piece of cheesecake to see what would happen. Still normal. Billy is now off his insulin and continues to maintain normal blood sugar levels. God healed Billy that day he and remains in good health today. Thank you, Jesus, for Your faithfulness to Billy.

In order to become a mailman, one must listen carefully in the secret place regularly. The Father has things to say to each of us. This is not why I go to my secret place every morning. I go to be with my Friend and sit in His presence. I go to feel His touch and hear His voice, to drink Him in and immerse myself in His Word. That is where all the treasures are.

By the same token, that is where He whispers in my ear and speaks of making amends; it is where He gives assignments. I have found that the two are interrelated. It is an opportunity for believers to participate in His wondrous Kingdom that He has given every believer access to. It is our inheritance; it is His will.

Isaiah 6:1-9

Matthew 5:21-24

Galatians 5:19

Kingdom Principle: Making amends to anyone we have hurt, be it superior or subordinate or child or stranger, opens the door to the supernatural nature of the Kingdom.

Prayer: "God, teach me to hear and listen to Your whisper in my ear. Teach me how to make a fearless moral inventory. Teach me to be obedient to the message You wish to send to one of your little ones. Amen."

Activation: In your quiet time with the Lord, ask Him if there is anything between the two of you that needs to be dealt with. Be still and listen. When He speaks of any offense, promptly admit to it. Make amends to the ones whom you have hurt. Now ask Him if He has any messages He wishes to send today and, if so, to whom? What does He wish to say? Sit quietly and listen.

What did you hear?

DAY 15 — ACTION VS. REACTION — DISTENDED BELLY

Have you ever seen those little steel balls hanging by filament in a straight line? If you pull the end ball out and let it fall, when it hits the string of balls, the one on the opposite end flies out. It is the perfect illustration of Newton's Third Law of Motion, "For every action there is an equal and opposite reaction." In the physical world, this law holds true every time.

Likewise, in the Kingdom of Heaven it also holds true. For every action in the physical realm there is an equal and opposite action in the heavenly realm, or in the supernatural realm.

In the book of Acts, there is a head scratching story about Paul and Silas being beaten and thrown into prison. They were taken to the inner prison where their feet were fastened in the stocks. Around midnight, in that foul place probably teeming with mice, rats, and roaches, Paul and Silas began to sing hymns of praise to God as the other prisoners listened.

Suddenly, there came a great earthquake which shook the prison to its foundation. Astoundingly, all the doors flew open and the prisoners' chains came loose. The story goes on to tell of the jailer, who assumed the prisoners had all taken this remarkable opportunity to escape. He drew his sword to take his own life. Paul cried out to the man to reassure him that all the prisoners were still present.

The jailer called for lights and rushed into the depths of the prison trembling with fear. He fell before Paul and Silas and asked, "Sirs, what must I do to be saved?" He and his entire household were saved that night and baptized. He took the two, washed their wounds, and led them to his house where he fed them at his own table, all the while rejoicing in his salvation.

It is extraordinary the things God will do to reach the lost. What this tells me is that physical praise and worship create a reaction in the heavenly realm. I firmly believe that Paul and Silas's worship caused an earthquake that opened the doors and created an opportunity to bring an unbeliever to salvation.

In like manner, your praise and worship in the sacred place impacts the rest of your day in a very concrete way. Whether singing Him a song of praise, or adoring Him by calling out His many names, you are storing up a reserve in Heaven that you can access when a need, illness, or situation may occur.

One day in Guest Chapel, the speaker was my old pastor and friend who taught me the truth about the Father's wish to be worshiped and the miracles that come from that. He gave a simple but profound message on the Father's love; many accepted Christ that day.

Afterward, we invited anyone who wished to come up for prayer. A woman came up crying about a pain in her belly. I noticed that her belly was so large that the buttons on her smock were pulled tight across her front. She appeared to be carrying twins but was not. Alarmed at her tears and the pain, I told her we ought to call 911 for immediate help. My guest speaker scoffed at me and instructed me to just pray for the woman. I laid my palm on her distended belly and began to pray for healing.

Suddenly her belly vanished under my hand, like a large balloon had just popped! I jerked my hand away. Her smock hung loosely on her frame. Dumbfounded, I was unsure of what had just happened. I was not sure that I saw what I saw. I turned to my old friend.

"Did you see that?" I asked my friend.

He smiled as he nodded in affirmation. He was not nearly as nonplussed as I was.

The woman grinned happily and skipped off to lunch in the dining room, evidently pain free. I, on the other hand, was still in shock. I had heard of this type of miracle before but had never seen one.

I kept asking my friend if that really did just happen. He laughed and assured me that it had. I never knew what malady the woman suffered from, and it really did not matter, but there was definitely a reaction to my action that day.

The daily praise and worship that I had offered to God caused a heavenly bank account to reserve those actions. The moment I prayed for the woman, the reserve was available for me to draw upon and set into motion a miracle.

Acts 16:22-34

II Chronicles 20:21

Kingdom Principle: Adoration and worship invites an encounter with our Lord. In His presence, the Kingdom releases itself into a reserve that can be drawn upon at any time.

Prayer: "Lord, teach me about this action and reaction in the Kingdom. Show me Your truth about praise, adoration, and encounter. Call to my remembrance the stories of old in the Scriptures that illustrate this principle. Amen."

Try this: Spend time in praise and worship every day for 2 weeks. Go through the following days with intention, looking for an opportunity to pray for a stranger. When you see it, act upon it. Then watch for the reaction.

What happened?

_____

_____

_____

_____

_____

DAY 16 — JOY — WANDA

In the Kingdom of God, the most precious commodity seems not to be silver or gold or even precious stones. In Heaven, gold appears to be a common construction material. But rather peace, joy, and righteousness seem to be the coveted commodities.

The book of Hebrews says it best, "But for the joy set before Him He endured the cross." We are His joy. Joy over us was so important to Him that He suffered indescribable torture to win it. That kind of sacrifice is extraordinary to me.

In the book of John, Jesus speaks specifically about how our bearing fruit in the Kingdom brings Him joy. Furthermore, He states that our bearing fruit will bring us joy. I can honestly testify to that in my own experience and in the lives of others who participate in the Kingdom. I have known no greater joy than seeing a little one come to know this Deliverer or be healed of a deadly disease.

In the book of Luke, Jesus sent the 70 out in pairs to preach the Gospel, heal the sick, and cast out demons. When they returned, they were full of joy and told Jesus all that they had experienced. In turn, Jesus was said to have "rejoiced greatly in the Holy Spirit."

The word "rejoiced" used in that verse translates from the original Greek as "leaping for joy, leaping and skipping." Leaping is an extravagant expression of joy commonly seen at sporting events; yet, our Savior did just that because He saw Satan fall from Heaven like lightning.

Jesus rejoiced at the work of the 70, just as He rejoices when we call upon His power to heal the sick, preach the Gospel, cast out demons, or simply give a cup of cold water to one of the least of these sisters and brothers of His.

One day in Chapel, I was preaching to the guests off the street. On the front row was a woman who was very drunk. Her skin was yellow and shriveled up like a raisin. My guess was that she had Hepatitis C, a common disease we see here at the Mission. I preached a message about Jesus and what He did for each of us. When I gave the invitation to meet Him personally, she prayed the prayer at the top of her lungs along with others.

Afterward, I explained that I would stay and pray with anyone for anything. The drunken woman came up with tears in her eyes.

"I have had Hep C for 15 years. This week, the doctor told me that I am at the end of the end. My liver is ruined. He put me on Interferon. What's to be done?"

I told her that we could go to God and ask Him. I prayed a short prayer over her, and she went to lunch in the dining room.

The following Monday as I approached my office, there sat the woman with Hep C from Chapel. Her eyes were as big as saucers. She was pink; she was plump; she was as sober as a judge. She looked so beautiful and healthy.

"Wanda! You look great! Did you go to a spa this weekend?" I jokingly asked.

"No, I went to my doctor. He did a scan of my liver and told me that my liver was inexplicably normal and healthy!"

We hugged and cried at the news. God had healed her of a disease that is rarely healed medically. She suddenly drew back and whispered, "Do you know what this means?"

"No, Wanda, what does it mean?"

"It means God loves me!"

I thought to myself, "Yes, Wanda, God loves you. He healed you in the midst of your drunkenness."

Some might say that, as a drunk, her health problems were all her own fault, that she was just reaping what she had sown. For me, though, my joy was made full that day to see God's grace and mercy on one of His little lost lambs. Thank God that none of us get what we truly deserve, or we would all be little piles of ash.

Instead, He used one little lamb to heal another little lamb so that our joy would be full. That is how the Kingdom of God works. We get to watch it unfold miraculously before our eyes. All we must do is be willing to participate.

Hebrews 12:2

John 15:1-11

Luke 10:17-21

Kingdom Principle: In the Kingdom, those who extend grace, help, healing, or deliverance to another experience uncontainable joy along with the miraculous.

Prayer: "Jesus, You rejoice at our joy when we take part in the Kingdom, bringing others into Your fold, casting out demons, healing the sick, or just showing kindness. Show me ways to take part in the Kingdom that brings You joy and brings me joy. Amen."

Assignment: Today, find one person whom you do not know who needs a touch from God. Encourage them in some way and pray for them out loud and in public. You will experience joy.

Write down what happened.

_____

_____

_____

DAY 17 – OBEDIENCE – WHEELCHAIR ON THE CORNER

I have come to realize that many times God orchestrates a "divine bump" along our busy path. In other words, as we go through our day, we may "bump into" someone who desperately needs a touch, a healing, or an encouraging word from the Lord. Next comes the nudge from Holy Spirit to approach the stranger and help.

Jesus spent most of His ministry "bumping into" people that came into His path. In some cases, He actually approached individuals to heal them, like the man at the pool of Bethesda and the woman at the well. Ninety-nine percent of His ministry happened outside of church with total strangers.

We have a choice to make. Will we initiate a conversation that might lead to something else, or won't we? We can choose to be obedient to the nudge by stopping the car, the cart, the shopping, the errands to fully engage the Kingdom, or we can say, "I am already so late!" and go about our busy day. Sadly, many times I have opted out of the encounter.

For instance, there was a period of time when everywhere I went, I saw people with canes, wheelchairs, crutches, or terrible limps. I felt the Lord nudge me to "bump into" these dear people and pray for them. For a while, I made one excuse after another as to why I could not take the time to stop and visit with them.

Inexplicably, as time went on, I realized I was not seeing any crippled people anymore, not one. I regretted my excuses, so I went to the Lord and repented for my disobedience. I promised that the very next person I saw who was lame in one way or another would receive my attention.

The very next morning on my way to work, I saw what appeared to be a homeless man in a wheelchair on a very busy downtown street corner during 8 a.m. traffic. I stomped on the brakes and pulled over. Miraculously there was an open parking place right next to the gentleman. I jumped out of the car and walked over to the corner where he was waiting for the light to change.

"Excuse me, but I could not help but notice that you are in a wheelchair. Are you hurt?" I asked.

"Yeah, I took a mortar in my thigh in Vietnam. I haven't walked since."

"Well, do you mind if I pray for you?"

"No, not at all."

I leaned over and touched his leg and began to pray God's blessing and healing on him. Suddenly, the power of God hit us both. He began to shout and wave his hands in the air. I joined in, and we looked, I'm sure, like a couple of drunken fools, singing and praising God right in the middle of morning traffic. It was glorious.

I was still very new to healing and did not know to ask him to try something he could not do before, but it did not matter. We both had an outrageous encounter with the Lord that day.

There is a Scripture in Psalm 103 that says, "The angels obey the voice of His word, and go about doing His will." It is said that my action to His Word releases angelic assistance. If that is so, what does my inaction do?

God lets us choose whether we want to be a part of His supernatural world or not. My choice not to participate through my many excuses is my choice. It has been my experience that those excuses dry up opportunities to see signs and wonders, such as blind eyes opening, the lame walking, the food multiplying.

Jesus said that we would do greater works than He did. That statement right there scrambles my brain. But if I, like a child, just believe that it is true, then it is true for me. If I do not believe it is true, then it is not true for me. I choose to believe.

I do not know if the gentleman in the wheelchair got healed. Again, I am just the UPS guy. I deliver packages from the Lord. This I do know. The gentleman had an encounter with the living God that day, and that makes it a good day.

John 5:2-11

Psalm 103:20-21

John 14:12-15

Kingdom Principle: Stepping out in obedience and approaching strangers to pray for them opens the heavens and releases the supernatural in the Kingdom.

Prayer: "Lord, would You open my eyes to the opportunities all around me today? Will You give me a nudge when You want to do something in someone's life? Will You remind me that I asked for the nudge and promised to stop and engage? Amen."

Activation: Today, look with purpose for a stranger whom God highlights to you. Pause for the nudge. Strike up a conversation with the individual. Look for the tell that needs an encounter. Then introduce God's purpose for the encounter.

What did you experience?

_____

_____

_____

_____

_____

DAY 18 – COURAGE – STROKE VICTIM

In the study of the Kingdom of God, there appears to be a particularly powerful rate of exchange that we, as believers, have access to. Courage seems to be looked upon as the gold standard in the heavenlies. There are myriads of stories in Scripture about men and women who risked everything, even their lives, to do what was asked of them. In the book of Joshua, God told the young warrior over and over to be strong and courageous while leading Israel into battle.

Esther was threatened with annihilation. Abigail bravely faced a very angry David and his men to smooth over the blatant snub by her husband. Both showed extraordinary bravery in the face of death. David and the apostles also faced incredible threats and danger. In each case, their courage unlocked a miraculous victory, deliverance, or healing.

One story in the book of Chronicles is about a particularly difficult battle in which the children of Judah had no hope of winning. Three foreign kings rose up against Jehoshaphat and Judah. Nevertheless, King Jehoshaphat and all the people fasted and prayed, and all of Judah came together to seek the Lord. The Lord assured them of victory, but the strategy was very odd indeed.

The king placed the praise and worship team in front of the troops to walk into battle without even a shield. It was a suicide mission at best. And yet, these priests and worshipers went out in Holy attire in front of the troops. They began to sing, "Give thanks to the Lord for His lovingkindness is everlasting." That must have taken extraordinary courage. The Lord set ambushes against the enemy army and rerouted them all. Because of their insane courage, Judah won the day.

The astonishing story of David and Goliath is another stunning example of courage. David was sent to the front lines of battle to take food to his brothers in the military. Apparently, David was too young to join the army. He was probably in his preteens. When he heard the giant Goliath hurling obscenities at the Israelites, he was outraged that nothing was being done about it. He bravely went up against Goliath with five little stones and a slingshot, knowing that the Lord would deliver the Israelites for he knew the battle belonged to the Lord.

As the stone was launched, it hit squarely in the giant's forehead and he fell on his face to the ground. Typically, the force of the stone would have driven the man backward, but clearly, he fell forward. He was supernaturally pushed to the ground from behind. The battle was indeed the Lord's and David was the catalyst to victory.

For me, it takes every ounce of courage to stop someone in a store and ask to pray for them. Yet, God asks it of me. Recently as I approached Walmart, I saw a gentleman standing by the curb leaning on a cane. His right side was clearly paralyzed, and his right hand was drawn up in a fist. Initially, I planned to walk on by to enter the store with my grandson who was nine. Yet, I knew I had to stop since I had just begun a page in this book on courage. Do I practice what I encouraged others to do or not?

I stopped and said, "Good morning," then commented on his cane. I asked him, "What happened?"

His words were slurred as he explained the massive stroke that he had suffered. His speech, limbs, and hand on the right side had been affected. Just then, a pickup rolled up and a gentleman got out and came around to help the fellow into the truck. I asked if I could pray for him. They both enthusiastically agreed. My grandson laid hands on the man. The helper also laid his hand on the man. I joined in and began to pray. People were coming and going all around us. Some stopped to listen.

As I finished, I encouraged the guy with the story of Mark on the scooter (Day 8) who had suffered the same type of stroke and was completely healed.

"Don't throw away your seed of healing," I said. "Hang onto it." Then men both smiled at me and we parted ways. Did he get a healing? I don't know. But this much I do know, he may not recover if I did not pray for him. My job was to be brave and courageous.

It does not seem to get easier to walk up to a stranger and ask to pray with them. The fear is magnified by years and years of upbringing that dictated social protocol: "Do not bother people, especially strangers. It is inappropriate." Nevertheless, the desire to see Heaven come down and change everything for that stranger motivates me to overcome my fear and my upbringing.

Is it scary? Absolutely. But, as one Christian leader said, "Just do it afraid." That is good advice in the Kingdom.

Joshua 1:6-9

I Samuel 17:26-50

II Chronicles 20:1-25

Kingdom Principle: Bravery and courage are a rate of exchange in the Kingdom of God that set into motion the supernatural.

Prayer: "Lord, thank You for the opportunity to take part in the Kingdom of God. Make me strong. Make me brave. Give me courage to introduce others to Your Kingdom, Your ways, and Your overwhelming love. Amen."

Launch: Today, approach a stranger who appears to be injured or ill. Strike up a short conversation, then ask if you might pray for him or her. Pray the Kingdom would come to them today.

Record the interchange and how God impacted that person (if known). How did it impact you?

DAY 19 – POWER – HIV

In exploring this realm of signs and wonders, I have discovered that when I read the Word, I must be careful to read without preconceived ideas or thoughts about a passage according to the last sermon I heard on it. What does that mean? It means that we as Christians tend to read the Word of God with denominational glasses. Different groups and denominations try to persuade other believers with distinct interpretations of the Word. How the Church interprets the verse is how we see it.

Growing up, I heard the Holy Writ interpreted in very cerebral ways. As a new believer, I read the Word through the opinions of the woman who brought me to salvation, with the eyes of a prepper (one who stores food water and guns to survive the really bad times in the near future). "The end is coming!"

By the same token, I also heard the interpretation of another group that says one must behave oneself or else.

Then there was the punitive way of looking at the Word, "Father's got a big iron skillet in His hand and He's not afraid to use it."

Of course, there is the more recent understanding, "It's a party! Free food and BMW's!" I soon learned to take off all the glasses and read Scripture with the heart of a child.

I stumbled onto the special verse in I Corinthians 2:4,5. It was such a simple verse that you could read right over it. But when I read it with my Kingdom glasses on, it changed everything for me.

Paul said, "And my message and my preaching were not in persuasive words." Well, there went the denominational approach to the Kingdom. He goes on to say, "but in the demonstration of the Spirit and of power." What does that mean? Demonstration of the Spirit? Of power?

I always thought those verses were referring to the Scripture that reads, "Thine be the kingdom and the power and the glory forever and ever. Amen." All that glory and power was in Heaven, or so I was led to believe. But now, with new glasses, I realize that it *is* in Heaven, but it also comes to earth.

Eureka, there it is, hiding in plain sight. "Thy Kingdom come, Thy will be done on earth as it is in Heaven." Good heavens!

How does that work, bringing the Kingdom to earth?

Are You asking me to do something that I am not capable of doing? To walk in power? Like Paul? I am no Paul. But then, Paul was no Paul either. He was a one-man black op wrecking ball for the government. Then Jesus wrecked *him* and gave him new glasses. He literally saw the light, and then the dark, and then the light again. He was never the same.

I deduce then that entrance into the Kingdom might sometimes involve a wrecking ball so to speak. For example, something must be burned away and a part of someone needs to die. For some it requires blowing some breakers altogether. Now who is the black ops guy? It would seem that the Holy Spirit might operate in that area as well.

There was a young man who came to us to get clean and sober. His complexion was the color of concrete. He had been HIV positive for 15 years. His lifestyle had rendered him a very sick man with no hope of recovery, save a ground-breaking new drug which had not materialized as of yet. Nevertheless, he worked a good program for twelve months and graduated. He came on staff, went into our chef training program, and worked hard in the kitchen. He was creative with the food budget and tried many new dishes to serve the guests. You might say he added a bit of flare to our food services department. But still, he was losing ground physically.

One day he came to me and asked that the staff pray for him. He was having a biopsy on a melanoma on his shoulder. At our weekly staff meeting, we gathered around him and prayed for healing.

The following week, I walked into the lobby of the Mission and saw a crowd of people crying. Alarmed, I asked, "What happened?"

No one paid attention to me. I put on my Director's voice and demanded, "What happened?"

The crowd parted and there was Ben sobbing. I feared the worst and went to him.

"What happened, Ben?"

He flipped his phone open and went to his voicemail. Then he selected a voicemail and put it on speaker for all to hear.

"Ben, this is Doctor 'P'. I have the results of your tests. Your melanoma is benign. But in addition to that, you are no longer testing positive for HIV."

I was stunned! HIV positive is not healed medically. And yet, here is a doctor confirming it. I hugged Ben and cried like a little girl. This little one had his life back. What a sweet and gracious God. He healed Ben and gave him a new life, despite his former lifestyle. Jesus wrecked Ben that day and burned his wires with His powerful love.

"I did not come in words of persuasion, but in demonstration of the Spirit and of Power." Sometimes, I am so undone by the Kingdom that I am speechless. Maybe that is for the best.

Matthew 6:9-13

I Corinthians 2:1–5

Acts 9:1-9

Kingdom Principle: The Kingdom is not predicated on wisdom, or brilliance, or education. It comes in power by the Holy Spirit.

Prayer: "Jesus, I am not eloquent or wise, but I am willing. Do what You must in order for me to enter the Kingdom in power. If something in me needs to be burned away, do it. Please do it! Amen."

Initiate: Today, make a list of characters in the Bible who experienced a cataclysmic encounter with God. Document what happened initially, and then what God called them to do.

What pattern did you discover?

_____

_____

_____

_____

_____

_____

_____

_____

_____

_____

_____

DAY 20 – CHARITY – YARD SALE

Jesus said a lot of things that cause Christians to scratch their heads in confusion. One such discourse is in the book of Luke where he said to His disciples, "Consider the lilies, how they grow; they neither toil nor spin; but I tell you even Solomon in all his glory did not clothe himself as one of these. But if God so arrays the grass in the field which is alive today and tomorrow is thrown into the furnace, how much more will He clothe you, oh men of little faith. And do not seek what you shall eat and what you shall drink, and do not keep worrying…your Father knows you need these things. But seek first His Kingdom, and these things shall be added to you. Do not be afraid, little flock, for your Father has chosen gladly to give you the Kingdom. Sell your possessions and give to charity."

In today's world, relying on God to provide all of these things is inconceivable to 99% of those who call themselves Christians. The reasoning in today's western world is that we must work hard to earn the money to obtain our needs and wants. Some believe it is the church's responsibility to provide those in need, while others believe it should be left to the government. After all, we tithe to the church and pay taxes to the government so let them handle the needs of the people. Evidently, Jesus had another way. A higher way. The Kingdom's way. If I am going to inherit this place, what is to be done with it, and what is my job description concerning it and my money?

My first clue seemed to be this statement, "Do not keep worrying," and "Sell your possessions and give to charity." That seemed a little excessive. But could it be that we, as individuals, might provide out of our own storehouses that which is God's to give? By giving it all to the church or the government, do we abdicate our own responsibilities of hearing from the Lord on what to do each day for those around us? I have been on a journey for many years to become a student of the Kingdom of which He speaks. One very important discovery was that we, as believers, are expected to participate with our possessions instead of mindlessly handing them off to someone else to do it for us, whether that be monetary or otherwise. I am not advocating to not pay one's taxes or tithing. I am just challenging the reader to look at things another way.

Early on in our marriage, my husband and I realized that in joining two families, our five children needed a great deal from us. Three had lost their mother to cancer, and two had been through a divorce. By the same token, we as a newlywed couple, desperately need time together. We hit upon the idea of a night class at the local college, giving us one night out a week. We settled on a photography class. Instantly it became our new passion. The photo shoots required outings. As a family, we packed up the kids and the car with the camera equipment, a large picnic basket, and sunscreen. It was wonderful time tramping through hill and dale, shooting up film, and posing the kids.

The dark room was a magical place where images inexplicably appeared on paper. We quickly decided that we needed a dark room at home to develop the myriads of shots we took. The problem lay in the cost of such an endeavor. And, like most Americans' solution to a cost issue, we planned a garage sale. We had so many duplicate items when we combined our households, especially appliances both large and small, washers, dryers, refrigerators, mixers, televisions, and stereos. With such large ticket items, we were certain we would be able to make enough to buy at least *some* dark room equipment.

The day of the sale was approaching when we received a call that one of my husband's employees suffered a house fire. No one was hurt, but everything was lost. The family was able to use a vacant house of a relative but had nothing in the way of furnishings. I began to be nudged. I knew what the Lord wanted us to do. I just did not want to do it. All of the furniture, appliances, and other "big ticket" items were desperately needed by this family. Depressed, I went to my husband to break the news about the Father's wishes. He agreed that we had to do it. We made the call and a trailer soon arrived to take the majority of our sale items away. The family was so very grateful, and we knew we had done the right thing, but still…

The day of the garage sale arrived. We put out our meager items. The sales were sparse. At the end of the day, we received a phone call from a woman concerning the sale. We did not recall placing our phone number in the ad. We quickly found the classified section of the paper to see if we had put it in the ad for the garage sale. Right there next to our ad was another yard sale ad reading, "Dark room equipment and cameras" and an address. We looked at each other speechless.

"Could we...?'

"Should we...?"

We counted the money in the cash box again to see if it had grown at all. It was still the same meager sum as before. Deciding it could not hurt, we picked up the cash box and drove to the address.

As we arrived, we were stunned. Strewn across the lawn was every conceivable piece of dark room equipment: an enlarger, pans, red lights, tongs, film canisters, photo paper, a timer, a huge heating press, and an impeccable medium format camera complete with tripod and film holders, similar to the one used by Ansel Adams. It was like Christmas morning.

A young man came out to greet us. He explained that his mother was a photojournalist of some distinction. This was her dark room equipment. She had recently passed away, and he had no use for it.

"How much for the enlarger?" we tentatively asked.

He crossed his arms and looked around, taking in everything laying on his lawn. Spreading his arms, he casually said, "For everything I would take $300.00."

We stared at him dumbfounded. It was exactly the amount in our cash box, and the camera alone was worth triple that at least.

We handed him the cash box and loaded everything into the car. As we made our way home, we marveled at the whole affair. We had given everything away, made an insubstantial meager sum from what was left, got a random call from a woman which compelled us to check the paper, which led to the yard sale ad, which led us to the yard full of equipment beyond our wildest dreams. This all cost exactly what was in our cash box. What are the chances of that? God has such a sense of humor.

For the first time in my life I understood the "charity" part of that verse. One access point into the Kingdom is charity. As believers, we all have access to the Kingdom of God if we choose to participate, but you might want to buckle your seatbelt. It's a wild ride.

Luke 6:38

Luke 12:22–32

James 2:15

Kingdom Principle: Giving always activates receiving.

Prayer: "Father, thank You for revealing to me another characteristic of the Kingdom. Today, I will give generously to charity. Amen."

Assignment: Sell a possession and give the income to charity.

Record your feelings about that.

_____

_____

_____

_____

DAY 21 – BOLDNESS – GAS STATION

In recent days, there has been a lot of doom and gloom amidst the body of Christ in America.

Many are upset at the divisiveness and agitation caused by the media over present-day issues, as well as foreign policies. The continuous shootings and bombings, especially in churches, have believers on edge. There is a great deal of fear as to where things are heading for Christians. The subject can be heard in many places, especially from the pulpit. Some seem to want to hunker down and wait it out until Jesus comes back and kicks some backsides.

Why some seem frustrated by the prejudice and condemnation aimed at believers is a mystery. Jesus told us it would be this way. He told us clearly of the persecution to come. He instructed us not to be anxious, but "the one who endures to the end shall be saved."

In the early church it was suicide to be a Christian, let alone preach this new life. The holy ones were so extraordinarily bold. Reading the book of Acts is like reading an espionage novel; murder, prison, disappearances, safehouses, even secret codes. Believers were being martyred on a regular basis. They counted it a supreme honor to be chosen to be a martyr. Today, in other countries, it is already taking place.

There is a passage in Acts that has inspired me so very much. I read it often to realign my prayers with the Father's will.

"And now, Lord, take note of their threats, and grant that Thy bondservants may speak Thy word with all confidence, while Thou dost extend Thy hand to heal and signs and wonders to take place through the name of Thy holy servant Jesus. And when they prayed, the place where they had gathered together was shaken and they were all filled with the Holy Spirit and began to speak the Word of God with boldness."

New believers prayed for more boldness, not for safety from danger, or prejudice when threatened with peril if they continued to spread the good news and perform signs and wonders.

Boldness releases dunamis power from the Holy Spirit to do great exploits, miracles, signs, and wonders. Is it frightening? Is it dangerous? Absolutely. What has that got to do with anything? Sudden death means sudden glory.

In the book of Matthew, the disciples ask Jesus to explain the end of the age to them and His coming back. He went into great detail about the signs at the end; wars, rumors of wars, tribulation, falling away from the faith, and lawlessness.

But more intriguing is His disclosure of His return and the judgement. The entire procedure centers around one thing, whether one fed, invited in, clothed, ministered to, or visited the less fortunate in the land. That's it. The sum total of the trial is predicated on these deeds. It is all mentioned again in the book of Revelation at the judgement seat.

Some say these are not the Christians, but the unbelievers. Maybe, maybe not. I am no scholar, but it does appear to be quite important to Jesus how one treats the little ones.

It is most unfortunate that there are lost and dying angry, hateful, hurting, and drug infested people out there who are lost sheep. It is unfortunate that few have had the boldness to leave the four walls of the church and go to the streets to gather such sheep.

One day I was filling up my car at the gas station when I noticed a beautiful young woman pulling up in an old boat of a vehicle. It was one of those big sedans where the trunk is the size of a double bed. There was a toddler in the backseat. She went into the store presumably to pay for her gas. I watched her come out, place the nozzle into the tank, and begin to fill the car up. In less than twenty seconds, the pump stopped.

"Something must be wrong with the pump," I thought. She began to withdraw the nozzle and put her gas cap back on.

"Excuse me, I noticed your pump already shut off; is it not working?"

"No, I only had a little cash to pay for a gallon of gas, but I was sitting on empty, so I put in what I could."

I thought to myself, "In that old boat, a gallon will be gone in the next block."

"Well, do you mind if I put some more gas in your car, just to get you further down the road?"

She looked a little shocked but agreed. I carry a debit card in my wallet that is connected to a separate bank account for just such emergencies as this. It is used to help strangers out of a predicament. It is my personal benevolence fund. I was introduced to this idea by a very wise and faithful believer. This way, when I see a stranger in need, I am equipped to help.

I must say, that old car had a bottomless pit of a tank. As it was filling, we talked. She lived with her sister to save on rent. They worked separate shifts. The sister's shift was in the day and the girl in front of me kept her niece. Then she took a night shift while her sister held down the fort. Still, it was tight for them.

It is the story of the working poor. They do not have access to higher education, so they work at minimum wage and do not make enough to make ends meet. Their lives get very complicated. One dead battery can blow the whole game for them. Our Mission and many churches have a benevolence fund for just such emergencies.

The girl looked at me a little suspiciously. "Why are you, a stranger, doing this for me?"

"Because once a long time ago a stranger saved my life. May I pray for you?"

We held hands right there at the gas pump and I prayed for a miracle for her. In this case, I prayed for a better job, with benefits, and for God to touch her there in that moment. She began to cry oceans of tears. All the pent-up frustrations and injustices melted away under Holy Spirit's hand. When the prayer was over, she smiled and hugged me.

My act of kindness was a small drop in this girl's bucket, and yet the kindness had a larger impact on her than the actual gasoline in her tank. Holy Spirit wanted to touch this beautiful one. He needed me to be alert and available to be bold with the girl. Was there an earth-shattering miracle that day? For the girl, there was. I was God's errand runner in that moment.

The question is, whose miracle are you?

Matthew 25:4-6

Acts 4:29

I Peter 4:14

Matthew 25:31-40

Kingdom Principle: Boldness to help the stranger releases miracles.

Prayer: "Father, will You use me in the Kingdom? Will You give me the boldness to step out of my safe world into a world I know nothing about and that I am a little frightened of? Will You open my eyes and show me today someone who just needs a touch from You? Will You let me be Your errand runner today? Amen."

Assignment: Today, place some cash in the back of your wallet to be used only for someone else's emergencies. Stay alert for an opportunity to touch someone with the power of the Holy Spirit. Then do it.

What happened today?

_____

_____

_____

Boldness to help the
stranger releases miracles.

DAY 22 — THE DESPERATE — DANE

In Jesus's Kingdom, we are constantly told to do things that are not within our power to do. Upon His departure from the earth, He gave us some alarming instructions, "And these signs will accompany those who believe. In My name they will cast out demons. They will speak with new tongues. They will lay hands on the sick and they shall recover." Any believer has access to these powers.

When I am in Homeless Chapel at the Mission, I tell the guests, "If you are a believer, you have healing in your hands. Lay your hands on those standing up for a miracle."

At first, they would not even let *me* lay hands on them. But over the years of preaching to them every week, they have come to trust me, and they are beginning to trust each other. Now, they watch with wonder as the person who they are praying for is healed, or they themselves are healed.

Unfortunately, many churchgoers, while they may hope to see such miracles, do not really expect to see anything change. Maybe that is because psychologically, they know that they have an alternative route to healing.

The health insurance cards that many of us carry give us access to health care and allow us the luxury of this alternative route should the miracle fail to materialize. Don't misunderstand me; I am grateful to have insurance and treatment.

Sadly though, the homeless are not afforded that luxury. Aside from free clinics, which are usually overcrowded, marginal, and take forever to even get into, this group of people has a desperation built into their ailments.

It might be that the desperate have a great deal more to lose "if this prayer does not work." My belief is that there may be a Kingdom principle to be learned here.

Last year, I tore my rotator cuff hiking with too much weight in my backpack: fly fishing gear, waders, boots, dinner, first aid kit, water, raingear, and dry socks. The orthopedic surgeon felt there was no alternative for me but surgery. We scheduled everything, and I went for prayer. I believed God would heal me without surgery. In fact, I felt a gift of faith surge up in me.

To my dismay, I was not supernaturally healed, and I went ahead with surgery (via that insurance card). I felt deflated and disappointed as I wore that brace for six weeks and dealt with terrible post-surgical pain. During this time of wearing the cumbersome "tool of torture," a homeless man named Dane came up to me in Chapel and asked for prayer for his shoulder.

"I finally found a job and I start tomorrow. The problem is, I just tore my rotator cuff again and now I can't do the heavy lifting. I will lose the job. I am desperate. Will you pray for me?"

The irony of the situation did not escape me, but those words that he uttered, "I am desperate," caught my attention. I looked at the shoulder in question and saw a severe sag. His arm hung limply; he had no range of motion and could not lift his arm out in front of him.

I am no doctor and have little knowledge of human anatomy, but clearly there was a problem. I laid my hands on his shoulder and prayed for a miracle for Dane. He left for the dining room to eat lunch.

The next afternoon, as I was preparing to leave for the day, Dane popped his head into my office.

"Look, Mrs. Taylor! God healed my shoulder! It works! I got up this morning and tried a pushup to see if it was healed. It's perfect. I worked all day and look! It's still good to go. I just had to come by and tell you."

I am a very little person in the Kingdom and will not even attempt to build a theology around what did and did not happen there. I was not healed, but Dane was. Understanding that outcome is for a far more educated mind than mine. However, it does not preclude me from doing what Jesus commanded, to lay hands on the sick and see them recover.

Mark 16:17

I Samuel 2:8

Psalm 72: 12-14

Kingdom Principle: The hopeless, desperate, and needy are precious in His sight and they are able to gain access to the Kingdom.

Prayer: "Jesus, You are my rock, my fortress, and my high tower. I run to You in my desperation. I run to You in my weakness. Lord, help me in my affliction. Amen."

Try this: Search for opportunities today to lay hands on anyone who will let you and pray for them. Do this for at least three people.

Write down how each person responded to Holy Spirit.

_____

_____

_____

_____

_____

The hopeless, desperate, and needy are precious in His sight and gain access to the Kingdom.

DAY 23 – THE BOOKS – STALLED TRUCK

In the book of Daniel, he makes mention of a dream and a vision he saw in his mind while lying on his bed. The dream was a convoluted unfolding of four winds and great beasts devouring and crushing things. Toward the end of the dream, he looked and saw a very different scene, one of thrones and the Ancient of Days, burning wheels, and fire.

I kept looking until thrones were set up, and the Ancient of Days took His seat; His vesture was like white snow and the hair of His head like pure wool. His throne was ablaze with flames, its wheels were a burning fire. A river of fire was flowing and coming out from before Him; thousands upon thousands were attending Him, and myriads upon myriads were standing before Him; the court sat, and the books were opened.

Daniel 7:9-10

Almost as an afterthought, he mentions "the books" that were opened. We have heard of "The Book," which is the book of life, but it is a little unclear as to what "the books" are.

"The books" are mentioned again in John's vision while on the Isle of Patmos.

Then I saw a great white throne and Him who sat upon it, from whose presence earth and heaven fled away, and no place was found for them. And I saw the dead, the great and the small, standing before the throne, and books were opened; and another book was opened, which is the book of life; and the dead were judged from the things which were written in the books, according to their deeds.

Revelation 20:11-12

Again, "the books" are opened "and the dead are judged from things which were written in the books according to their deeds." That one sentence gives one pause. What deeds?

I have discovered mention of these books elsewhere in scripture. Psalm 139 mentions the books that were written about us when we were just "unformed substance."

For You formed my inward parts; You wove me in my mother's womb. I will give thanks to You, for I am fearfully and wonderfully made; wonderful are Your works, and my soul knows it very well. My frame was not hidden from You, when I was made in secret, and skillfully wrought in the depths of the earth; Your eyes have seen my unformed substance; and in Your book were all written the days that were ordained for me, when as yet there was not one of them.

Psalm 139:13-16

In verse 16, the word *"ordained"* could be translated as *"predestined,"* i.e. molded into, as a potter molds what he wishes out of clay. Everything we are destined to do in the Kingdom are in the books. All the hopes, dreams, and plans that God has for our lives are there. It is our choice whether we do those things or not.

One day I was late for work; it was already 9:30. I may have been driving "with great haste." As I drove down the freeway, I noticed a woman sitting on the tailgate of a very old truck. The hood to the engine was up. I kept going. The Lord spoke to me and said, "Jena, what do you all do at the Mission?"

"Well, we help people who are in need and cannot help themselves."

"What about the woman with the truck?"

"Well, I am really late for work. It's already 9:30."

"Your point being?"

"Fine! I'll turn around and see what I can do."

I exited and drove back to the truck. I parked on the access road and hobbled over the trash strewn grass in my heels to the edge of the freeway where the truck was stopped.

"Excuse me, do you need some help?"

The woman jumped off the tailgate and came toward me. "Oh, thank God you stopped! I have been stranded here since 6:30 this morning! And not one person would stop. I took my son to work, and on the way home the truck just quit. I left my cell phone at home."

I knew this was way above my pay grade, so I retrieved my cell phone and dialed the Mission. There was a wonderful man on staff who took care of our fleet of vehicles and could fix anything.

"Ron, we have a situation. A truck is broken down and I need for you to bring your tools, a sack lunch, and a bottle of water to this location."

As I rang off, a vehicle rolled up behind the truck. It was the woman's husband. He had begun to worry about her and came looking for her. As we waited for Ron, we talked and visited about the difficulties they had been through lately. This just seemed to be one more addition to an extensive list of disappointments and failures. I suggested we pray. On the side of the freeway, we joined hands and prayed for God's intervention into these lives. Both husband and wife began to cry. Holy Spirit met them there on the side of the road and healed some hurting hearts.

After 15 minutes, Ron pulled up to take over. Now rendered useless, I gave them my card and left for work. When Ron returned, he let me know that it took a bit, but they eventually got the truck running and on the road, again.

It dawned on me that in Ron's book it was written that he would rescue a stranded motorist today. He had fulfilled one of his many destinies on the earth.

I never heard from the couple again but was glad I obeyed the Lord and stopped. I, too, got to participate in a work of Holy Spirit on the earth. It made me wonder how many opportunities I had passed up over the years, opportunities that were supposed to be mine, but someone else was called to step up and, instead, it was written in their book.

That day, Jesus taught me the first of many lessons on the impact of one small act, good or evil, upon the Kingdom.

Here is the question, what is written in your book?

Daniel 7:9,10

Psalm 139:16

Revelation 20:11-13

Kingdom principle: Stopping for the one in front of you, especially if you are late, opens the door to the Kingdom.

Prayer: "Jesus, it is my greatest desire to do the things You have written in my books. I want to work the works You speak of, so I may receive my full inheritance. Will You whisper in my ear, and point out the works I am to do? I promise to turn the car around and go back. Amen."

Activation: As you go about your day today, make yourself alert to those around you. Look for an opportunity to do an act of kindness, a miracle, or a sign. Look for an opportunity to join in on the Kingdom of God. Then step up and do it.

Journal what happened.

_____

_____

_____

_____

_____

_____

_____

DAY 24 – DELIVERANCE – PARANOID SCHIZOPHRENIC

There is a verse in the Word of God that documents Jesus summoning his 12 disciples and giving them authority over unclean spirits in order to cast them out and heal every kind of disease. Just prior to this, He demonstrated that authority in the demoniac of the Gadarenes, a fascinating story of a completely insane man who could break every chain that the leaders tried to restrain him with. Interestingly, he is recorded as history's first cutter, slashing himself with sharp stones. He roamed naked among the tombs. In today's world this man would be placed on some heavy antipsychotic medication to subdue him. Sadly, the drugs only subdue; they do not heal.

It is interesting to note that Gadara was an infidel city in Decapolis, where the main means of economic growth was swine. This animal was unclean to the Jews and considered abhorrent.

Yet, Jesus purposely made it His destination. A good Jew would never subject himself to such close proximity to pigs. Jesus set up this encounter with a man who was out of his mind, to deliver him personally from the thousands of demons that plagued him. Further, He had a more far reaching goal, to bring the Kingdom of God to a lost and twisted region. When Jesus cast out the demons and the man sat fully clothed and in his right mind at the feet of Jesus, the towns people were so frightened that they demanded that Jesus leave. When the newly reformed demoniac begged to go with Him, Jesus refused, but sent him as the first missionary to the region to tell what God had done. In other words, Jesus was using the least capable in the Kingdom to usher in the Kingdom. What an extraordinary story of redemption and the ways of God.

A young man, aged 19, came to the Mission to overcome his addiction. We are a homeless shelter that offers a program, free of charge, to help those on the street start a new life of sobriety and redemption. Paul had been diagnosed as a paranoid schizophrenic with bi-polar disorder and was on some heavy antipsychotic medication. We knew of and had encountered two very distinct personalities within him. One was slightly depressed and quiet, even meek and very withdrawn. The other was truly the most malevolent person I had ever encountered. He was vicious and dangerous and prone to violence, with a very dark personality.

Paul's history of physical abuse as a child was extreme. We were afraid we could not keep him because of the potential danger to everyone else staying with us, especially the women and children.

One evening after a Board meeting at the Mission, I found Paul sitting outside my office. As I approached, he called out, "Mrs. Taylor! I believe that if you pray for me right now, God will deliver me from my mental illness tonight."

I was so very tired. It had been a particularly long day, and I had absolutely no faith to believe for this young man's healing. Yet, he was so desperate to be set free; he was bold in his declaration. I gathered some of the other students who were in the program and asked them to lay hands on Paul. Holy Spirit whispered in my ear the names of the demons who had taken up residence in the young man. One by one, they came out. It was actually one of the easiest deliverance sessions I had participated in. I think Paul was so desperate and so determined, that God honored his extraordinary faith. The demons that had tormented him all his life were sent to the dry places. When we said, "Amen," Paul looked up at me and smiled broadly. His face was transformed. He was filled with a kind of glow; for the first time I saw that signature dimple that formed every time he smiled. I was elated. God was able to use one woman and a handful of addicts to set this captive free. It proved to me that God can use anybody in the Kingdom.

A week later, Paul came to my office and asked me to remain silent as he took himself off all his meds, because God had delivered him. I was extremely alarmed at this prospect. Although I had seen a huge change in him, I was responsible for the safety of all the other guests and students, about 200 at any given time. Finally, I did agree to not to tell the Men's Team.

"If I see that dark personality again, I am calling you on it," I warned.

In the following weeks I saw Paul thrive and even cut up a little bit. I constantly saw the dimple with his beautiful smile. I was truly excited that God had changed this young man. To be sure, I asked his instructors how he was doing in his classes. They confirmed that he seemed happy and engaged, even funny at times. I asked them to arrange a new assessment and diagnosis by the Panhandle Mental Health Department. The psychiatrist found no split personality or bi-polar traits; he was deemed mentally healthy. He had been off his meds for three weeks.

The doctor declared, "If he has been off his meds for 3 weeks, then he does not need them."

Like the man at the Gadarenes, God healed this young man completely. The Kingdom opened itself to an addicted lost soul who believed. It goes against everything we know and believe in today's world; yet, God showed His glory in this little one.

Paul went on to finish the program and graduate. He selected a white tuxedo with white patent shoes for his celebration wear. In his mind, God had washed him and made him white as snow. I learned a very important lesson from this young man. Never allow man's belief system to dictate what God will or will not do in the Kingdom.

Mark 5:1-20

Matthew 10:1

Luke 11:20

Kingdom Principle: Faith gains admittance to signs and wonders, even small faith.

Prayer: "Jesus, forgive me for putting any parameters around You when it comes to difficult cases in the Kingdom. Help me in my doubt and unbelief. Make me brave enough to step in and pray for impossible situations. Amen."

Launch: Today, step out of your usual circle of friends and church members and seek out someone whom you believe is desperate. Strike up a conversation with the individual; ask if they need prayer for anything. Lay your hands on them and pray for them. Ask them if anything feels different or ask them to do something that they could not do before.

Write down your experience and your feelings.

DAY 25 – THAT WHICH WAS LOST – COLLIER

Most people have experienced a loss in their lives at some point or another. Whether it is a business, a home, or a loved one, the experience leaves one crushed and bruised. Many times, the loss is irreparable; the loved one passed away, or the keys are in the lake.

At other times, a frantic search turns up the missing item. One day I misplaced the house key. It was tied to a ribbon to make it easier to find, but I had looked all day for the thing, carefully inspecting every surface and the floor with no success. Frustrated, I stopped and sat down. I knew the Holy Spirit knew where the key was. I became still. My mind got quiet and returned to peace. I asked Him to show me where it was. I waited. Within two minutes I heard, "The key is in the kitchen trash." I jumped up and ran to the kitchen. There in the trash was the key on its ribbon. The relief was instant.

Most every wife has lost her wedding ring, and she frantically turns the house upside down to find it. The sense of loss is great no matter how much or little the band cost. When she finds it, the sense of joy and relief is just as great.

In the book of Luke, Jesus responded to the religious leaders of His day when they complained that He associated with sinners, and even ate with them.

Jesus responded with three stories about loss, and the joy when that which was lost was found. He used the example, for instance, of a shepherd with his sheep. When one is lost, he leaves the 99 to find the one, and having found it, lays it on his shoulder rejoicing. And when he has come home, calls together his friends to rejoice with him that he has found his lost sheep.

Again, He relayed a parable of a woman who having lost a coin lit a lamp and swept the house until she found it. And when she did, she called together her friends and neighbors to rejoice with her.

The most heart rending was Jesus's story about the son who demanded his inheritance before his father had died and left to squander it all on drugs and sex. When the money was gone, the boy found himself in dire straits. He found a job feeding pigs, an odious position for a Jew, as pigs were unclean to Jews. He was also starving and found himself eating out of the pig troughs.

In other words, he had hit rock bottom. He reasoned that if he could just get home, he could hire himself out as a servant to his father. He really had no other choice.

He got up and went to his father. The story records that when the boy was still a long way off, his father saw him, had compassion for him, then ran and embraced him and kissed him. The son ran through his prepared speech of not being worthy to be a son anymore.

The father brushed all this aside and threw the boy a party, "for that which was lost was found, and that which was dead had become alive."

Jesus loves redemption, reconciliation, and reunion. He goes to great lengths to orchestrate it.

At the Mission, we see this very story unfold in the lives of the addicted who have lost everything and have nowhere else to go. The loss is especially crushing when a loved one has become estranged because of the addiction.

Collier came to the Mission to try to put his life back together and become clean and sober. He had lost everything, including his family. He worked hard at his program and was diligent in his classes and duties. He had a good attitude.

As the months went by, he thought of his family and especially his daughter whom he had not seen for 11 years. He gauged her to be about 20 years old at this point. He began to pray that, somehow, he could find her and be reconciled.

One day Collier was manning the front desk in the front lobby of the shelter while the receptionist took a break. There were large windows that overlooked the parking lot, and he noticed a young woman walking toward the front doors. When she entered the foyer, she introduced herself and said she had come to volunteer.

"I know who you are," Collier responded. "You are my daughter. You're Teal."

The girl was confused and did not know what to think. Finally, recognition dawned, and she flew into his arms. There were lots and lots of tears and hugs. There was instant forgiveness and reconciliation.

The story circulated through the Mission that day. I caught wind of it right before I began to preach to the lunch crowd in chapel. What a wonderful report. Collier was on security duty in the service and as I related the account to the guests he grinned sheepishly. They clapped and cheered for his good fortune.

It was at that point that I learned the girl was, at that moment, volunteering in the dining room. I asked Collier to go get her so that we could all celebrate together.

As she walked into Chapel, I was stunned. I knew the girl! I had met Teal 11 years ago when her baby brother was born. Her baby brother is my grandson!

I remember the 10-year-old girl she had been all those years ago, and how she had grieved that she did not have a father who wanted to be with her. Teal and I had become good friends while she was going to college in a nearby town, and we both shared a passion for missions. I had been able to contribute to her mission trips over the years. She was a little evangelist and continues to do that work.

It was only the previous week that she had come to the Mission at my invitation to sign up for volunteer work and take a tour. What are the odds that Collier would be sitting at the front desk when Teal walked across that parking lot? What are the odds that he would even recognize the young woman as his daughter?

Jesus went to great lengths indeed to see these two reunited. That which was lost was miraculously found. Hallelujah!

Matthew 18:12-14

Luke 15:8-10

Luke 15:11-32

Kingdom Principle: The Kingdom of God lifts its gates to those who put their confidence in Him.

Prayer: "Father, when I have lost something or someone, please remind me that You know exactly where they are and how to bring them home. I place my hope and peace in You. I choose to put my confidence in You for their return. Amen."

Try this: Write down the relationship, job, or item you have lost. Every day remind Jesus of what He said about the lost coin, sheep, and son. Place your confidence in Him that He will do the same for you.

What happened?

_____

_____

_____

_____

_____

_____

DAY 26 – IDENTITY – FEATHERS

In the process of accessing the Kingdom in our prayers, there are some belief systems, identities, and constraints that will block our entrance into the world of miracles, signs, and wonders.

There is a beautiful illustration in the book of Mark which gives evidence of such things in the Kingdom. There was a man named Bartimaeus who was blind. He begged for a living. A little-known fact of historical Jewish practice has to do with gaining the right to be an official beggar. There were certain steps to take in order to receive a disability check of sorts. If a person were blind, lame, or incapacitated in some way, he could go to the synagogue and show his disability to the Rabbi. He would then be "certified" by them and prove that he was in fact, not a con artist so it would be lawful for him to beg. Evidently, the proof of this certification was a certain type of cloak.

As Jesus and a large crowd passed by Blind Bartimaeus, he cried out in a loud voice, "Jesus! Son of David, have mercy on me!" Many in the crowd tried to quiet him. I suppose they felt he should remain as he had always been, blind. After all, he was "Blind Bartimaeus." How could he be anything else? But he cried out all the more.

As a child, I was horrified that Jesus did not stop and pull the fellow up and heal him. I was further offended when Jesus did finally decide to do something. He made the poor man come to Him. For crying out loud! You are going to make a blind man come to you?

Reading further, we learn a very important fact that changed everything. When the people informed Bartimaeus that the Master was calling for him, he threw off his cloak. Why?

In order to be healed, he had to throw off his old identification as a blind man and psychologically become a seeing man. His self-identity had to change first. He could not hug his blindness to himself anymore. His action of throwing off the cloak that identified him as blind and getting up go to Jesus healed him. Jesus knew this.

In like manner, in order to see the Kingdom and enter into our own healing, we must throw off our psychological identity as a cancer patient, stroke victim, diabetic, or any other illness. We cannot hug our disease to our bosom any longer or wear it as a badge of honor.

By the same token, if we want to see the Kingdom, we must not carry with us our preconceived doctrines and belief systems about what the Kingdom can and cannot do. We must throw off the cloak of our psychological identity with a certain belief system, be it denominational or otherwise. The tricky part is, we cannot go over the edge and see red angels on green bicycles either.

An example of this conundrum confronted me in my own search. Recently, there was a film crew who traveled the earth to film and document the revival that was breaking out in the Church and on the streets across the continents. They filmed salvations, healings, and every sort of sign and wonder.

It was all so exciting, but there were a few videos that I thought were in the red angel, green bicycle category. I turned my nose up at stories of angel feathers, gold teeth, oil appearing out of nowhere, and gold appearing on surfaces and hands. I was having none of it. I stated such opinions loudly and with gusto.

As was our habit in the morning, my husband and I would arise early, dress warmly, put on our headphones, and head out the door. We were learning Spanish, and each lesson was exactly thirty minutes long. We had established a route around our neighborhood that would take us down the street to the park. We would circumnavigate the park, head back down a different street, around a Church, and eventually arrive at our door in exactly thirty minutes. It was dark when we started out but by the time we reached the far end of the park, the dawn was breaking.

One day on our walk, as we left the park and moved down the block, I noticed a white feather in the street beside the curb. It looked odd in its whiteness in a rather dirty gutter. I dismissed it and tried to concentrate on the Spanish lesson. Two feet further there was another white feather. In two more feet was another white feather. This went on down the entirety of the block, white feathers lined up like soldiers in a perfect row. We turned the corner at the Church. I hoped that was the end of the very odd parade of plumage. That was not to be the case. The feathers turned the corner with us and marched along the next block in the same way. All the way home, someone had painstakingly placed each feather two feet apart. It was disconcerting, but I resolutely refused to believe the obvious. This was NOT a sign and wonder.

The following week I came home from work and our home was filled with feathers. They were upstairs, downstairs, on the stairs, and on the furniture. I decided my husband had tracked them in. I picked all of them up and tossed them in the trash.

A few days later, I glanced out our bay window to the back yard. There were white feathers everywhere. I decided that they were from someone's down pillow. I gathered what I could and threw them all away. My resolute theological stand on "feathers" was wavering. I became confused and uncomfortable. I did not want to become one of those spiritual nut jobs who see pink orbs and manna falling from Heaven, but I could not deny the obvious.

The following morning in my quiet time in the living room, the Lord spoke to me.

"Why do you kick against the goads? Am I not God?"

I knew what He was referring to. It truly was a battle to repent for my prejudice against the signs.

"Papa, if the feathers are from You, would You leave one more feather as a sign? Amen."

I got up to go get ready for the day. An hour later I came back down to turn off the lamps and leave the house. There on the carpet beside my quiet time chair was a large white feather. I wept. From that point on I accepted what I could not embrace.

Do I understand the whole feather thing? No, but I know enough to bow to the sovereign nature of the Father. I will not demand by what authority He does these things. He is indeed

God, and as a dear Roman Catholic said to me one day, "He's God! He can do whatever He wants!"

Since then, I have had feathers float down in front of my face in meetings or surround my entire car in a parking lot. At one conference, I saw a white flake float down in front of me. I held out my palm; it gently landed on my fingertips. It dissolved into nothing. I turned to the girls sitting behind me with wide eyes.

"Did you see that?!" They solemnly nodded their heads.

While writing in a workbook at a signs and wonders conference, liquid gold drops appeared on the words I wrote, and on my hands. I knew then that I was down the rabbit hole.

I have seen a cloud hanging in the air while we prayed in Chapel. Photographs have captured bright orbs of light over people's heads as well. At times we have seen them with our naked eye. One day as I prayed alone in the middle aisle of the Chapel, I opened my eyes to see a physical person kneeling in the fourth row second seat. It startled me to such a degree that I jumped and shrieked. She had a flowered shirt on and a knitted shawl and blonde hair. She suddenly disappeared before my eyes.

Is it possible that these are signs from the Sovereign One? I was robust in my denial of such things, that is, until God sat me down in the time out chair gave me a talking to. Like the signs on a freeway that point to the exit, these signs are just that, signs that point us to something else, or rather someone else. To me, the signs are intimate displays of encouragement and assurance that He is indeed present and does see our days on the earth. Much like a scavenger hunt if we search, we will find these wonderful objects of His glory.

The Father is God and I am not; I am a little person who wants to know Him and everything about Him.

Mark 10:46-52

Matthew 21:23-32

Exodus 16:13

Kingdom Principle: There are signs on the earth that point to the Kingdom of God if we look. These signs are given to assure and encourage the believer that God is intimately involved with us.

Prayer: "Holy Spirit, thank You for your tenderness and gentleness. Thank You for changing our hearts in an instant. Will You come and change my heart where it needs changing? Amen."

Initiation: Today, go to a quiet place. Put on praise music. Go before the Lord sitting, standing walking, and kneeling. Ask Holy Spirit to come and brood over you and show you any "cloaks" of identity that you might be clinging to. Then wait. If the Lord shows you something, repent of it and make a physical act of throwing off the offending self-image.

What happened to you? Write down every sensation and feeling, everything the Lord may have spoken to you. What did you discover?

_____

_____

_____

_____

_____

_____

_____

There are signs on the earth that point to the Kingdom of God if we look. These signs are
given to assure and encourage the believer
that God is intimately involved with us.

DAY 27 — GO — PICKLE HUNT

In searching the teachings of Jesus, there is a clear message to us about His intentions. He said, "Go." In Matthew, He summoned His disciples and gave them authority over unclean spirits, to cast them out, to heal every kind of disease, and every kind of sickness. He then sent them out to preach the Good News in the villages and towns in this tiny area. Who knew they would turn the world on its ear?

Several years ago, a tradition was born at the homeless shelter here. The guys who lived with us getting clean and sober began to go out into the downtown area and the mall on "pickle hunts." I don't know why they called it that, but the goal was to find someone who needed to know Jesus and love them into the Kingdom. This endeavor was not organized in any way. It was just a handful of homeless guys who had lost everything, obeying the instructions of Jesus.

One day, the guys decided to walk the streets and find a pickle. They found several people who needed prayer, so they stopped and prayed with them, but had not found their pickle. As they passed the county jail downtown, they saw a young man walking out dazed and confused. The guys struck up a conversation and quickly learned that the young man, Beau, had been in jail for meth possession and reckless driving for thirty days.

He had literally lost everything; his job, his truck, his apartment, and his girlfriend. They encouraged him to come eat a hot lunch with them at the Mission. Since he had nowhere to go and nothing to do, he agreed.

At lunch, they told him all about the year-long program to get clean and sober offered at the Mission. The program was free of charge and he liked that idea. He literally had nowhere else to lay his head. He joined the program.

The staff watched this young man dig in and work hard on his program. He did his chores without complaining, participated in classes, and volunteered wherever there was a need. He came to know Jesus and came to understand his addiction. As time went by, he helped other men join the program and turn their lives around. After a year of hard work and dedication, he graduated and rejoined society. He got a job and worked hard.

Beau became a pickle hunter himself and brought many men and women to Jesus. In the Kingdom, the least likely can become the most effective saints. Those that are last shall be first. In the book of Mark Jesus said, "Go into all the world and preach the Gospel to all creation." Our students took this seriously and obeyed the command.

The mall was another place that the students liked to go to encounter Kingdom moments. The guys would actually sit in the van in the mall parking lot and ask Jesus to show them who they would be appointed to encounter. A young woman on staff would walk them through the process of hearing or seeing what God wanted to do. They would write down words and colors that they saw, discuss it, then head in.

Jesus always showed them who to approach. Men, women, even children were prayed for and encouraged. Did they all get healed? Saved? I do not know, but they did experience the love of God, which is every bit as much of the Kingdom as all the rest.

One day in particular, the guys went to the mall and walked through the same process. One "saw" a little girl with a debilitating disease. They found her with her mother in Dillard's and gathered around her to pray. Other shoppers noticed and stopped. Soon a line formed with all kinds of strangers that wanted prayer as well.

One student saw a brown shopping bag and orange juice. This seemed odd indeed. Nevertheless, they looked for someone with a bottle of orange juice and a brown shopping bag. They saw no one. It was time to head back to the Mission, so they left to the exit closest to their van. As they headed through the food court, one of the students yelped.

"Look! The brown shopping bag at the Orange Julius counter!" Indeed, there was a woman with a brown shopping bag buying an orange juice. They knew it was her. They approached her and introduced themselves as from the Mission.

The woman burst into tears. The students nor the staff member knew what just happened or what to do. Eventually she calmed herself. She explained that her brother was at the Mission and had just lost his son to suicide. She had driven to Amarillo to comfort him and help make funeral arrangements.

Driving into town, she had stopped at the mall for some necessities and refreshment. The students instantly knew to whom she was referring. It was Eric, their fellow student, that had received the news about his son. Everyone began to cry in the middle of the food court, hugging and comforting one another. The women asked if they could lead her to the Mission. She did not know the way. Everyone piled into vehicles and made their way back to the shelter. Initially there was dead silence in the van as each pondered what had just happened.

"My gosh! Can you believe the odds of what just happened?"

They all agreed that it was unimaginable. They were dazed with the crazy stories of what God did that day.

You know what is really crazy? A leader in the revival movement actually prophesied that homeless men would bring revival to America. At the time I scoffed.

"He does not know the homeless very well, they are a mess," was my thought. And yet, here I was, watching it before my very eyes. In the Kingdom of God, any person willing to "GO" will do.

Matthew 10:1-8

Matthew 28:18

Mark 16:15

Kingdom Principle: The least likely will be the ones who are called to bring the Kingdom to the world.

Prayer: "Jesus, help me be willing to lay aside my busy day for a moment and look for my pickle. Show me Your wishes and desires and lead me to that situation. Make me brave enough to follow Your lead, no matter what. Amen."

Suggestion: In your busy day today, ask God to show you the pickle hunt. Then ask Him what he wants to do with this individual. Be courageous and approach the person. If they reject you, bless them. As you walk away, pray for their "next time." If they engage, access the Kingdom and see what transpires.

Journal the results of the hunt.

_____

_____

_____

_____

_____

_____

_____

_____

_____

DAY 28 – COMPASSION – VETS

On many occasions, Jesus was said to be moved with compassion for the blind, the lepers, demoniacs, even the hungry. Our humanness does not repel Him. In the book of Mark, there is a very short story of a leper coming to Jesus and falling to his knees before Him and saying, "If you are willing, You can make me clean." Moved with compassion, Jesus stretched out His hand, touched the leper, and said, "I am willing; be cleansed."

There is a video of an episode of "Britain's Got Talent" in which a fellow walked out on the stage. He was overweight and his clothes were rumpled. His teeth were a mess. It was said that he was a mobile phone salesman. When asked to tell what he was going to do, he simply said, "I am going to sing opera."

The judges could not hide their disdain and doubt about this mousy little man singing opera. Nevertheless, the music began. Suddenly, he was transformed, when he began to sing, the entire theatre went mad. It was stunning. Simon cocked his ear to catch any failure in pitch. It was perfect. No one was more shocked than Simon. It was said after the show, "I think what we have here is a little lump of coal that is going to turn into a diamond, a frog that is going to become a prince."

Instantly, I thought of the men and women who walk through our doors every day. They are lost, disheveled, dirty, and sometimes under the influence. It causes me to weep uncontrollably. Compassion for them wells up inside of me and I fall to my knees and cry out to God on their behalf. I realize that each one is a little lump of coal who had lost his way to becoming a diamond. I weep and pray until I am completely spent. The compassion I feel is different from human compassion. It is far more powerful, almost consuming. I know that what I feel for these little ones in my charge is what Jesus felt when He walked upon the earth - a divine compassion far more powerful than man's.

One day in noon Chapel, the homeless off the streets filed in to listen to the message and eat a warm meal. It was my turn to preach. As a whole, they looked beat up, worn out, and a little listless. A few had already been drinking. I start most Chapel services with a Sunday School joke. It puts them at ease; they laugh no matter how bad the joke is. They change into a fifth-grade class with one-liners shouted out from the group. They have decided that I am a safe person.

That day, God had given me some prophetic Words for some illnesses in the crowd.

"There is someone here who has a tumor on his left lower abdomen. God wants to heal you today. Who is that?"

A gentleman in a wheelchair raised his hand. I recognized him by his Vietnam veteran hat. He works the underpass where I have seen him panhandle for money. His wheelchair was new, perhaps a "prop." His hand was shaking as he raised it. I walked over to him and knelt down. I asked him to tell me about the tumor. His words were slurred and garbled. I looked at the head of our security team to get a line on this guy. Bill, being addicted and homeless himself for fifteen years, knew all the guests by name and their stories. He had a supernatural compassion for them. Bill smiled at me and nodded. That is code for "he's a mess." Nevertheless, he was God's special mess and the Lord wanted to heal the gentleman. I felt that compassion flow through me at that moment and knew it was Jesus's compassion for the man. Bill and I laid hands on the bulge in his abdomen and prayed. I asked the fellow to let us know what the doctor found on his next scan.

One day, in Homeless Chapel, a woman came up to me crying. The left side of her face was red and swollen, and there was a large tumor below her ear. She told us she was a Navy Veteran.

"Please pray for my ear. It hurts so much," she begged through her tears. "But please don't touch it. It is so painful."

Moved with compassion, Bill, once again joined me in prayer and laid his hand just behind the bulge. I, too, was moved from the pain I saw in her face. I laid mine gently on the tumor, cupping my palm so that it was barely touching. She wept as we prayed. We saw nothing happen.

The following week, the woman came to the Mission with a bouquet of flowers for me. The tumor was gone, as well as the swelling and redness. She was completely healed. She was jubilant! God had touched her and made her whole again.

Is there a divine compassion that unlocks the doors to the supernatural? I suspect so. I do know this; it has a different feeling to me than human compassion. I cannot describe it, but I know it to be true.

Matthew 9:36

Matthew 15:32

Luke 15:20

Kingdom Principle: When human compassion becomes divine compassion, the Kingdom of God is unlocked and the supernatural is accessed.

Prayer: "Jesus, I ask You to give me a divine compassion for these little ones who come to us for help. Please don't ever let my heart be hardened to their needs. Amen."

Activation: Ask God to show you divine compassion for the little ones. Learn to love them and touch them with prayer and compassion.

What happened?

DAY 29 – NEEDY – MAN ON THE BICYCLE

There is a certain truth in the Kingdom of God that has been overlooked by most but is exquisitely powerful. It is a sign and a wonder mentioned many times in Scripture, but most powerfully in Isaiah. It refers to the fast. However, this fast has nothing to do with going without food for an extended period. In this fast, God asks the believer "to break the yoke of the oppressed, to feed the poor, to bring the homeless into the house, and to loose the bonds of wickedness." It appears that this type of fast is involved in helping others who are in a bad way.

"Then your light will break out like the dawn and your recovery will speedily spring forth." The whole of Chapter 58 goes into great detail of what He will do for those who adhere to this truth. There are ten very specific things that God will do for us when our fast embarks on a journey of helping others in need of assistance.

Long ago, as my second marriage dissolved, I had to move to another city and start over again. I was deeply oppressed by my seeming inability to have a good marriage. I felt like a double failure, which somehow disqualified me from being active in the Kingdom any longer. I would simply have to look on from the sidelines as other saints walked out a victorious life. As a believer, I knew that I was redeemed and my ultimate home was Heaven, but the crowns that I would throw at His feet would be few. So, I settled into a life of the subpar Christian. Of course, I went to church every Sunday, even taught third grade Sunday School, but on the whole lived the life of a defeated believer.

Every morning, I would drive my daughter to the high school that was located downtown on a wide street that funneled all traffic to the center of the city. Each day I would see the same drivers making their way to work. One lady would eat a doughnut as she drove. One guy would always be smoking a cigarette; another was a gentleman who, in his suit and tie, rode a bicycle to work. As autumn turned to winter, nothing much changed for the morning migration, except the man on the bicycle. I noticed new additions to his wardrobe, such as an overcoat, mittens, and toboggan. I worried for the fellow, but he seemed undaunted. One morning, however, it was sleeting badly. We were all moving slowly to avoid an accident. There up ahead on the shoulder of the road, the guy on the bicycle was fighting to keep it upright on the ice. "That's it! He's going to lose control of that bike. I am stopping!" I pulled over and stopped the car, an enormous old Grand Wagoneer that got a mere eight miles to the gallon.

"Sir, could I please give you a ride to work? I am worried about you on the ice."

He shivered uncontrollably as he stopped the bike and agreed to load it into the back of the Wagoneer. He got into the backseat, his teeth chattering as we talked. As it turned out, he lived in the apartment complex next to mine. He was a financial advisor for a firm downtown. As I stopped at his office building and we removed his bicycle, I handed him my card.

"Sir, if you ever need a ride to work, please don't hesitate to call me. I will stop on my way downtown and give you a ride. He thanked me and walked the bike into the building. I went on to the high school and dropped my daughter off.

I did not really think of the incident again, until a few weeks later I received a note in the mail with an unfamiliar return address. As I read the note, I was shocked.

Dear Friend,

I don't know if you remember me, but I was the man on the bicycle that you helped during the sleet storm last week. I wanted to thank you for stopping to help me.

What you do not know is that I am Pastor of a Church in town. Last week, my sermon was on Jesus's parable of the Good Samaritan. Your act of kindness was my example of living out that parable in today's world. That freezing day, of all my friends, relatives, and congregation, it was a little white woman who stopped to help me. Thank you again for living that out.

"God bless you."

I was absolutely shocked. I had no idea that the fellow was a pastor, or that my stopping was remotely newsworthy, or that my new friend would find it odd that "a white woman" would pick him up. I did not care one whit about any of that. What I cared about was the realization that God had allowed me to participate in the Kingdom, despite my failures and shortcomings. Apparently, divorced white women can be of some use. I was so very happy. I thanked God for His mercy. For the first time in a very long time I had a place in the Kingdom, the official "Texas State Roadside Assistance Service."

I immediately went out and bought jumper cables, a gas can, a first aid kit, as well as the aerosol spray that temporarily aired up a tire. I created an assistance box and placed it in the back of my boat of a car. For the first time, I thanked God that I owned that enormous thing. I placed a one-hundred-dollar bill in the back of my wallet for emergencies. I was ready to be of assistance.

Now, most normal people would sternly warn me of the danger of such a plan, that I was putting my life at risk. I did not care at all. "Sudden death, sudden glory." All I cared about was being useful again.

Over the course of the next few years my joy was stopping for stranded motorists, calling the tow truck, going to town for gas, or loading everyone up in that Wagoneer and taking them to their home. Only once did I stop to render aid and felt uneasy. After cracking my window to ask what the problem was, I sensed a malevolent entity. I immediately drove away.

There were two people who were in desperate need of help in this story, the fellow on the bike on the side of the road, and me. That man changed my life and gave me back my dignity. Isaiah was right. My "light broke out like the dawn, and my recovery speedily sprung forth." Thank you, Papa for Your wonderful truth.

Isaiah 58:3-12

Luke 10:30-37

Isaiah 25:4

Kingdom Principle: Serving the helpless, stranded, sick, and homeless somehow opens the Kingdom of God.

Prayer: "Jesus, I am so grateful to You that Your Kingdom invites the likes of me to participate. Although my resume is dismal, You don't seem to mind. Use me in any way You wish. I will go, send me. Amen."

Launch: Today, go before the Lord and ask Him how He wishes you to participate in the Kingdom outside of your church. Once you hear His direction, prepare for that specific endeavor. Make the call, find your volunteer opportunity, and stock your vehicle. Do whatever He instructs you to do. Make it a practice.

Write down your experiences.

_____

_____

_____

_____

_____

_____

_____

_____

_____

DAY 30 – PHYSICS – COWBOY

In order to enter the Kingdom of God, the biggest part of the battle we must fight is between our ears. We were raised in a Newtonian universe where the laws of physics never change. In fact, I know that I can rely on them every time.

For instance, gravity will always hold me to the surface of the earth. I have no fear of floating off into space. Molecules act the same way when heated or frozen. I can rely on water turning to ice for my Coke, and the chair on which I sit not melting into a puddle.

However, in the Kingdom of God, it appears that Newton and his laws all fly right out the window. Jesus multiplies the bread, walks on water, instantly opens blind eyes, and reshapes a withered hand.

My husband surmises that when we lay hands on the sick and pray, the heat or cold we feel, the kick of the organ under our hands, or the electric shocks emanating from our fingertips indicate another form of physics at work. My highly uneducated guess is that it has something to do with quantum physics, of which we know little; but again, the more I learn, the less I know.

Our littleness of knowledge tethers us to the universe we do know. Barbara Taylor, an Episcopal priest at Piedmont College says it best,

"In many places, it is still possible to hear God described as a Being who behaves almost as predictably as Newton's universe. Pull this lever and a reward will drop down. Do not touch that red button, however or all hell will break loose. In this clockwork universe the spiritual quest is reduced to learning the rules in order to minimize personal loss (avoid hell) and maximize personal gain (achieve salvation)."

I fear we have put God in a very small box, and in doing so, missed a great deal of the wonders of the Kingdom.

While attending a conference on cultivating revival, I quickly noticed how tethered I was to Newton's laws and how small my spiritual box was, even though we had, at this point, seen many miracles and healings at the Mission. By the third day, my box blew up completely when I saw little children running through the audience healing the sick in very unorthodox ways such as a simple high five and a "be healed." Testimonies of healing came from several people who were high fived. I wept for hours on the floor, unable to do anything else. The following days, I continued to weep over the littleness of my mind and its inability to grasp these new laws. I was wrecked. In some small way, my mind and my thinking were transformed.

What does that tell me about the Kingdom? Its laws may be quite different from those that govern our physical realm. We must change the way we think and approach the supernatural realm with a completely different mindset. We must blow up our spiritual boxes. Signs and wonders are to be accomplished by every believer, even the little ones. The words of Jesus float back to me, "Truly I say to you, unless you are converted and become like children you shall not enter the Kingdom of God."

When I was first learning about the Kingdom, but not really seeing it, God came to me in my quiet time and told me that there would be an individual in Guest Chapel that day who had an old back injury that was being reinjured and causing constant pain.

He told me to pray healing over the small of his back. I was trepidatious to say the least. What if no one raised their hand? What if they DID raise their hand? Then what? It was all a bit worrisome in my head.

Sure enough, there was an old cowboy in a starched white shirt, pressed jeans, and boots who raised his hand when I mentioned the old back injury in Chapel. He was a feedlot cowboy presently out of work. The injury was from a bull ride in a rodeo twenty-five years earlier. Work at the feedlot kept the injury alive.

"How did you know?" he asked, clearly confused. He asked it several times as I walked back and laid my hands on his back to pray. He stood up and twisted this way and that.

God healed him instantly. What kind of physics happened to his spine that wiped away twenty-five years of pain? That part is still unclear to me, but God's grace and mercy toward this fellow was absolute. That morning, God had that old cowboy on His mind and told His little one about it in her quiet time. That alone is extraordinary.

For weeks, the cowboy came to the Mission for lunch, always with a smile and a "thank you." He always had on his starched shirt and pressed jeans. Thank you, Papa, for allowing me, a little person, to participate in this extraordinary Kingdom.

Romans 12:2

Matthew 17:14

I Corinthians 2:4-6

Matthew 18:3,4

Kingdom Principle: When one comes to God as a child, the Kingdom opens, and a supernatural side of physics come into play.

Prayer: "Lord, I want to enter the Kingdom. Make me as a child and teach me the childlike faith I must have to come in. Blow up my spiritual box and transform my thinking. Amen."

Exercise: Seek out a conference, workshop, organization or mentor who walks in signs and wonders. Pray and ask God which one to attend or contact. Make an appointment or register to go to the conference. Determine to make a spiritual and financial commitment to learn all that you can. Put the date on your calendar, pack your bags, and go.

Note: My initial trip was downtown to a homeless shelter where I learned volumes of Kingdom principles from the homeless, the poor, and the addicted. That might be a good place to start.

Document where you are going, who you are seeing, and when you are leaving.

DAY 31 — TRANSFORMED — ALEX

The extraordinary story of Jesus being transformed into a brilliant shining being before the eyes of Peter, James, and John is baffling. Other stories in the Bible of brilliant angels radiantly glowing catch our eye. Moses was reported to have come down from the mountain with such a blindingly radiant face that he was required to cover it with a veil. What happened that such men would be so dazzling? What part of quantum physics is this?

I am told that in the sixties, Dr. Iverna Tompkins in her research on light particles, developed a light spectrometer that actually measured microscopic light particles emanating from the human form. She observed race, gender, and age, taking note of the number of light particles she saw in each subject. Her findings were telling.

She discovered that the number of light particles swarming an individual were contingent upon his or her mood. If the subject were negative or depressed, lonely or angry, the light particles, dubbed "Biophotons," were few and far between, thus exuding what we may refer to as a dark countenance. We have all seen these brooding, dark individuals.

If, however, the subject's mood is joyful, happy, or positive in his or her emotions, the light particles increase to such an extent that they put off millions of particles of light. Hence, the glowing bride, or radiant pregnant woman. Even the man who has fallen in love is awash with the light.

Looking back at the stories in the Bible where individuals took on a radiant glow begs the question: Were these so awash with light particles that it caused a brilliant radiance to shine forth? What caused Jesus to be transformed that day on the mountain? What was Moses doing that made his face shine so brightly? Was there a tear in the veil between this world and the other?

On closer evaluation, it would appear that the common denominator to this radiance is an encounter with the Lord and His miracles. There are so many stories in Scripture of these divine encounters such as Abraham on that starry night, Joshua and the Lord of Host, Jacob and the ladder of angels, Daniel by the river. Each was transformed at these encounters.

There are still more stories of modern-day ordinary men and women who encounter the Living God and are never the same again. Here at the Mission, we are privileged to see it often, as well as the radiant glow afterward. It truly is a wonder to see.

One day, a man was dropped off at the Mission by his aunt. He was not, as they say, a happy camper. I was fortunate enough to be in on his interview with the Men's Team. Alex was an angry man who did not want to be in this place, but his family forced the issue of his drinking. I began to ask the usual questions about his wanting to become clean and sober. He was having none of it.

"I am not staying." (I wish I had a nickel for every lost soul that has said that.)

"Okay, what is your drug of choice?"

"Vodka."

"And how much Vodka do you drink?"

"About two gallons a day."

"Alex! That is not medically possible!"

"Oh, you build up to it."

That was shocking to me. His addiction had to consume every waking hour of his day. I knew that his addiction would kill him soon.

I asked him what health issues would preclude him from working his chores while in the program.

"I have late stage cirrhosis of the liver and I am jaundiced, but I am not staying."

"Well, you are here with us now, so may I pray for you?"

"I am not a religious man."

"Okay... so may I pray for you?"

Alex rolled his eyes as if to say, "Get this woman out of my face!" His sense of politeness prevailed, and he agreed to be prayed for. The team laid hands on him and I laid my hands on his liver. We began to pray for healing. Suddenly his liver kicked me as a baby kicks in the womb! Surprised, I jerked my hand away.

"Did you feel that?" I asked.

"I did! But I am not a religious man."

"Well, let me know how that turns out!"

For the time being, Alex stayed with us. Twenty days later, Alex went to a doctor's appointment at Texas Tech Medical Center to have a check up on his cirrhosis. They ran the blood work, then the intern came into the examination room.

"Alex, your liver enzymes are reading normal, and we know that is not true. So, I am going to grab your doctor."

Alex's doctor decided to do a sonogram. As he proceeded with the examination to look at the liver, he turned to Alex and said, "Alex, I have seen your liver and all I can say is you are a walking miracle. This liver is normal!" God did the impossible to Alex's liver. He healed it. Alex had a new chance at life.

He began to weep at what God had done for him, even in his defiance. He ran to the lobby and called his family to tell them the good news, the miraculous news. In the following days, he began to learn all he could about this God who had saved him and even healed him. He fell in love and was transformed. The jaundice was completely gone, and within a month the huge belly caused by cirrhosis was flat. He could not stop grinning. He literally glowed.

That is the Kingdom at work here on the earth. Alex's body, world, and mind were all transformed in a millisecond. He left the kingdom of darkness and walked into the marvelous light, never to be the same again. And yes, his biophotons are still off the charts!

Matthew 17:1-8

Exodus 34:29

II Corinthians 3:18

Luke 11: 34–36

Kingdom Principle: Divine encounter is the gateway into transformation and the wonders of the Kingdom.

Prayer: "Jesus, I pray for your brilliant light to transform me as you and Moses were transfigured. Let me know the intimacy of Your presence where I, too, am changed. Amen."

Action: Set aside a daily time to be in the Lord's presence. Make a commitment to keep this appointment with Jesus every day. Determine that no one interrupt this sacred time.

Write down your appointed time on your calendar. Believe that He will meet you there and visit with you face to face. Each day write down what happened in the presence of the Lord.

Divine encounter is the gateway into transformation and the wonders of the Kingdom.

DAY 32 – CHANGED – BILL

In the Kingdom of God, there is a phenomenon that often takes place in a nanosecond. It is that moment when a person is suddenly engulfed by the Person of the living God and is instantly and forever changed. It is an astonishing thing to watch. Just like the story of Moses and the burning bush in which God utterly changes him from a broken, frightened man to a fireball of faith performing the impossible.

Time after time, we have seen it happen here at the Mission. There are those who come to our doors with no shred of hope or future left, those who come to us from prison, or the streets. Some are being badly beaten by boyfriends or best friends and have reached rock bottom. There is nowhere else to turn, and no one else to turn to.

They come hoping for a meal, a warm bed, or just safety, knowing they will not be judged or mistreated. Here, the transformation, the encounter with the living God, changes them from broken, frightened men and women to fire breathing dragons for the King.

There is another type of transformation that takes place over time. In the book of Romans, Paul commands us not to be conformed to this world but be transformed by the renewing of our minds that we may prove what the will of God is, that which is good and acceptable and perfect. It is a lifetime process by which we are changed.

The day one is utterly changed by salvation is only the beginning of the journey. I am so very grateful that God did not let me remain a brat but was faithful to break every bone in my body in my journey to change. I am a very slow learner, but I am getting better every day.

In yesterday's story, Alex was changed in every way. He stayed in the program to get clean and sober and to learn a new way of life. In one month, the huge belly caused by cirrhosis of the liver was gone. He was working hard to learn everything he could about this God who had healed him. The most telling sign of the changes taking place was the new way he thought about everything, with faith and not doubt or disdain.

One day, Alex received a call that his brother-in-law, Bill, was in the hospital. Bill was a raging alcoholic as well and was in a coma. He, too, had late stage cirrhosis of the liver and was jaundiced. His organs had begun to shut down and he was at the end of the end. Alex, in his newfound faith, reasoned that if God had healed him, He could just as easily heal Bill.

He gathered up eleven other students who were also in the program to achieve sobriety and were equally as excited about their own transformations. He asked them to accompany him to the hospital to pray for his brother-in-law.

When they arrived, they gathered in a circle on the front lawn of the hospital and began to pray for God's power to come. They proceeded to Bill's room. He was still in a coma and looked terrible. He was profoundly jaundiced with carrot colored pallor. The men gathered around the bed, laid hands on the unconscious patient, and prayed.

Suddenly, Bill woke up. He looked at the crowd and said, "Hey, what are y'all doing here?" Alex explained their mission, gave the briefest version of the Gospel, and led him in the salvation prayer. When one is dying, one is a ready student.

As they visited with Bill, they noticed a pink dot appear on his nose. They were mystified as they watched it spread across his face. The jaundice was disappearing right before their eyes. The pink continued down his neck and covered his arms. Bill was healed. There was a great many high fives and laughter at the recovery before their eyes. Two days later, Bill left the hospital a new man.

Alex's transformed mind changed his reasoning. He was learning to think Kingdom thoughts, not medical diagnosis thoughts. He was also learning to not fear addicted thoughts. In fact, his mind was so renewed that when he was slated to go to a wedding in Las Vegas, he knew to prepare himself to think and act differently while surrounded by every conceivable temptation. In the moment that he was actually approached by a waitress asking if he would like a cocktail, his answer was ready, "No thank you." He returned to the Mission elated at his success at sobriety on the road.

Alex graduated from the program at the Mission and went back to work in the restaurant industry, this time clean and sober. He spread the Gospel everywhere he went. Old customers could not believe the transformation.

Thank you, Papa, for healing this young man, delivering him, and remaking him into an extraordinary powerhouse for the Kingdom.

Exodus 3:1-16

Romans 12:2

II Corinthians 3:18

Kingdom Principle: Transformed people transform other people into the Kingdom of God.

Prayer: "Papa, teach me how to renew my mind so that I can be transformed in my thinking. Take my thoughts and give me Your thoughts on every subject and crisis. Amen."

Activation: Today, select a problem or illness you are dealing with right now. Now picture Papa on the throne wringing His hands in worry over your problem. Silly, isn't it? He never sits on His throne wringing His hands over your crisis or illness. He is perfectly confident about the outcome.

Take your situation before the Throne and ask God to transform your thinking about that problem, so that it matches His thinking on the problem. Find a verse that proves what His thinking is, such as Romans 8:28, or Psalm 138:8.

Make notes on these scriptures. Write them on 3X5 cards, and place them on your dash, or desk. Meditate on these truths transforming your thinking.

DAY 33 – TOUCH – DOMINGO

I have made it my quest to grasp, even in a tiny way, the concept of physics, quantum or otherwise, as it has to do with miraculous healing. What happens to the diseased body when believers lay hands on it? What is taking place on a subatomic level that makes a huge diseased liver become physically normal? I have turned to scientists who have begun to discover and unlock some of these mysteries:

"From the quantum angle, an electron is not simply an electron. Shifting <u>energy</u> patterns shimmer around it, financing the unpredictable appearance of protons, mesons, and even other electrons. In short, all the paraphernalia of the subatomic world latches onto the electron like an evanescent cloak, a shroud of ghostly bees swarming around the central hive. It is not a discreet individual, but a part of a complex network of relationships."

~Paul Davies

As believers, we know that Jesus created the universe and He created humans in particular. As we all learned in eighth grade science class, all of creation is made up of molecules. In the cloud, molecules float rather loosely apart, enabling objects to pass through them easily.

In a liquid state, they move more closely together. It is still possible to pass through that state, but with more resistance. In a solid state, molecules are more tightly assembled, and only Jesus has walked through that state.

However, human surface is not really solid. Our molecules are just packed together more closely. Are the electrons in our molecules swarming with this shroud of energy? Could our surface be swarming with this "shroud of ghostly bees" on our electrons?

When a believer in the power of the Holy Spirit lays hands on the infirm and prays, what supernatural event happens on a subatomic level? Could it be that a believer's swarming subatomic paraphernalia bump into the diseased swarming subatomic paraphernalia, and supernatural energy and light of the Holy Spirit transfer to diseased shrouds and the individual is healed? Is this the source of the feeling of cold, heat, the kick under our hands, or the electrical shocks we sometimes feel while praying?

In the same way, when Jesus laid hands on the sick, did His energy and light transfer to the patient? There is a passage in the book of Mark in which the villagers recognized Jesus and brought their sick to the marketplaces, entreating Him if they could just touch the fringe of His cloak. Everyone who did was cured. Did the swarming energy and light cling to Jesus's cloak? Did just a touch of the garment change their bodies?

In the story of the woman with the issue of blood, the woman touched the hem of Jesus's garment. "Immediately, He perceived that 'power' from Him had gone forth." Jesus stopped and asked, "Who touched Me?" Did He feel that miraculous "kick" of the organ? Or the enormous heat or cold? Or did He feel the electrical shocks?

These are all phenomenon we at the Mission have felt at times. And why is it that when I place my left hand onto the diseased area of an individual and pray, it begins to send electric shocks through my left hand, but not with my right hand?

Of course, this is all just kindergarten conjecture and questions, but it is interesting to ponder. All I know is that my job is to pray for the little ones.

When Alex was healed of cirrhosis and jaundice, and then Bill, his brother-in-law, was healed, word got out.

A man named Domingo came to the Mission and, speaking only Spanish, asked the receptionist if it were true, that two people were instantly healed of cirrhosis of the liver. She confirmed that it was indeed true. He asked if we could lay hands on him and pray for his cirrhosis, jaundice, and the huge belly that protruded over his belt. The woman instructed him to come the following morning to Staff and Student Chapel and we would pray for him.

The next day, Domingo was already waiting for us as we filed into Chapel for our service. He immediately came forward. In Spanish, he told us of his diagnosis and asked us to pray. I called Alex forward and we both laid our hands on his swollen liver. The rest of the congregation stretched their hands toward him. As we prayed, his liver flopped like a fish under our hands for several minutes. Alex and I exchanged glances and smiled.

"Domingo, I am pretty sure you're healed, buddy." Still the liver continued to flip this way and that for several minutes. We continued to hold our hands over it until the flipping stopped. We all praised God, and off he went.

The following week in Guest Chapel, I was relating this incredible story to the guests off the streets. I told of the healing of Alex, Bill, and possibly Domingo. Our head of security stepped to the back row and said, "You didn't even recognize him, did you?"

Confused, I walked to the back row. Seated there was a gentleman I did not recognize until I noticed the teardrop tattoo on his left cheek. I looked closer; it was Domingo. The jaundice was gone. The huge belly was gone, and he broke into a huge smile at my surprise. God had healed this man! Instantly, as the light and energy of Holy Spirit collided with the diseased area, it was made brand new. Jesus, Your universe is astounding! And You allow us to participate in this universe in extraordinary ways. Thank you!

Mark 6:56

Mark 5:25-30

Acts 9:17, 18

Luke 13:11-13

Kingdom Principle: Holy Spirit is the supernatural power in the Kingdom. We, as believers, work in symphony with Him as conduits of His power.

Prayer: "Jesus, I do not know much about physics and what must happen to an organ when it is healed, but this I do know. You healed the sick. You commanded us to heal the sick. Whatever goes on at subatomic levels is beyond my ability to understand. I trust You and I trust Holy Spirit. I will simply be Your conduit. Amen."

Activation: Volunteer at a homeless shelter for several months. Once a week, go serve in some capacity. Interact with the guests. Get to know their names. Visit with them. When you have established a connection, ask if you may pray for their illnesses.

What transpired?

DAY 34 — ONE BODY — CANCER

It would appear that In the Kingdom of God, we believers are all connected somehow. In the book of I Corinthians, Paul speaks of one body, the Church. "For even as the body is one and yet has many members, and all the members of the body, though they are many are one body. So also, is Christ. For by One Spirit we are all baptized into one body."

It all sounds very mystical, but we are greater than the sum of our parts. We are more than a membership of believers. Paul goes into great detail of each of our parts fitting together making up the whole body in a wondrous way, with Christ as our head.

When, however, "the knee is mad at the ear and will not forgive him until he admits that he is wrong" or, "the nose is offended because the ankle got a raise and he did not," the whole is damaged. In the body of Christ, our parts are all governed by the head which is Christ.

When we grasp that our choices, both good and bad, affect the whole body, regardless of how secret we keep them, we would do well to tread carefully.

Conversely, when one member of the body acts kindly to another part of the body, whether they deserve it or not, the whole body is affected.

So, how does this fit together in the Kingdom? In Genesis 1, God says those incredible words, "Let there be light," and there was light. Only, in the original Hebrew, it is a little more complicated than that. The word used in this text is *hayah* which means to exist, to be, to be done.

Some commentaries propose that the text might rather be translated, "I am the light," or "I am He who is the Light." This includes the expanse, the waters, the vegetation, stars, creatures, and man. That is shocking to me. Nevertheless, Jesus said in John, "I am the light of the world."

So far, so good. In the book of Matthew, He said a confounding thing to His listeners, "You are the light of the world." It would appear that in some way we are connected to the Father, to the Son, and to each other.

"According to quantum theory, subatomic particles that decay into two particles become a set of twins, a single system with two parts, spinning in opposite directions. No one knows which is spinning 'up' until a measurement is made, but according to the laws of physics, they must always balance each other. Now imagine those two particles flying apart - one of them heading around the dark side of the moon while the other lingers in the laboratory above the nimbus of Einstein's hair. If Einstein could nab that one and reverse its spin, he theorized, then the other particle would have to reverse itself too - even if it were light years away. According to the laws of quantum physics, this is exactly what happened. Because the two particles were in a state of "quantum entanglement," they would behave in complementary ways, no matter how far apart they were. Once two particles have interacted with each other, they remain related regardless of their physical distance from one another. In some sense they stay in contact through space and time. The point seems to be that they do not behave as two separate particles, but one."

~**Barbara Taylor**

I am reminded of the mother who suddenly feels fear for her grown child hundreds of miles away, or the twins who meet for the first time at age 52 and are wearing the same blouse. Or the husband who has a funny feeling that his wife is having an affair. After all, Paul wrote that they are one flesh.

The point is that on some subatomic level, we are all connected to each other while we remain separate; much like the myriads of kernels on a corn cob.

After the church service one Sunday morning, several of the elders and their wives were visiting when a man walked up and asked for prayer. He had cancer which had metastasized everywhere; into his brain, lungs, back, and belly. He was in late stage, but still taking chemo. The elders (the heavy artillery) spread out in front of him laying their hands on every available body part. We wives (think M-16 or AK-47) spread out behind him, and laid hands on his back.

As the men began to pray, I felt as if I would be knocked backward by the Holy Spirit. It was as though we were all engulfed within a thick presence. A sense of elation filled me. We all commented in amazement on the palpable power of the presence of Holy Spirit after the gentleman walked away.

The following week, the man found us and reported that he had gone to his chemotherapy session, and they did a tumor marker test to see the level of tumors. There were no tumor markers. The doctors scheduled a scan. There were no tumors either. This man whose body was riddled with cancer was instantly healed at the hands of a very small group of believers.

The body of Christ, being one, acted in symphony and one was healed by the whole. It is still a mystery, but I wholeheartedly accept it. When we act as one, the whole world can be changed. It is my prayer that we as believers begin to grasp that truth.

I Corinthians 12:12-27

John 8:12

Matthew 5:14-16

Matthew 19:4-6

John 17:20-23

Kingdom Principle: When we as believers act as one body and in one accord, the Kingdom of God falls upon us.

Prayer: "Holy Spirit, give me a revelation of us believers as one body. Teach us how to act in symphony. Amen."

Galvanization: Study the body of your congregation. Do you act as one? Are you connected as one family? When you pray together, do you see things happen?

Write it down:

_____

_____

_____

_____

_____

_____

_____

_____

_____

_____

_____

DAY 35 – LAY DOWN YOUR LIFE – TERRIFYING AND AMAZING

In the Kingdom of God, there is this overriding theme of oneness. This is a bit of a stretch for us in the western Church. We are trained to be fiercely independent; it could be said that we take pride in our autonomy.

The Kingdom instructs us that there is no greater love than to lay down our lives for a friend. There is a subculture we could take a few lessons from here in America, the homeless. I can already feel the angst and trepidation in the reader at such an outlandish statement. Do not misunderstand me. This people group can be quite naughty but keep an open mind.

In the book of Ephesians, Chapter 4, there is an admonition "with all humility, and gentleness, with patience showing forbearance to one another…there is one body, and one Spirit…one Lord, one faith, one baptism, one God and Father of all."

As a longtime observer of the homeless, I have watched countless acts of kindness that they show to one another. They will share their last cigarette, what's left in the bottle, or give the boots off their own feet to another. Don't get me wrong, it is not all rainbows and bunnies in this subculture, but their scores for acts of kindness are far higher than most Christians.

There is a custom among the staff at the Mission. Every January, we go around the table in our first staff meeting of the new year and tell of the "terrifying and amazing" things we individually plan to embark upon for the coming year. This tradition came out of a quote I found.

"If it is terrifying and amazing, you should definitely pursue it." (Author Unknown)

I challenged my staff to just try to do something amazing. The first year, only a handful of us did it. In the years that followed, other staff members jumped into the game.

One year a staff member decided that for his terrifying and amazing thing, he would go homeless for a week in another city of which he was unfamiliar. He wanted to better understand this people group and know, to a certain extent, how they felt, thought and acted. His wife was not happy with me.

We made plans for him to be accompanied by one of our recovering graduates who had previously been homeless and was more familiar with the streets. They both grew their hair and beards out, packed their backpacks (cell phones for emergency purposes only, as one was a diabetic), found some more appropriate clothing in our sorting department, and headed for Oklahoma City.

They parked their pickup in a friend's driveway and piled into the friend's truck. They then proceeded into downtown and were dropped off. At that moment, they had no idea which way to go. As the friend drove off, the staff member was gripped with terror. What had he been thinking? This was not safe. Every fiber of his being told him to call his friend to come back and pick them up. Instead, they started walking.

That night, they found a warehouse that looked somewhat safe. They walked around the back and made camp (I use that term loosely). They found an old mattress and the staff member took it, covering himself with his old blanket. They were both exhausted. In the middle of the night, he was awakened by a tap on the shoulder.

"Excuse me, but that's my mattress." Michael jumped up and apologized. The fellow took his place. Michael moved to the ground, and they all drifted back to a fitful sleep.

The next morning, introductions were made. George was a Vietnam vet who suffered from PTSD (Post-Traumatic Stress Disorder) and had taken to the streets to cope. For the rest of the week, George treated the two as royal guests, showing them the ropes, who to avoid, and where to get a meal.

He made introductions to the other men on the street and looked after Michael and his companion. They were warmly welcomed.

By the same token, businessmen and shoppers completely ignored them as if they were invisible. The staff member began to feel his self-confidence and identity slipping from him. He was becoming psychologically unsettled.

As he observed his decline, he was amazed at how fast it was happening to him. He also knew that in a few days his friend would be picking him up and he would go home, get cleaned up, and go back in his office working on finances. These people would still be out on the street with no hope of such a thing.

"I've got your back, man," George would say. He was a little crazy but so kind and helpful. I am certain that George will receive extraordinary rewards in Heaven for the kindness shown to two undercover agents who were not who they said they were. It makes one pause and wonder how many "undercover angels" we unknowingly serve.

Ephesians 4:4

Hebrews 13:2

John 15:12-14

Kingdom Principle: Acts of kindness are the rate of exchange in the Kingdom.

Prayer: "Father, teach me the truth of being one body. How do I pursue one body among others? Give me a heart for all who are in the body, not just my church friends. Amen."

Activation: Today, look for an opportunity for a terrifying and amazing moment. Perform an act of kindness for a stranger. Strike up a conversation with him or her, make them smile. Do them a favor.

Addendum Activation: In addition, begin to plan your own terrifying and amazing act for the year. Try something you have never done before but always wanted to do. Begin making plans to carry that out. For instance, go sky diving, take a course, try karate, ballet, or cooking classes. Write a book or plant a garden. Do anything that would be terrifying and amazing for you.

What Happened?

DAY 36 — THE GLORY — TISSUE

The book of John records Jesus's reference to something called the "Glory" in His high priestly prayer.

"And the glory which Thou hast given to Me I have given to them that they be one just as we are one."

I have often wondered if this Glory of which He speaks is a catalyst for divine healing, miracles, and wonders. How does this Glory come upon us? I have found the Glory most often in one place, the place of focused prayer and worship in secret. It is a place of purity and light, warmth and elation. It is absolute euphoria, and altogether different from corporate worship.

In the book of Matthew, Jesus gives explicit instructions about this place of Glory.

"But you, when you pray, go into your inner room, and when you have shut your door pray to your Father who is in secret, and your Father who sees in secret will repay you."

If the believer understood that and pursued the inner room, he could quite possibly step into the glory of the Kingdom. That deep intimate time in the inner room changes an individual, as well as circumstances.

There is an astonishing story in the book of Acts that describes something extreme about the Glory. Paul saw and felt and heard the Glory on his travel to Damascus. The Glory utterly changed him. He went on to see extraordinary things in the Kingdom.

"And God was performing extraordinary miracles at the hand of Paul, so that handkerchiefs and aprons were even carried from his body to the sick, and the disease left them, and the evil spirits went out."

Could the Glory that Paul experienced at his conversion naturally be sloughed off onto anything he wore or touched, like dust particles? Paul was a man, just like you and me, but his grasp of the laws of the Kingdom were to such an extent that it defies our imagination. Nevertheless, I have determined in my heart to believe all that is written in this wonderful book and to practice the Kingdom despite its very odd behavior and my very narrow understanding.

I, too, am able to receive the Glory, as can any other believer activating the divine in their lives, should we choose to pursue it. I have learned this; the activation requires a deep abiding relationship with my Savior. I do not mean that in order to walk into the glory I have to "do the time" in prayer. That's just charlatanism, like the magician in the book of Acts. Christians go into the inner room to be with the One that they love.

There is a word in the old testament that denotes a "knowing" as in Adam "knew" Eve. The connotation is a deep abiding; knowing as a familiar friend, a kinsman, a beloved. In the book of Exodus there is life verse of mine. It is the cry of my heart.

"Thus, the Lord used to speak to Moses face to face, just as a man speaks to His friend." This is the friendship of which I speak. This is the intimacy that has changed me over and over.

It reminds me of a miraculous story that happened several years ago. During altar ministry at church, a woman came up to me and asked for prayer for her brother-in-law who was dying of cancer in another city. The doctors could do nothing more for him, so they sent him home to put his affairs in order. The cancer had spread over every area of his body.

We prayed together for a supernatural healing for him. I had never done this before but felt we should take one of the Kleenex tissues made available at the front, pour anointing oil on it, lay our hands on that, and pray. We did, and I encouraged her to send it to her sister to lay it on her husband's body.

Many months later, I ran into the woman; she related the outcome of that tissue sent to her sister. When the sister received it in the mail, she carefully laid it on the site of the original tumor. Day by day, the man began to feel better. When he went back to his doctor for another scan, all cancer was gone from his body. He was healed.

The Glory attached itself to a humble Kleenex, traveled to a dying man's home, and healed him. Do I understand how that worked? Did I grasp the physics of it? Absolutely not. I just had a dear friend to whom I could go for help. He told me what to do. I did it. Thank you, Father, for Your friendship and Your glory.

Acts 19:11

John 17:22

Matthew 14:36

Mark 5:28-34

Exodus 33:11

Kingdom Principle: The Glory is in the inner room. In the inner room, the Kingdom comes upon us.

Prayer: "Jesus, it is astounding to me that You would even want to give us the Glory. Will You teach me how to enter the Glory, and handle the Glory without misusing it? Amen."

Do this: Begin to research the word "Glory" in the Old Testament and the New Testament. Make reference to its characteristics. Look up the original meaning in the Greek and Hebrew. Research commentaries on the Glory.

Record the reference, the Greek or Hebrew translation, and every meaning and nuance of the word. Write down one nugget that you discovered that you did not already know.

JENA RAWLEY TAYLOR

DAY 37 – THE TENT – SCREWDRIVER

Most believers have, over the years in their walk with Christ, chosen a verse or verses from Scripture that are their "Life Song." They live by them and fix them as a North Star to guide them. Exodus may be an unlikely book to choose from, but out of it came my North Star. Exodus 33 records a habit that Moses had of going outside the camp to enter the tent of meeting, "and the pillar of cloud descended upon the tent, and the Lord would speak to Moses."

Intimacy with God became my obsession. The hour or so that I set apart for my time in the tent was non-negotiable and was not to be disturbed. My timeslot of choice was when no one else was up yet. I felt that I had Him all to myself.

He indulged me in my myriads of questions. He spoke to me and showed me "great and mighty things I do not know." Every morning was a treasure hunt that unearthed gold, diamonds, and pearls of truth that I have never seen before in the Word. He gave me instructions and showed me the color of the shirt or the location, or the gender of those He wished to touch with His Glory. It must be noted, however, that the primary purpose of time in the tent was not to see the signs and wonders later in the day. The primary purpose was to be with Him, to abide with Him, to sup with Him, the God of the universe. Having said that, the Glory does the rest from there.

I was once told by, what could be called a general in the Kingdom, "The Glory is in the secret place." Among those today who have walked in every miracle and wonder over the years, every one of them have an extended and daily time in "the tent." Why anyone would not go to the tent is beyond me, but I understand that Satan will do anything to prevent Christians from going in there.

"I am so busy; I have 4 little children; I work out in the morning; I am not a morning person." It is true that we in the western world are very busy. The questions could be posed, "How desperate am I? How badly do I want it?" I had my struggles too, as a young mother with a career, until the day I walked past my living room with an armload of laundry. Seated in one of the grouped wingbacks, I saw Jesus watching me. I knew exactly what He wanted. I literally said out loud, "I'm coming! Just let me put this load in the washer." That night I realized that, sadly, I did not make it back to the living room that day but stayed busy with everything that "needed to be done." The reality of that struck me hard. That is when everything changed for me, and it became non-negotiable. That was 35 years ago. Now, I thank God for that day and its lesson.

One morning recently in my tent, I asked the Father if He wanted to heal anyone in Chapel that morning. I saw the human anatomy and specifically the left side above the waist was highlighted to me. I knew God wanted to heal someone's left side above the waist in Staff and Student Chapel. As I looked out over the crowd, I noticed a lot of homeless guests had joined us (I suspected it was because it was 7 degrees outside). One young man was slouched in the second row and appeared to be badly hungover or going through withdrawal. Either way, he was miserable. He was pale and hunched over with his forearms on his knees. I feared he might lose his breakfast at any moment. When I mentioned the left side, he perked up and raised his hand. "Oh, that's me!' I asked him what was wrong.

"I was in a street fight and stabbed right here with a screwdriver; it never healed. It hurts all the time." He lifted his shirt and showed the scar. It was clearly not healed. I asked the other men around him to lay their hands on him and pray. They did so, and when they said, "Amen," the young man looked up and smiled broadly. I asked him to check himself to see if anything felt differently.

"Man! I feel great! My headache is gone, I don't feel sick, and my side doesn't hurt anymore." Color had returned to his face, only the color was no longer a sickly shade of green. He showed no apparent signs of discomfort.

In His grace and mercy, God reached down and healed an imperfect man. Being flawed did not disqualify him from God's perfect grace. Thank You, God, for healing this little one. And thank you for the tent.

Exodus 33:7-11

Matthew 13:46

Jeremiah 33:3

Luke 10:38-42

Kingdom Principle: Hangovers do not block the Kingdom from coming.

Prayer: "Lord, with all that is within me I want to meet You in the tent. Please help me find a time that is set aside every day and is non-negotiable. Like Moses, I want to know You. Help me do this. Amen."

Suggestion: Look over your daily schedule and select a time slot that can be set aside every day for tent time. Determine how many minutes you feel comfortable with to stay in the tent. You may start with thirty minutes and work your way up. Select a place that is sacred to you and where you will not be disturbed. Make a commitment to the Lord to meet Him there every day. Now, just do it.

Note: I had to have a friend call me every day at 5:00 a.m. to get me out of bed and into the tent. After two weeks, the habit was set and she did not have to call me any longer. Accountability is a wonderful thing.

Everyday write down what transpired in the tent. Start with the date, then a verse that jumped out, a revelation, or a question. Every day, go back and read what you wrote the day

before. You will not remember half of what you wrote, and the reread will be a new diamond, ruby, or pearl for the days to come.

DAY 38 — THE MOUNTAIN — BABY

One-on-one intimacy has always been the goal of the Father. He is extremely relational. In Exodus 33, Moses had quite a conversation with God about His intentions. "Who are You, and what do You want? Show me Your Glory." God granted this request. He placed Moses in the cleft of the rock and let him see the Glory pass by him. Moses was interested in far more than his "ministry," his name in lights. He wanted to know the nature of this God. In the same way, many today approach Him in order to know Him. In Exodus 34, there is the most astounding text, a text that reveals the secret to the universe. Moses went up to the mountain to visit with the Lord. He stayed forty days and forty nights; he neither ate nor drank. When he finally came down, he did not know that the skin of his face shone because he had been in the presence of the Lord. According to Scripture, the glow stayed on Moses's face for a very long time. Evidently the shining was so bright that it required putting a veil on his face.

In today's society, it is hard enough to stay forty minutes in the presence with no food or water, let alone a day, and certainly not forty days. Yet, most of us would give a great deal to have been with Him so long that our face shone. Why was Moses up on the mountain so long? The Lord was laying out in detail the blueprints for the tabernacle, an extraordinary revelation.

What's the point? These things take time. The deeper things of the Lord take time and effort. Most are happy to just skate into the pearly gates and are not remotely interested in a relationship; that is until they get into a jam (ask me how I know this). Participating in the Kingdom of God on the earth is a different playing field altogether. And yet, all are invited to participate. It is a choice we make. Keep in mind, when the tabernacle was built, all were able to see the cloud and the fire hover over it.

For those who wish to go deeper, all it takes is relationship. Out of that comes not only the deep abiding, but the signs and wonders.

There was a young couple who loved God with all their heart. They had a little baby girl born with a condition where there were too many blood vessels in the back of her head. As she grew, her head became very large. They had been to all the specialists, and all agreed that, although this could not keep growing like this, it would be too dangerous to operate. It might cause more damage than was already present. The family was heartsick, and without answers for their precious little girl.

One evening the whole family, along with friends, were invited to a birthday party at a trampoline and games establishment. The kids were having a blast diving into a huge pit full of foam balls and jumping on massive trampolines. The noise level was deafening. I sat to the side watching, as did this young mother with her baby girl whose head was noticeably enlarged. We chatted a bit, and then I asked her how the child was doing. She explained all of the complications of surgery, and the lack thereof. I asked if I could pray for the little girl. The mother agreed. Right there in the midst of the shrieks of glee and the noise that only a steel building with thirty kids inside can make, I laid my hands on the child's head. I prayed a simple prayer of healing. Weeks later the family was slated to go back to Dallas for more tests. To the doctors' shock and amazement, the myriad of blood vessels was gone, and the child was normal. Oh, my goodness! Thank You, Papa. You gave this family joy unspeakable. Their little girl was made whole. I am undone by Your Glory as it passes by me in the healing of a child.

That is why the mountain is non-negotiable for me. It is my sacred time to reconnect with my God and sit at His feet. I am not a spiritual giant; I am a little person, "boots on the ground" so to speak, but I get to see the Kingdom come to the earth. It is my very great treasure, my pearl of great price.

Exodus 34:1-30

Matthew 13:44-46

John 2:11

II Corinthians 4:17

Kingdom Principle: Time spent in the presence of God pulls back the veil between the two Kingdoms, and God's Glory is revealed.

Prayer: "Papa show me Your glory. Show me Your Kingdom. Amen."

Exercise: Each day this week, try a new space to worship and pray in, a space you have never been in before. Try sanctuaries, chapels, parks, walking trails, underwater (with a snorkel), a museum, an inner room, or a crowded street corner.

Document where you experienced His glory and in what way.

_____

_____

_____

_____

_____

_____

_____

Time spent in the presence of God pulls back the veil between the two Kingdoms,
and God's Glory is revealed.

DAY 39 — GENTLE TOUCH — RAYMOND

There is a phenomenon amongst the creatures upon the earth that is quite common, yet inexplicable. That is the healing power of touch. When our parents kissed the scratch, the bump, or the cut made with one's brother's pocketknife (it's Texas, everyone over the age of seven has a pocketknife), it actually feels better. When tragedy strikes, and a friend enfolds the bereaved in a hug, it is comforting. It has even been recorded in the world of animals. We have seen monkeys grooming one another, cats curled up together, horses nuzzling their owners.

I have met people with a gift of touch. Their particular hugs seem to make the world right again. It is recorded in several Scriptures how Jesus's touch healed the people. In the book of Luke, it is written that all who were sick with various diseases were brought to Him; and laying His hands on every one of them, He was healing them. In the book of Mark, it is recorded that He healed many. All those who had afflictions pressed about Him in order to touch Him.

These wonderful stories bring the matter of touch and its healing power to a new level. Even more astonishing is a passage in the book of Matthew in which Jesus summons His disciples and gives them authority to heal every kind of disease and every kind of sickness.

Staff and Student Chapel was about to start, and we all began to gather. Raymond, our Men's Director, was slated to speak. I was a little nervous about this because the day before, he had had two wisdom teeth cut out. I knew he would still be in a great deal of pain. As I entered the Chapel, he was standing at the podium looking a little green. The left side of his face looked like a very large balloon. As I walked to him, my maternal instincts kicked in and before I knew what I was doing, I cupped his jaw with my hand (which could be construed as unprofessional).

"Are you able to speak today? You look a little worse for wear." He wanted to try, even though his head was pounding. He was slightly nauseated and neuropathy in his feet was being very uncooperative. I took my seat. His sermon was well done, even funny. He seemed to be doing just fine. He did not seem so swollen any more. I made a mental note to apologize to him afterward for the touch.

As I approached him later and began to make amends, he explained. "I have to tell you, when you touched my jaw, all the pain vanished. My head stopped pounding, but the crazy thing is, all the neuropathy in my feet is gone. My back hasn't felt this good in twenty years! Thank you for the touch."

I was astonished. I cannot say that I had ever seen that happen. I did not pray, or even think of praying for him. And yet, the man was supernaturally instantly healed. I never cease to be amazed at God's goodness to us, or His apparent affection for us.

Luke 4:40

Luke 9:1

Matthew 8:15

Mark 3:10

Kingdom Principle: When one has been in the Glory, even a simple touch can heal the body.

Prayer: "Lord, open my eyes to who needs a touch from You today. Whether the need is healing, deliverance, or comfort, make me aware enough to stop my day and give them Your wonderous touch. Amen."

Put into practice: Go to work or a store today, Lowes, Walmart, Target, or the gas station. Look for someone who needs a touch. Once you identify the one in need, ask Father to come into the aisle, by the pump, or to the checkout line. Begin a conversation with them about the weather, their hair, or screwdrivers. Just let things unfold. If you receive a prophetic Word, tell them. If you notice a limp or impairment or injury, ask gently about it. Ask if you can pray for them and ask if you might touch the area. Watch what Holy Spirit is doing. Sometimes, it results in a hug of comfort. Sometimes it results in a miracle.

What happened?

When one has been in the Glory,
even a simple touch can heal the body.

DAY 40 – POOL OF BETHESDA – VIRGINIA

Chronic or long-term illness is particularly hard to watch as the individual wastes away slowly. Even with prayer, nothing seems to move the Spirit to heal the seemingly helpless person. Yet, Jesus told us, "Heal the sick, raise the dead, cleanse the lepers, and cast out demons." When that does not happen, we question God. As humans, we want to understand the "why" of anything confusing. Why doesn't God heal my loved one? The common reaction is to blame God. But Scripture is clear. Jesus said, "The devil comes but to kill, steal, and destroy. But I have come so that they may have life and might have it abundantly." When someone is prayed for over and over again with seemingly no results, I have learned to conduct a "forensic investigation." The goal is to find the obstruction, and hopefully help remove it.

One such case was a man who was so sick he could not move himself. It is recorded that he had been in the condition for 38 years. Each day, he lay by the pool of Bethesda for it was said that when the angel of the Lord came down and stirred the waters, whoever was able to step into the pool first would be healed.

One day, Jesus saw the man lying there and knew he had already been a long time in that condition. He said to him, "Do you wish to get well?" Now that may seem like a silly question, but the man's response to Jesus is quite telling. He began to explain his predicament. "I have no one to put me in the pool when the water is stirred, but while I am coming, another steps in before me." In other words, when asked if he wanted to get well, he made excuses why he could not get well. Even today, many people are so focused on their illness and why it is impossible to get well, that no amount of prayer can break through. The sick can impede their own healing.

Jesus said to him, "Arise, take up your pallet and walk." Immediately the man took up his pallet and walked. The key to the story is that later, when the man ran into Jesus again, Jesus said to him, "Behold, you have become well; do not sin anymore, so that nothing worse will befall you."

In this man's case, the issue was secret sin. Over the years, I have discovered several other obstructions that can hinder a healing. The most common is unforgiveness. Another is fear. Resentment, anger, and a religious spirit also play a part. Some people wear their long-term illness like a badge of honor. That, too, will hinder the healing process. In order to see the sick set free, these hindrances must be gently and lovingly removed. It is a delicate process that must utilize kindness and understanding, with no judgements.

There was a beautiful woman I knew who suffered one such long-term, terminal disease. Many people prayed for her, but nothing budged. Slowly, but surely, she deteriorated until her arms and legs were paralyzed and her organs were malfunctioning. This went on for years, until she was forced to use a motorized scooter operated by her mouth.

One day it was reported that she was back in the hospital with renal failure. Things looked grim. My sense of it was that there had to be some obstructions to her healing. I went to the Lord for direction and asked what to do. His answer was very clear. Go to the hospital and gently walk her through the idea of hindrances to her healing.

The next day, unexpectedly, the woman called me from her hospital bed. As uncomfortable as I was with speaking to her about her obstacles, I knew that I had to go. As I arrived at her door, another couple whom I did not know walked up. The three of us trooped into the room. I felt very uncomfortable. That discomfort was exacerbated by the presence of strangers. I did not want to pursue this in front of others. Nevertheless, Holy Spirit pressed me to proceed.

To build her faith I began to tell several stories of God's grace to heal cancer, scoliosis, strokes, paralysis, and even HIV. She began to get excited, as did the couple. They had never heard such stories. Their faith to believe began to build. I then broached the real matter at hand, "Sometimes we can block our own healing with things like unforgiveness, resentment, jealousy, or self-pity. Are you willing to explore something like that?"

"Absolutely!"

We walked through the possible blocks; she acknowledged the issues and repented. We cast out the offending demons and moved to the next issue. Holy Spirit came into the room and wrecked us all. It was so sweet to see her set free. I finally laid hands on her and prayed for miraculous healing. The infection around her feeding tube was instantly healed. Thank you, God.

The following morning, she texted me to say that the test results on her kidneys was truly a miracle. She was no longer in renal failure. We rejoiced. I reminded her to keep her seed of healing and continue to believe for the rest of the miracle. A week later, she stunned everyone when she WALKED into a women's conference at church on her own. What a glorious day for her! Papa, You are remarkable. Thank You for Your love for us, even in our mess.

John 10:10

John 5:2-14

Luke 13:10-14

Kingdom Principle: Removing hindrances to healing will open the door to the Kingdom.

Prayer: "Jesus, show me how to find the obstacles in my own life that keep me from walking into Your destiny for me in spirit, soul, and body. Amen."

Try this: Explore all the possible obstructions that may be hindering your healing such as unforgiveness, fear, identity, a religious spirit, offense, jealousy, resentment, anger, unbelief, your thought life, or self-pity. Repent and ask God to forgive you and cleanse you from all unrighteousness. Now, the spirit attached to the sin has no more legal ground to stay. Cast him out in Jesus name. Pray for healing.

What happened?

DAY 41 – FEAR – LUMP

Over the years, I have come to realize that although a person believes in healing, certain attitudes will impede or block the miracle. The most common attitude is fear. Countless times I have seen people come for prayer, desperate to be made well, but they are so gripped with fear and worry no amount of prayer seems effective. "Do not be afraid," is a commandment throughout Scripture repeated over and over. In fact, it is repeated 46 times. Joshua is instructed by the Lord to be strong and courageous again and again. The prophets declared it; Jesus commanded it.

A few years ago, I was at my yearly gynecological exam, when the doctor found a lump in my right breast. He guided my fingers to the spot where he felt it. Sure enough, I could feel the offending lump. It was about the size of a pea, and hard. He ordered a mammogram right away. As I walked through the days and nights until the test, I reached up a thousand times and felt it. Fear gripped me. My husband had lost his first wife to breast cancer. It did not seem right to put him through that again. We had already been through so much. I did not tell him about the lump.

I was knowledgeable enough about healing that I knew to decree my Scriptures and shake my fist at the devil while standing on the promises, but deep down I was frightened.

One day I was listening to a fellow who knew a great deal more about healing than I did. He was addressing fear.

"You love Jesus; you turn your affection toward Him every day. You focus on His affection toward you. Then you are diagnosed with something terrible. Fear strikes with a vengeance. You get on the Internet

and find out all the terrible things that could happen from this diagnosis. You are overwhelmed by the possibilities. What has happened in the spirit is that you have turned your affection and focus away from Jesus and bowed the knee to the demon god of fear, worshiping, so to speak, at the altar of a demon."

~**Bill Johnson**

I was rocked to my core. Everything within me rose up.

"Whatever happens, I will NOT bow the knee to a demon god! That I will not do! Live or die, sink or swim, come or go, I will not walk through eternity having bowed the knee to a demon god of fear!" I became ferocious about it. I willed my affection back to my Father. When the spirit of fear would begin to speak to me at 3:00 am and I would feel for the thousandth time the lump, I would get mad and turn away from the chatter. I was resolute. Looking into eternity, it was easy not to be duped by demonic chatter. This I would not do. I would not bow the knee, regardless of the cost.

I told no one of the upcoming tests. I did not want them to bow the knee either. Finally, the day came, and I went for the test. The technician asked me to point out the offending mass. I felt for the lump but could not find it. I pointed to the general area. She ran the test and said she could find nothing unusual, but because it was a doctor who had found it, she asked the resident oncologist to come in. He too ran another test.

"I just do not see anything remotely wrong here. There is not even a fibrous lump. There is nothing here," he said. He looked a little confused as to what in the heck my OBGYN had felt. I knew what I felt over and over. I knew that it was a miracle. Father had healed me.

When I mention this possible impediment of fear to those who ask me to pray for them, they say, "I can't help it. I just become overcome with fear."

Yes, you <u>can</u> help it. It is like a bird that flies through your barn. You see it and hear it, but you don't let it build a nest on top of your head. You do not entertain the thoughts. You must take captive every thought to the pulling down of this stronghold. God will not do that for you. It is your responsibility to keep the barn cleaned out.

It has been my experience when the demon comes at 4:00 in the morning and whispers in my ear, it sounds like first person Texan. It sounds as though this is my thought. It is not. It is a demon that has come in disguised as me. I have learned the hard way to take captive the thought and command the demon to get out in Jesus's name. Demons are very legalistic. They know exactly what they can and cannot do. They must obey the name of Jesus so they must leave. Here is the important part. That demon will be back and try again to stir up fear, resentment, jealousy, or whatever you are battling. It has worked for all these years and he hates to give up such a willing prisoner. Each time, I cast him out again. My experience has been that he will try about ten to fifteen times. When I stand my ground every time, he finally gives up. I always turn my attention and affection back to Father.

Initially, I had to ask Holy Spirit to whisper in my ear and remind me this is not my thought. It is a demonic thought. I must take it captive. This one truth changed a great deal for me.

Joshua 1:1-9

Leviticus 19:4

Deuteronomy 11:16

Luke 12:7

II Corinthians 10:3-5

Kingdom Principle: If one bows the knee to a demon god, the Kingdom of God cannot be accessed.

Prayer: "Jesus, when fear overcomes me, will You whisper in my ear to take captive the thoughts? Remind me not to bow the knee to a demon god, but to turn my trust and affection back to You. Amen."

Galvanization: Today, make a list of things that you fear such as failure, loss, illness, or general anxiety. Sit quietly before the Lord. Repent for bowing the knee to a demon god.

Thank Him for forgiving you. Now, in Jesus's name, cast out each demonic entity that has built a nest on your head. Once they are out, ask Holy Spirit to rush in and fill you up. I do this on a regular basis like a medical checkup. The stinkers will sneak back in sometimes.

Journal what happened:

DAY 42 – DELIVERANCE – LESLIE

When addicts come to the Mission to get clean and sober, they are usually carrying incredible wounds from their past. Many have stories of abuse, abandonment, brutality, and extreme neglect. Their stories are horrific. They include rape, incest, or beatings beyond our comprehension. There is a hurt so severe and deep that to cope with life, they had to numb the pain somehow. At whatever age they discovered alcohol, or drugs, they discovered a new best friend to make the pain go away. By the time they come to us, the numbing agent has taken complete control, and whatever shred of life they may have had is decimated.

These precious individuals are then open season for the demonic to rush into the void to deliver the final blow.

Such was the case with Leslie. She was living the life of a drug dealer's wife. She became familiar with the underbelly of society and all the perverse and demoralizing things that go with that. At one point, she and her husband had a gun aimed right at them in their own living room. Prolonged drug use can begin to deteriorate the brain both physically and spiritually to the point that the user does something wildly demented. Eventually the day came when her husband, in a terrible state of mind, took his own life. She was accused of causing the violent act. Her devastation drove her to drugs for comfort, which then proceeded to destroy her completely. She heard of the Mission and the work we do with the addicted. Desperate, she came to join the twelve-month program of classes and therapy to achieve sobriety.

One of the courses we offer is Art Therapy. Creating art has been known to raise endorphin levels in the brain. That chemical is extraordinarily helpful in creating a sense of wellbeing so desperately needed in the process of getting clean and sober. In addition, we introduce the spiritual side of recovery, and what Jesus did to help people become free from their past.

One day I introduced the concept of demonic entities that had come into the students' lives through trauma and drug use. We walked through the general concept, then identified the demonic entities that may have snuck in during the course of their lives.

Jesus was quite clear on the concept. When He walked on the earth, He cast out demons on a regular basis. He commanded us to do the same by His authority, and in His name. In the book of Mark, the last words spoken by Jesus were about the demonic. He said, "And these signs will follow those who believe in My name they will cast out demons, they will speak with new tongues…they will lay hands on the sick and they will recover."

I handed out a list of common demonic entities who may be resident in them. The students were to circle the ones they thought may be a problem for them. For instance, a person struggles with his temper, and wants to get it under control, but try as he might, he simply cannot overcome the outbursts of anger. That would be a clear indication that there is a spirit of anger who has foothold in this precious person's life. As believers, we have the legal authority to cast them out in Jesus's name. In order to teach them how to get the buggers out, I asked them to name one that they particularly struggled with. The guys always yell out "lust," so we went after that one together. Manifestations of the demonic leaving the person vary. The spirit of lust is particularly demonstrative. The guys start to manifest with loud burps, groans, mucus, and eventually throwing up in the trash can. I encourage them not to feel shame or embarrassment. It is just part of the process. Someone then yelled out another and we went after that one.

Suddenly Leslie, who had only been at the Mission for two days, began to scream. Alarmed I asked what was wrong.

"My feet are dancing!"

"What?"

"My feet! They're dancing! You don't understand. I am Roman Catholic, and I did not believe anything you were saying about the demonic, but it is my second day here and I did not want to be kicked out, so I did what you said, and my feet began to dance. You must understand that I am physically unable to do this."

Several years prior, she had been involved in a car wreck. Her leg from the knee down was crushed and the surgeons had to screw a steel rod unto her tibia bone from the ankle to the knee for stability. The pain was terrible. She explained that she had never been able to walk on it very well without extreme pain. She certainly could not dance. They fused her ankle. She jumped up and began to dance for the first time in years. I was dumbfounded. I have never seen anyone physically healed miraculously through deliverance, but God is God and He can do anything He wishes. For my part, I am a ready learner.

Later that day at the Mission, she visited our Chiropractor who volunteers once a week to come and adjust the students in our programs. She danced into the room and said, "Look! I can dance!" He was confused. She explained what had happened that morning. The doctor had her lie on the table and began to check for the steel rod.

"Girl, God healed you! The rod is gone, and the screws are gone. Let's see that dance again."

Leslie met her God that day. She has never looked back. She has since graduated from the program and is an entirely new person. Papa, I am so grateful to you for your kind affection to this little lost sheep. You did not abandon her in her darkest time but "bent down, drew her out of many waters and set her on a broad place." Hallelujah!

Mark 16:17

Matthew 8:28

Matthew 9:32,33

Psalm 18:16

Kingdom Principle: In order to fully intercept the Kingdom, one might need to do away with the demonic entities that have taken up residence in one's life.

Prayer: "Oh God! You are my God, and I am your pupil. Teach me the nature of Your divine Kingdom, and how to traverse through it. Show me Your glory in the earth. Amen."

To do: Search out the Scriptures to find how many ways Jesus healed the sick or performed miracles through touch, mud, and distance.

Record every different method of the miraculous that you found in the Gospels.

DAY 43 – OPPRESSION – BETHESDA

When Jesus walked on earth, He went about doing good and healing all who were oppressed of the devil. In the book of Mark, there is an account of an evening when the people brought to Him those who were influenced by the demonic. With one word, He cast them out of the afflicted and healed all who were ill.

What does it mean to be oppressed? We have seen in the past instances when one country oppresses another country, or one individual oppresses another individual. The original Greek word used in the Scriptures is "*kadadynasteuo.*" It means, "to exercise harsh control over one; to use one's power against one; to oppress one." In Jesus's time, demonic beings exercised harsh control over the people's lives.

In today's society there is still this oppressive entity who "uses his power against people." In most cases, they have no idea that they are being led around by the ear and influenced to act in certain destructive ways. In other words, they indeed are held captive. The good news is that Jesus came to set the captives free. In like manner we, too, are commanded to do the same.

At one time, we were contacted and asked to come to an outreach center in town to preach on healing and pray for the sick. Three teams loaded up and came to the center for the weekly church there. I laid out some simple truths about healing, then began to call out different conditions that God had spoken to me about that morning. As I spoke, people with those conditions came forward. A young woman with an oxygen tank and tube came forward with COPD. She was instantly healed. Another with a hernia was healed as well. A young man came forward for healing in his back and legs. He looked very dark and brooding, His eyes looked like lifeless coals. As it turned out, he was consumed with grief over his wife leaving. The Lord showed me several specific secret sins that oppressed the man. I whispered in his ear, "Is there any secret sin that you are practicing?" He declared that there were none. Knowing what the sin was, I challenged him again. Again, he denied it. "You are watching sex videos and looking at porn," I declared. "Oh, yeah, there is that," he admitted. He confirmed he struggled with those. He repented, we cast them out, and he literally changed before our eyes. His complexion grew lighter and lighter, his eyes began to brighten and sparkle. He even began to laugh. Jesus set this captive free. We then went after the healing. Both his back and his knees were healed. He was an utterly changed man.

There was a man in the congregation who did not believe one word that was being said. In his heart, he scoffed at what was happening. I had no idea that the man was struggling. Just at that moment, the Lord urged me to say to the congregation that there were actually things that could block a healing, such as doubt and unbelief. Those words hit him like a stone. He was propelled forward to one of the teams.

He was shaking uncontrollably and teetered like a very inebriated individual. He explained that he had a tumor in his brain that caused the imbalance and the trembling. The team was a little unclear on how to proceed with a man who did not believe in signs and wonders in modern times. Finally, one of the team members spoke and said the perfect thing.

"I tell you what, let's just go to the Lord and hear what He wants to say to you today (he knew that theological arguments never got anyone healed)." The team laid their hands on the man and invited Holy Spirit to come and touch this dear person. Like a tender hen brooding over her chicks, Holy Spirit came and brooded over him.

"I can feel Him!" he exclaimed. The team knew to just let Holy Spirit work. Tears began to roll down his cheeks as he stretched out his hands to receive. Still they waited. Finally, the man opened his eyes and smiled.

"Wow!" was all he could say. The team asked how he felt.

"I feel great!" It is then that the team realized that he was no longer shaking, and his balance was normal. The man looked down at his hands and realized that they were steady. He walked around with no sign of teetering or stumbling. Everything was normal. He began to cry and could not stop.

What a glorious day. The man was set free in more ways than one. Holy Spirit did just what needed to be done.

Acts 10:38

Matthew 8:16

Mark 1:3

Luke 4:14-19

Kingdom Principle: Condemnation does not lift the veil to the Kingdom. Kindness leads the little ones into the presence of God.

Prayer: "Jesus, give me a compassionate heart for those who are oppressed by the devil. Show me how to lead these lost souls into Your glorious presence so that You can wash over them with peace, joy, and a sense of hope. Amen."

Encounter: Today, watch for an opportunity to lead a stranger into the presence of God. Be a conduit for His love and peace to poor over them. At all cost, avoid a theological debate. Concentrate on presence, as opposed to arguing.

What transpired?

DAY 44 – FORGIVENESS – BEVERLY

I have learned over the years that there are attitudes that I must guard against if I really want God's hand on my life in the area of healing and the miraculous. One such impediment to a healing is unforgiveness. There is a particular Scripture that brings me to tears every time I quote it, and I quote it often. "…but for the joy set before Him, He endured the cross, despising the shame…" I am no theologian, but to me the joy set before Him was each of us. That includes me, you, and my abuser. I can only imagine how distasteful it must be to Jesus to have endured torture, hell, and the grave for my perpetrator, only to have me undo that sacrifice with my unwillingness to let it go. Shame? Yes, shame on me.

In the Word, Jesus is quite clear on the subject. I must forgive seventy times seven. No matter how many times I am betrayed, lied to, or tricked, I must forgive. Jesus further points out what will happen if I do not forgive. I will not be forgiven. In addition, I will be turned over to the tormentors. Why is He so adamant about this? We cannot be free of the tyranny of the evil one unless we forgive. It remains an open access point for the enemy to sneak in and wreak havoc in our lives. In the act of forgiveness, we triumph over the works of the devil.

When someone comes for healing, and God whispers that there is unforgiveness, I ask the person, "Is there someone you need to forgive?" The answer given usually is, "I am struggling with forgiving my husband, my father, my son, my sister." The truth is that if we struggle with forgiving someone, we are the ones in prison, not them.

"Yes, but someone needs to take the blame for what was done to me! Someone needs to pay!"

Yes, and He did. Jesus Christ stepped up and said, "I will take the blame. I will pay the price for the betrayal, the abuse, and the brutalization." He did that on the cross. When He uttered those three words, "It is finished," 800 hundred billion failures disappeared. Your slate was wiped clean and your perpetrator's slate was wiped clean as well.

Some people have said, "I have tried to forgive, but the memory comes back. I get upset all over again."

A very wise man taught me how to become free from the need to punish my perpetrators.

"Picture forgiveness as a scale from one to one hundred, one being that you want to want to forgive, all the way to one hundred, which is total forgiveness. If you can get to number one, and you want to want to forgive, Jesus will miraculously come to your number one, pick you up, and carry you all the way to one hundred. He can bring you to total forgiveness and do it supernaturally. You will finally be free of the burden and the consequences. Thank you, God, for setting me free.

At the Mission there is a weekly Staff and Student Chapel service where guest speakers come to encourage us all. Aside from staff and students, guests off the streets will join us occasionally, as well as members of the community from other churches.

On one occasion, our Board President, Paula, brought a very small and timid lady named Beverly to be healed of debilitating scoliosis. She was so crippled by it that she was doubled over and could not lie on her back or raise her hands up above her shoulder. On this day, our speaker was a particularly fiery fellow who "mixes it up" as they say. By the close of the service, many of us were lying on the floor in the presence of the Lord. When I was able, I turned to look back at the rest of the congregation. Ten feet away Beverly was lying on her back on the floor crying. Paula motioned for me to come and pray for Beverly. As I crawled across to her, Holy Spirit whispered, "She has unforgiveness in her heart. There is a demon wrapped around her spine."

Gently I asked, "Beverly, is there someone you need to forgive?"

"No…No, I'm good," she replied.

I do not remember what came next, but Paula tells me that I got up over her and pointed at her and yelled, "Beverly! Who do you need to forgive?!?" She began to tremble and cried out her betrayer. We walked her through the scale of one to one hundred. Jesus faithfully carried her to total forgiveness.

Having settled that, we meandered our hands into the small of her back and began to pray for healing. Instantly, her spine rolled and popped like a wave in the sea.

Paula yelped at the feeling of the motion under her hand. We were certain that Beverly was healed. She jumped up and straightened, then began to walk at a fast pace around the Chapel, waving her hands above her head. She was laughing and praising God for what He had done for her. She boldly walked up to the speaker and declared that she had been healed.

"Yes, I can see that, because the snake I saw wrapped around your spine when I walked in is gone," he replied. We all whooped for joy.

That afternoon, she realized that the following day she had an appointment in Dallas with her surgeon who was to operate on her back. She called to cancel the appointment. She was told that if she kept the appointment or not, she would be required to pay $350.00 for the visit. Beverly decided to go. The following day, she presented herself at the appointment. When the doctor walked into the examination room, she began to tell how Jesus had healed her scoliosis. With obvious doubts, he said, "Well, let's take another image of your spine and see just what has happened."

After he looked at the new images of her back, he came back to the examination room and sat down.

"Beverly, in my field, if we operate on scoliosis and see a 2-degree improvement in the spine we consider that a success. If we are able to see a 6-degree improvement, we call that a miracle. You have an 8-degree improvement in your spine since the last time we met. I am not touching your back. One more prayer and you will be perfect!"

The man was of another faith, but he could not deny what he saw when he compared the new image to the old one. Right there on the floor of the Chapel at a homeless shelter, Beverly forgave, and God healed her instantly. Oh, God! How mighty are Your works in all the earth! And we are filled with joy.

Hebrews 12:2,3

Matthew 18:21-25

Ephesians 4:22

Isaiah 53:3-6

Kingdom Principle: The door to the miraculous is shut tight when there is unforgiveness. Forgiveness is the key to unlock the door.

Prayer: "Jesus, thank You for taking the blame for all of my sins. And thank You for taking the blame for all of my abusers' sins. What You went through for us is outlandish. Is there someone whom You took the blame for that I have not forgiven? Whisper in my ear. I pledge to You to forgive that person after what You endured to set him free. Amen."

Suggestion: Go to your tent. Settle into His presence. Become open and honest with Him asking if there is someone you harbor resentment or bitterness towards. Listen for the whisper. If anyone comes to mind, go to the scale of 1 to 100. Determine where you are on the scale. Ask Jesus to come capture you and supernaturally take you to 100. Say out loud, "It is finished." Determine in your heart that when the demonic comes and brings it up again you will not be shaken but stand firm at 100% forgiveness.

How did that go?

_____

_____

_____

The door to the miraculous is shut tight when there is unforgiveness. Forgiveness is the key to unlock the door.

DAY 45 — GRATITUDE — MY FATHER

Growing up, my father had lots of mottos by which he guided his life and the lives of his four children.

"Do not criticize, condemn, or complain."

"Leave the campsite cleaner than you found it."

"Always treat others with respect, especially the underprivileged and minorities."

"Noblis Oblige (Noble Obligation)."

"You are responsible for the lives of those who work for you or serve you in any way."

"Love God and do as you please." (This motto was a trick. It sounded liberating until my father would add, "If you love God, doing His will is what will please you.")

My father was a noble man, faithful to his God and to his family. He was an artist, well known for his intricately carved altar crosses, some as tall as 2 stories. He carved communion rails, pulpits, and altars in the European cathedral style. He was happy and fulfilled.

Then his world and all that he loved was wiped away. His wife, my mother, was diagnosed with cancer. In order to seek out medical care and support, he brought her to Texas. It was too late. She only had a few weeks to live. From her hospital bed she took my father's hand and said, "Walter, I am ready to go home now. In an instant, I will be in the arms of Jesus. There is one last thing I want to do. I want to sleep next to you and hold you one more time in our own home."

In the early stages of Alzheimer's, he was dazed and confused, but the family was galvanized into action. Within a week, we bought, remodeled, painted, wallpapered, and carpeted the house across the street. We moved her favorite furnishings in, arranged the flowers, and hung the paintings she so loved. It took an army of workers, but she got her wish to pretend for one week that all would be well.

Then she was gone. She was my dearest friend with whom I shared everything, and she was gone. My father's grief was cataclysmic. In an instant, his gallery, foundry, friends, church, and his true love of 65 years were swept away by a monumental tsunami. He stood in the ashes and rubble of his life and grieved.

I was designated as his caregiver. I learned quickly that life as I had known it was also gone. I was crushed under the burden of caregiving and sorrow. In order to survive, I had to lock my own grief for Mother's sudden death into an airtight box and bury it.

In the coming days, all I could see was the growing burden of Dad's Alzheimer's, and his continued mourning. I railed against it all and told my sister, "I just want my life back to normal."

Her reply? "This is your new normal."

I kicked and screamed at the goads. Eventually, dad had to move in with us. His disease had become too advanced to leave him to his own devices. For four years, I bristled at the responsibility, shaking my fist at the heavens.

"What are You smoking up there?!?" (I strongly urge the reader NOT to do this. It just prolongs the agony.)

My father had a new motto, "Just when you think it cannot get any worse, it does."

And it did. My husband's mother also died, and his father, who also had Alzheimer's moved in with us. His was so advanced in his disease that he could not remember that the love of his life had died. Every morning he would come to breakfast asking, "Where is Gwen? I can't find Gwen."

We would have to explain all over again that she had died. The horrid grief would wash over him again. He was inconsolable.

It was a nightmare with no end in sight. Two old men traversing the recesses of their dark and convoluted minds, along with all their meds and walkers and braces and dirty clothes and doctors' appointments. Life as I had known it was whisked away in the wind. I was bitter and resentful, and profoundly depressed.

One day I picked up a book called <u>One Thousand Gifts.</u> It was not a particularly spiritual book, but one that unraveled one of the greatest powers in the Kingdom - the power of intentional gratitude. The author had found herself in an unbearable grief that lasted for years. She could not overcome it. In fact, she had become obsessed with it, addicted to it. An acquaintance had challenged her to ease the burden by starting a journal listing 1,000 gifts she could be thankful for. The story is her journey out of her own oppression simply by being grateful.

I promptly went out and bought a bound journal and began my own journey into 1,000 things I was grateful for. The change in me was nothing short of supernatural.

David said, "Enter His gates with thanksgiving, and His courts with praise. Give thanks to Him. Bless His name." He knew how to walk into the Glory.

Paul said, "Devote yourselves to prayer keeping alert in it with an attitude of thanksgiving." In other words, be intentional in your gratitude. It literally changes everything.

I began to watch for things I could write in my gifts journal.

1. Watching my sons praise the Lord with hands lifted high.
2. The morning light flashing on the bird's wing as he flies.
3. The sweet smell of a baby just out of his bath.
4. Being held in the night by my husband.
5. The ticking of the clock early in the morning.
6. Finding revelation in the Word, as though a treasure had been left there just for me to find.
7. Watching my boys rock their babies.

8. Healing me because I asked You to.

9. The life and mind of a very great clergyman. The Church triumphant in the face of death, the body of Christ raising its voice proclaiming the greatness of God.

10. The sheer joy of a three-year-old.

11. A well-cut cocktail dress.

12. Being disciplined by the Lord privately and not publicly.

13. Brilliant golden leaves shimmering down outside my window in the crisp fall air.

14. Cake batter.

15. Human history.

16. Pansies, grape hyacinths, and tulips.

17. Preaching the Gospel.

18. A sense of peace despite it all.

19. Crickets.

20. Standing three feet from a Van Gough, tears running down my cheeks from its beauty.

21. Crepe Myrtle.

22. A gift of a hand signed Picasso and the thought that went into that gift.

On and on I went, filling page after page with beautiful things in my life that I had been overlooking. The transformation in me in the midst of my private hell was extraordinary. The bitterness and resentment melted away. My private hell disappeared. I began to enjoy life again. I was made utterly new by this one act. Thank you, God!

Psalm 100:4

Colossians 4:2

Philippians 4:6

Kingdom Principle: Intentional gratitude unwraps the joy and peace of the realms of God.

Prayer: "Jesus, thank You for the gift of gratitude. Thank You for not leaving me under that heavy dark blanket of anger and resentment but liberating me from my own coffin. Amen."

Action: Purchase a journal or spiral notebook. Begin your list of gifts that have been all around you all this time. Be intentional every day to find the beauty, the joy, the verse, the smile, or the comment that lies in your path. Write it down. Do it every day. Eventually go back and read your list.

What happened?

_____

_____

_____

_____

_____

_____

_____

Intentional gratitude unwraps the joy
and peace of the realms of God.

DAY 46 — ABIDING — WICHITA FALLS VISITORS

There is a certain phenomenon in the Kingdom of God that prevails over all things. It is an agricultural phenomenon that paints an exquisite portrait of the Kingdom at work. Jesus says, "I am the vine, you are the branches. He who abides in Me, and I in him, bears much fruit, for apart from Me you can do nothing." *Abide* is a lovely Greek word which means to remain or dwell with, giving the connotation of "over a period of time." Jesus goes on to say if we abide in Him and His words abide in us, we may ask whatever we wish, and it will be done for us. In other words, we are close friends. We have a relationship. We are so connected; we are literally living extensions of Him. And apart from Him, we will literally shrivel up and die, just as one of our arms or legs would do if it were no longer attached to our body. When He says, "You can do nothing...," He means literally nothing. We cannot take our next breath without Him, let alone produce anything.

However, when we are walking and talking every day together, He can trust us with our requests. He can trust that we will not ask for stupid stuff, like a Maserati, unless a Maserati would further the Kingdom. We are simply no longer interested in those types of things. Nevertheless, it has been my experience that when we are no longer interested in the things of this world, that is precisely the moment He will drop something like a hand signed Henri Matisse print or an Al Mar pocket knife with a pearl handle into our laps for no apparent reason.

This abiding is much like a good marriage. One does not have to connect with a spouse. One wants to. There is a longing for the morning coffee together, the call in the middle of the day, sometimes three calls, just to hear the voice of one's beloved; the homecoming in the evening with easy conversation over dinner; holding each other in the night, and weekend mornings in bed, just sharing thoughts and theories, and hearts. We are abiding. And our deepest desire is to provide whatever the other needs or wants.

At the Mission, staff members are asked to spend time with the Lord every day in the Chapel. Many find the Chapel to be their favorite space on the earth, because He tabernacles there. His presence is constant there. The moment one walks in the door, He engulfs the person. Difficulties and issues are washed away. Only peace remains. We don't have to go to Chapel, but those of us who do count it a privilege and a pleasure. Those who choose not to go simply have not experienced the supreme joy of His closeness there. We are abiding. Many propose this is why we see so many signs and wonders, miracles, and healings. In our abiding, the Father is happy to give us whatever we wish.

Recently, a couple traveled from Wichita Falls, Texas to come and see what manner of things were going on at the Mission. They had heard stories of wondrous healings. They stayed for three days and drank in as much as their poor brains could hold. During the course of the visit, they shared their difficulties with some physical issues they were facing. The husband had fallen twenty-five feet from a scaffold and landed on his hip years ago. It was a source of constant pain and made climbing stairs unbearable.

He could only accomplish it by holding onto the railing and pulling himself up each step. He had to wear a lift in that shoe. The wife had a hip replacement that had left her with one leg significantly longer than the other. Looking at her from behind said it all. Her left hip was so much higher than her right, so much so that a casual glance would make it clear. It caused her whole body to be out of alignment constantly. The pain was constant as well.

On the final day, I had introduced the couple to a Board Member who was a Chiropractor. He came every week to pray over and adjust every student and staff member. He always prayed for healing for his patient first before adjusting them. Then, he would check them. Many were divinely healed and no longer suffered from their malady.

Dr. Hand (appropriate name for a Chiropractor) immediately noticed the difficulties of this sweet couple. He prayed over each, and each was healed instantly. The husband ran to the stairs to try it out. He climbed the stairs without touching the railing. He was amazed. His wife was no longer lopsided or feeling any pain. She cried. All they wanted to do was go to Chapel and praise the Lord. They stayed so long that we checked the security cameras to make sure they were okay. They were sitting on the first-row crying.

God wrecked them both, and they encountered His love there. Thank you, Papa!

John 15:1-11

John 15:13-17

Exodus 33:11

James 2:23

Kingdom Principle: Abiding with the Lord continually unbolts the door to the domain of the supernatural.

Prayer: "Lord, teach me this wonderful sense of abiding with You as a dear companion and friend. I just want to be Your friend. I want to know You. Help me make time in my busy day to stop and come abide with You. Amen."

Suggestion: Create or seek out a sacred space where you are able to go and abide with the Lord. Make a sacred time that is designated only for Him. Determine in your heart to guard this space and this time. This week commit to going there and becoming a companion. When interruptions come, ask yourself, "If I were here with the President would I allow this interruption?"

What did you discover about your friendship with God?

DAY 47 – RELIGIOUS SPIRIT – TEETH

Over the years of studying the miraculous, there appears to be a pattern concerning hindrances to miracles and healings. Why do some people come again and again to a church to receive healing and nothing happens? The questions begin.

"Why doesn't God heal me?" Or, "Why did God take my wife?" Or, "If it's God's will." Or the all-time worst, "God gave me this illness to make me stronger."

I have heard it said that if there is a failure or disconnect from signs and wonders, healings, or deliverance, it is never on God's side. Saying, "This disease was sent to make me stronger," is not scriptural. Jesus never refused to heal anyone so that they could gain strength or insight when He walked on the earth.

As frail humans, we want to understand the "why" of it all, and the because. So, we manufacture a religion to explain what we do not comprehend. Jesus said, "Peace I leave with you. My peace I give to you; not as the world gives to you. Let not your heart be troubled, nor let it be fearful."

To understand the failures and the "why's," many people begin to create a doctrinal explanation around the "why." A religious spirit is only too happy to accommodate that. We have heard people say, "It is not always God's will to heal." Or, "Healing is not for today. It was only given to the Apostles." Or worse, "It was a demonic spirit that healed him." I have spoken at conferences on the subject of divine healing, and I could feel the majority of the crowd stiffen and fold their arms in disbelief. Very few people were healed afterward. Jesus experienced the same thing in His ministry. Because of the offense, He was able to do only a few miracles.

Pastors have come to me and asked, "Why do you see so many healings at the Mission, while we see very few?" A religious spirit hates miracles, signs, and wonders. He is very legalistic and knows exactly what his legal rights are with any given individual, or Church; he is very territorial. If leadership believes that it is not always God's will to heal, then a religious spirit has every legal right to see that that doctrine is enforced.

If, however, the belief is that healing, deliverance, and salvation are all three in the atonement of Jesus Christ, it is not difficult to wrap one's head around it. For example, years ago when Martin Luther received the revelation of salvation by grace, the Church was set free from the tyranny of a religious spirit. Because of that, it is easy to see people come to a heartfelt salvation. In fact, we expect it. Only recently have most of us received a revelation of the full atonement, "saved, healed, and delivered."

The key word in Scripture is the word *sozo*, a Greek word that translates interchangeably to be "saved, healed, delivered." The Scriptures record Jesus saying, "Your faith has saved you." In other places, He is quoted as saying, "Your faith has made you well." The Greek word in those two scriptures is the same, *sozo*. It is interchangeable.

In addition, the 53rd chapter of Isaiah documents the same. "He was pierced through for our transgressions, He was crushed for our iniquities, the chastening for our well-being fell upon Him, and by His scourging we are healed."

For years I was taught that this chapter was not about Jesus, but Hezekiah, a king of Judah. As a new believer, I thought, "Wait a minute! Hezekiah had nothing to do with my transgressions, my iniquities, or my sickness. Nor was it recorded that he was ever beaten or scourged." Jesus did that.

The important thing to take away from all of this is Jesus took the full brunt of our messed-up lives and erased the consequences in one stroke. All we have to do is reach out and take the gift by faith.

One day a friend called and asked if she could bring her college aged granddaughter to the Mission for prayer. The girl had had an accident on a trampoline when she was little, whereby her teeth were pushed up into her gums. Years and years of orthodontic surgery had resulted in infection after infection. She was presently experiencing a new infection with extreme pain. The surgeon told the girl that the surgeries had failed; she would have to start all over again. She cried and thought she could not go through anymore.

She came to the Mission Chapel service for prayer. During praise and worship, the Lord told me to ask the students with problems in their mouths to come lay hands on the girl and pray for her miracle. Massive drug use destroys their teeth and gums, so most have terrible issues with their mouths. Six came forward, one of which was brand new to the program and had only arrived the night before. She was not even detoxed yet. They all gathered around and laid their hands on her. Each prayed the simplest childlike prayer. The little newcomer's prayer, even though she was still detoxing, was especially sweet. When they finished, I asked each of them to check their mouths for any improvement. The newest girl noticed that the pain in her jaw was completely gone. She had been on the streets for so long that she had numbed the pain of the abscess with drugs and alcohol. Detoxing had brought back the pain with a fury. Now the pain was completely gone.

That night, the granddaughter noticed the pain in her mouth was gone as well. The infection was gone.

What does that tell me about the Kingdom? Healing is available to all who seek it. God sends the gift every time. If I believe it is for me here and now, I may receive it. If I do not believe it is always His will to heal, I will not receive it. It does not take a famous spiritual giant to heal the sick. Signs and wonders are to be accomplished by every believer, even an addict still detoxing.

Luke 7:50

John 14:27

Mark 9:22-24

Isaiah 53:5

Kingdom Principle: If one believes signs and wonders are for today, the Kingdom is opened. If one does not believe it, the Kingdom is locked down and inaccessible.

Prayer: "Jesus, I believe when You walked on the earth, You healed every disease and every sickness. You never said "no" to anyone. I believe You send the gift of healing every time. I want to receive it. Lord, I believe, help me in my unbelief. Amen."

Do this: Look up every Scripture in the Gospels using the word SOZO. Do a word study on the original meaning in the Greek. Find the pattern in these verses concerning God's will to heal.

What did you discover?

_____

_____

_____

_____

_____

_____

_____

_____

_____

_____

DAY 48 – PRIOR PRAYER – DANIEL

In the book of Mark, there is another puzzling story when a man, desperate for his son's life, brought him to the disciples in hopes of a miracle. They were unable to do anything to help the boy. Scripture goes on to say that a group of scribes gathered to argue with the disciples and a large crowd had assembled.

So, let's look at the story. A large crowd had gathered, the disciples started arguing with the scribes, and the boy was manifesting a powerful demon rolling on the ground and foaming at the mouth. Complete chaos had broken out and crowd control had become an issue.

At that moment Jesus, who had taken Peter, James, and John up to a high mountain and was transfigured before their eyes, returned from the summit. The story reads that the entire crowd saw Him and they were amazed. One suspects that there may have remained an incandescent glow that had not entirely departed from Jesus.

Jesus asked a simple question, "What are you discussing with them?"

The father of the boy cried out to Jesus for His help.

"If You can do anything, take pity on us and help us!" This poor father was frantic, as any parent would be. Jesus was his last hope.

Remember, Jesus had just been to another dimension and he was glowing. He had crossed over and somehow conferred with His old friends, Moses and Elijah. His perspective was elevated above all the foolishness that was erupting around Him. A little irritated He essentially says, "You just don't get it. It is so easy and so doable. Just believe."

The poor father cried out, "I do believe; help me in my unbelief." That was probably the most honest prayer ever uttered in history.

Jesus saw the crowd rapidly gathering. He rebuked the demon and commanded it to come out. The demon gave it one last hurrah by throwing the child into terrible convulsions and making him as a dead corpse. Jesus took him by the hand and raised the boy up. I am sure that the father of the boy was beside himself with joy.

The disciples were perplexed, "Why could we not cast it out?"

The response is crucial to catch. "This kind cannot come out by anything but prayer." In other words, no theological debate will ever accomplish a miracle, or bring true salvation for that matter. The disciples arguing with the scribes was futile and only muddied the waters. Further, this kind is not your everyday garden variety demon, and only having been in prior prayer, in the presence, in the Glory with an elevated perspective can one see this kind come out.

The phenomena of supernatural elevated perspective one can only get with time in the inner room, in secret. "And when you have shut your door pray to your Father who is in secret. And your Father who sees in secret will repay (discharge what is due and promised under oath) to you."

The Father is in secret. That is where you will find Him. That is where He sees you, in secret. Out of that comes the "transfiguration" that allows a random moment to turn into a miracle.

One of the Mission's outreaches to the homeless and working poor is to provide every possible item they might need, from clothing and shoes, to housewares, furniture, even large appliances. People in the community are so good to donate massive amounts of new and used goods to our In-Kind Donations Department so that every week men and women are able to "shop" in our free store. It is the Walmart of the very poor.

One day, a family came to the Mission in need of a bed and dresser. This family belonged to a culture in which the whole family goes together to the store, the emergency room, and the Mission. On this outing, even the old grandfather came. He was ensconced in one of the club chairs in the front hall waiting when Madison, one of our staff members, walked by and noticed the gentleman. She noted how twisted and gnarled his hands were, as well as his legs.

He had a cane with him. She stopped and began to visit with the old man. He explained that he was crippled with pain all over his body from rheumatoid arthritis. Madison asked if she could pray for the man. He agreed, so she laid her hands on his joints and prayed for healing.

Having received the needed furniture, the family came to retrieve the old man. He hobbled off with no apparent improvement.

The following day, the old man appeared at Madison's office door. His cane was missing. Shocked, Madison asked him to sit and tell her what had happened. The man began to relate how nothing had improved from the prayer she had prayed on the day before. However, when he awoke the following morning, he felt wonderful. All the pain and stiffness were gone. He rose to see if his legs would hold him. They did. He felt young again. God had healed this dear soul.

"I just threw that old cane in the closet and came to tell you the good news!"

Madison had been in the secret place, and her transformed mind was able to see the possible, not the impossible. The Father, who is in secret, rewarded her with the elevated perspective that she needed to heal the old man.

Mark 9:14-29

Matthew 6:6

Mark 9:1-8

Kingdom Principle: Prior prayer in the secret place produces an elevated view of the Kingdom where signs and wonders are unleashed.

Prayer: "Father, today will You bring me to the elevated place where I might see and believe from Your perspective? Will You show me the Kingdom from above and not from below? Amen."

Activate: Create for yourself a secret space, a place that is special to you. It could be a closet, the backyard, or a guest room where you may meet with the Father in secret. Spend time every day in this secret place. Build an account of prior prayer that can be drawn upon at any time.

Having done this for several weeks, go out and find the one you are to spend your prior prayer on.

What happened?

DAY 49 — TRAUMA —
CHAPEL OF THE HOLY SPIRIT

The homeless population in any city faces difficulties that are a bit foreign to the average citizen of a town. Many suffer mental disorders originating from abuse, physical or otherwise, brutality, or massive drug use. In order to keep everyone safe in our 200-bed facility there are protocols to follow. A security team is ever watchful. Nevertheless, things do erupt from time to time.

One guest, a military veteran, was particularly difficult. He was a regular and I had previous conversations with him in Chapel. He was bright and articulate but challenging. We have learned over the years that it is the nature of the beast. Hence, the security team. In order to keep everyone safe, all are wanded with a metal detector when they enter the building to check for weapons; bags are searched for contraband.

The team has never carried weapons or sticks. The greatest hope is to talk a disgruntled guest off the ledge in calm and assuring tones. These little ones are, after all, very near to God's own heart.

Nonetheless, on February 14th in Staff and Student Chapel, our veteran pointed a gun at the congregation and took thirty or so hostages, including some from the security team. One young female staff member shielded her two young friends with her body and pushed them out the door to safety when the gunman demanded they sit with the others. Many were able to run to safety elsewhere in the building. It was a long and tense ordeal. Zip ties were produced, as well as blindfolds, and a young mother was instructed to zip tie everyone's wrists. She was shaking and could not manage it. One of our students stepped forward and offered to help, thus creating a diversion enabling six other hostages to take the gunman down. The gunman was able to get several shots off, miraculously missing their mark and hitting the mural of Jesus on the front wall where the young mother was standing, but remarkably she was not shot. One hostage wrestled the gun away and ran with it out into the hall. He was mistaken for the gunman and was shot twice by the swat team who had been summoned. He was hospitalized and is doing well. The gunman was led away to the police cars.

The aftermath of the shooting was filled with various levels of trauma by all who were involved. Crisis intervention counselors were called in to help staff and students regain some level of wellness. Our building was a crime scene and we were not allowed back in for several days, but we all felt the need to have a worship service to praise God for His goodness to us throughout the whole ordeal. We moved everyone out to our Mission Ranch located ten miles north of town. Previously an Episcopal church camp, there was a dear little Chapel, named "Chapel of the Holy Spirit." We scheduled the service the following morning. Local pastors came to be a part, as well as therapists and members of the community. The Chapel was packed with about a hundred people.

As we began singing praises to God, a wave of the Holy Spirit rolled from the back of the Chapel to the front, and everyone began to shout simultaneously. We could not stop, as the wave washed over us, again and again. We wept and shouted and danced uncontrollably. We were utterly baptized in joy. Holy Spirit washed each of us clean that day. The following week, we held services in the little Chapel again. The Holy Spirit rolled over us again; signs and wonders and miraculous healings all took place in quick succession. People were wrecked all over the floor. Laughter and weeping broke out. No one wanted to leave.

It was as though the trauma opened a door to revival. And even back in our regular Chapel, the presence of His Glory is thick still.

In Scripture, I began to see a pattern of trauma followed by extraordinary revival. The story of the Road to Emmaus in the book of Luke documents disciples filled with sorrow at Jesus's death, only to discover that their traveling companion was Jesus Himself. They raced back to Jerusalem with joy to tell the others. As they arrived, Jesus also appeared, and they were all filled with joy.

In Acts 2, the disciples of Jesus hid in the upper room waiting for what they did not know. They were missing Jesus terribly. Similarly, a rushing wind came into the room and tongues of fire rested upon their heads. They spoke in new tongues and spilled out into the street where Peter preached to the crowd and 3,000 were saved. The Church was born that day. Signs and wonders followed. Even the persecution of the early Church acted as a seed pod broken open and flung on the winds to the entire planet.

We were finally allowed back into our Mission. Bullet holes were patched, blood was mopped up. The only fatalities were the ice machine in the adjoining kitchen, and a file cabinet in the sound room. The one thing we could not piece together was how the gunman got the weapon into the building in the first place.

We were forever changed that day. Holy Spirit rose up in us in supernatural joy and I learned that trauma can be the door to the Kingdom of God if we let it.

Luke 24:13-53

Acts 2:1-41

Acts 3:1-10

Kingdom Principle: A dastardly act of violence can be a corridor to the Kingdom.

Prayer: "Father, thank You for covering the congregation that day with Your wings; for protecting the little ones. Thank You for healing us with the power of the Holy Spirit and ushering us into the Kingdom. Amen."

Meditation: Look back over your own life. Was there a time when a loss or trauma actually brought you closer to the Lord?

Write down what you remember:

DAY 50 — A SWEET TOUCH — MR. WHITAKER

Sometimes, Jesus uses us and our flawed earthly vessels despite ourselves. Peter was such a train wreck a lot of the times. However, in one minute he had that glorious revelation of who Jesus really was. Jesus commended Peter and commissioned him to start the Church. The next minute he was arrogantly rebuking Jesus for all that nonsense of being handed over to the Jewish leaders to be murdered. Jesus actually said to Peter, "Get behind Me Satan!"

Again, Peter declared to our Lord that he would die for Him; the next minute he was swearing at a slave girl, denying he even knew Jesus at all.

And yet, when Peter got wrecked by the Holy Spirit on the day of Pentecost, he boldly preached to thousands, endured imprisonment, healed the sick, raised the dead, and was finally martyred.

Staff members at the Mission are strongly encouraged to pray once a day in our Chapel for thirty minutes. We all have our unspoken time slots that we prefer. Some staff members pray together. I prefer to be alone. I don't like double dates. At any rate, we have discovered that all this prayer all day long has created a tabernacle of sorts in which God comes to dwell. Our little Chapel at our little shelter has become filled with His presence. Just walking in the door, one is hit by the presence of the Lord. He has manifested Himself by a cloud of smoke hanging in the air by the mural, as well as brilliant balls of light, or angels visible to the naked eye. But most of all, there is an overwhelming sense of refreshing, and renewal. Whatever worries and troubles we come into the Chapel with are gone by the time we leave. They are replaced with a supernatural sense that all is well, despite what may come our way.

Two couples came from a nearby West Texas oil town named Canadian to visit the Mission and take a tour. They had heard the stories of divine healing and wanted to hear more. As we sat together at lunch, I was telling the story of Alex and how his liver was healed instantly. While I told the story, I mindlessly placed my hand on the side of the gentleman sitting next to me to illustrate my point. "I just laid my hand right here and Alex's liver kicked me." I do not know what I was thinking. We are careful about casual touch at the Mission, because we do not know what traumas the person may have endured at the hands of another. But there I was, touching a stranger on the side of his abdomen. Sheesh!

We spent the afternoon touring the Mission, and even prayed for the gentleman's wife. We said our goodbyes and they promised to come again.

About a month later, the gentleman whose side I touched returned to the Mission and visited with our Development Director and brought a donation. He told his story:

"Michael, I did not want to say anything until I was sure, but ten years ago I ripped the ligaments in my side bucking hay bales." A rancher bucks a lot of hay bales over the years. "It never really healed, and I kept reinjuring it. But that day last month when Mrs. Taylor laid her hand on my side, it was the exact location of my injury. For the first time in ten years, the pain was gone. And it has been gone ever since. It doesn't hurt, even when I hoist hay bales."

I unknowingly touched the very spot on his body where the old injury was. Why? I guess God wanted to heal him that very day. Despite my mindless touch, or because of it, the man was healed. Texas ranchers are a tough crowd. They don't necessarily believe just anything unless you have some cold hard facts. The cold hard fact was that Jesus healed him right then, right there. He was never the same again.

While I was amazed at this inadvertent healing, I knew that my time in the Chapel with the Holy Spirit for weeks and weeks on end had built up a reservoir of supernatural power at the Mission.

I have found that there is a link between healings and my personal prayer time in the Chapel here. I suppose so many people praying daily in there causes miracles to happen despite us. I feel certain that this was what had happened to me. I went to Chapel to be with Holy Spirit over and over again. Holy Spirit went with me to the sick over and over again, and they were healed. Hallelujah!!!

Mark 8:31-33

Mark 14:29-30

Acts 2:14-21

Matthew 8:1-3

Kingdom Principle: The amount of time spent in intimacy with God face to face is in direct proportion to the level of the phenomenal signs and wonders one sees.

Prayer: "Jesus, thank you for the power of the Holy Spirit upon us to change us and make us whole. Thank you for using us despite ourselves. Use us again. Amen"

Try this: Find a church whose Chapel is open to the public. Designate a weekly time to go. Show up every week. Do not miss.

How'd it go?

_____

_____

_____

_____

_____

The amount of time spent in intimacy with God face to face is in direct proportion to the level of the phenomenal signs and wonders one sees.

DAY 51 — THE PAINTING — ANN

On many occasions in the Bible, God had the prophets of the Old Testament and the believers of the New Testament do some really odd things. Hosea was instructed to marry a prostitute. Elisha was told to throw a jar of salt into the poisonous waters so the waters could be made pure.

In the New Testament, Agabus took Paul's belt and bound his own feet and hands to show the way Paul would be bound and taken into the hands of the Gentiles. In like manner, He has asked me to do some pretty strange things.

Many years ago, a friend whom I had not seen in a very long time approached me at a conference. She told me of a dream she had had in which a man stood before one of my paintings staring at it. He was instantly healed of his disease. That did not compute for me. It was such a bizarre notion, that I dismissed the dream and never gave it another thought.

Twenty-five years later in my tent time, I heard the Lord say these words, "I am imparting to you a supernatural power of peace and hope. Your paintings are like prayer cloths sent to heal the body and the soul when sent with that power upon them."

Instantly, I remembered the dream. I sat stunned. I was still not able to conceive how this could be remotely possible. The Lord spoke again.

"Jena, what are prayer cloths made of?"

I responded that they are commonly made of cloth and oil, sometimes a tissue and oil in a jam.

"And what are your paintings made of?"

"My paintings are made of canvas and oil paint." Revelation mowed me down in a split second. It still seemed crazy. People would think I was insane, but I knew it was His voice that I was hearing.

A few weeks later, a little grandmother came for women's shopping, a benevolence program where clothing, housewares, shoes, and even toys are made available to women and children free of charge. They gather in the Chapel right after the noon service and wait to be escorted to shopping.

I was visiting with the ladies and children, when the little grandmother asked me to pray for her daughter, Ann, who had severe migraines and seizures almost daily. They had been to the emergency room on several occasions. Nothing seemed to help the woman. The thought of the prayer painting came to me.

I asked her to come to my office where I took one of my prints on canvas of Jesus at the well and explained what I thought we should do. I retrieved my anointing oil and drew the sign of the cross on the back with it, along with a healing Scripture. We prayed over the painting. I instructed her to take it to her daughter to be placed where she could look at it. The little woman cried and hugged my neck.

A few weeks later in women's shopping, the woman approached me and told of how the print was placed on the mantle for the daughter to look at. She had not had a migraine or seizure since that day.

We hugged and cried at what God had done. We rejoiced at His goodness. He used a rather odd and somewhat unorthodox method to heal one of His own. Was it really just a "pretty prayer cloth" that healed the girl? The image of Jesus at the well? Or all of the above? I have no idea. I am just a foot soldier doing what I am told. I am learning to trust Him and obey Him even when His instructions make no sense. Thank you, God!

Hosea 1:1–3

II Kings 2:19–22

Acts 21:8-12

Kingdom Principle: Trusting God's wisdom over human wisdom will unzip the Kingdom of God.

Prayer: "Father, I am continually amazed at Your works and the vast wonders of the Kingdom. Thank You for showing me such extraordinary wonders. Thank You for letting me participate in the wonders. Amen."

Do this: Write down some areas in your life in which you struggle to hear God's instructions. Trust Him enough to obey those instructions. Select one area and focus your prayers of trust and obedience on that one area every day.

What happened?

_____

_____

_____

_____

_____

_____

_____

_____

Trusting God's wisdom over human wisdom will unzip the Kingdom of God.

DAY 52 – THE BOX – HOLY SPIRIT

I have heard it said that God is better than we think, so we have to change the way we think. This profound phrase is a rewording of Paul's admonition in Romans 12. "Do not be conformed to this world but be ye transformed by the renewing of your mind, that you may prove what the will of God is, that which is good and acceptable and perfect." In order to grasp the Kingdom of God, we must be transformed. In order to be transformed, we must renew our minds. What does that mean? It actually means in the Greek a *renovation*, which makes a person better than in the past.

Picture your mind, your way of thinking, as a box. In that box is your upbringing, your culture, your way of thinking, and your way of life. Everything that has happened in your life created your box. Suddenly, something happens that is so cataclysmic that your box cannot hold it and it literally blows up, because it is too small to contain this new concept, this new culture. Box blowing is, I have learned, necessary in order to see and grasp the Kingdom. The Kingdom will not fit in our box; our box is far too small. So, if we wish to see and understand it, we must allow our box to be blown to bits.

While attending an international conference for those that work and run gospel rescue missions, I was to speak at a breakout session on signs and wonders, an altogether new concept for this conference as it was by far predominantly evangelical in its belief system. I arrived at the hall in which I was to speak. It was a lovely room with floor to ceiling windows on one side and a glass wall into the large expanse of lobby on the other side. Great glass double doors slid wide open to enlarge the space. A monitor introduced herself and told me that she would monitor my time. She was a lovely woman about my size - five feet on a good day. I placed my notes on the table at the front and began to pray. I felt elated and full of joy. And as sometimes happens when I speak, I began to feel faint.

"Not now, Holy Spirit. I need to seem normal right now. Not crazy."

I fell to my knees. The monitor was beside me in an instant. Oh dear, God! Not now!

"Are you alright?"

And down I went on the floor. I heard her speaking to me and then men came to me. They helped me to a chair and asked me if I were diabetic.

"No, I am fine, really."

They handed me a peppermint to suck on. I was somewhat embarrassed as I knew that these people would not understand being slain in the Spirit. I prayed again and stood up.

"Hello, I am Jena Taylor and I would like to tell you a story. There was a woman named Wanda on the front row of Chapel very drunk…."

I continued to tell miracle story after miracle story. The guests all became excited to hear such astonishing things and clapped and shouted. I glanced at the double doors and the wall of glass. People were lined up along the glass. The doors had been thrown open so that they could hear better. On and on I went describing the miracles and the glory of God and His Kingdom; the people were like sponges, drinking in the healings and the signs and wonders. This was all foreign to most and I knew it was risky, but I felt called to tell the story of God's mighty power on the earth. Finally, I saw my monitor raise her hand. I finished but asked if anyone wanted prayer. I mentioned that I would stay along with my staff and we would pray. A line formed. The first in line was a beautiful young Jamaican woman who suffered from migraines. We laid hands on her and prayed. Tears coursed down her cheeks as the migraine left. On and on we went, and every single man and woman wept as we laid hands on them and prayed. Some were healed and some were not, but they were all touched by Holy Spirit. After an hour, people were still joining the line. Finally, after two hours we had prayed for the last one. I reflected on the tears. I had heard of a baptism of tears but had never seen it. It was just so moving. I wanted to touch their tears.

I almost felt like a missionary bringing the Good News to a people that did not know such good news. I think some boxes got blown up that day. But no matter, God touched His beautiful sons and daughters. Praise the Lord!

Romans 12:2

Habakkuk 1:5

I Corinthians 2:9

Kingdom Principle: In order to enter the Kingdom, some of our doctrinal boxes must be blown up, so that the new Kingdom paradigm can be grasped.

Prayer: "Lord, in Your grace will You blow up my box, my traditional way of thinking? Will You transform me? Will You renew my mind? I wish to have Kingdom eyes. Let me see the wondrous things that You are willing to do in us. Amen."

To do: Search out and find a mentor who is further along this road into the Kingdom. Ask them to teach you everything they know about signs, wonders, and miracles. Shadow this person for several days.

What did you discover?

_____

_____

_____

_____

In order to enter the Kingdom, some of our doctrinal boxes must be blown up, so that the new Kingdom paradigm can be grasped.

DAY 53 – THE WORDS – CUPCAKES

In this Kingdom of God that we are seeing more and more of, it seems that it might require a real shift in the concept of who we are once we accept the gift of salvation. Most people are happy to be saved and going to Heaven, but beyond that there is little interest in who we are in Christ and what we have been commanded to do. From the very first book in the Bible, any student who wishes to see it may discover the path to the shift. It is the Word.

Let us start by looking at the first words. The creation story has been fascinating to me. I have heard the story all my life, and yet every time I read it I find something new in the words that I missed before. I began to translate every word in the first five verses of the Bible and found some extraordinary truths about the Kingdom.

In the first verse the author uses the Hebrew word *bara*, for the word created. "In the beginning God created the heavens and the earth." (*Bara* has an emphasis on the world that was created out of nothing.) The Latin term is "*creatio ex nihilo*." How does God do this? In verse three we learn that the vehicle by which creation took place was by word of mouth. It was spoken. And yet, the original meaning of the word means to think it, declare it, and create it all in one act. Brilliant!

Then God said, "Let there be light," and there was light. Since the sun, moon, and stars are not spoken into existence until the fourth day, one must look to the original Hebrew to discover what nature of light we are reading about here. The original Hebrew word was *owr*. The translation is fascinating. It means illumination, enlightenment, brightness, happiness, cheerfulness, or life. Sounds like Heaven to me. It calls to mind Jesus's statement, "I am the light of the world." Then He said, "You are the light of the world."

The Hebrew translation for "let there be" is the Hebrew word *hayah*, which means to exist, to be, to become. It refers to God as the "I am He who exists." In other words, the translation would be rendered, "I am He who is the light. I am He who is the expanse. I am He who is the water, the land, the creatures, and the man." For me, this changes everything. It would indicate that Adam had the divine nature in him before he fell. When Jesus, the man, won the battle over death, hell, and the grave, He restored that divine nature to us. With that in mind, it is not a leap to realize that I am able to do what Jesus did which is heal the sick, raise the dead, cast out demons, cleanse the lepers, and multiply the food. After all, I am the light of the world. Jesus said so. Therefore, I must realign my thinking to what He said, not what I have been told by others.

Several years ago, it happened that I was to preach to the guests off the street before lunch on my birthday. I decided to throw a birthday party. I asked the team to go buy about 75 cupcakes to hand out to the guests as a treat. As Chapel was filling up, the security guard would let us know the count that day. It quickly became apparent that we did not have enough cupcakes for everyone. There were 98 people in the service. Panicked, I told the team to go get some of the girl scout cookies out of the food pantry, but Madison, my assistant had other plans. You may remember Madison from Day 12.

"Let's just pray that Jesus multiply the cupcakes!"

"Fine, you pray, and I will go get the cookies." It is amazing how fast one can revert to old thinking patterns. As Chapel began, the platter of 75 cupcakes sat on the table from which I preached. There was not a cookie in sight as I had requested. I plowed ahead with the message. As the guests filed into the dining room, we handed them a cupcake. Miraculously, each guest got one. When everyone had received one, there were three left over.

The simple faith of a young woman to believe what Jesus said, "You give them something to eat," produced the miraculous multiplication of food, with leftovers.

I learned a valuable lesson that day. If Jesus utters the words, I must believe the words above all else, even in the face of the impossible. A young woman taught me that.

Genesis 1:1

Genesis 1:2-5

I Peter 2:9

Matthew 14:13-21

Kingdom Principle: When we have faith to believe that what He said is true, we are able to walk in our divine nature and speak into any circumstance and see it change.

Prayer: "Jesus, reveal to me the full extent of the power in Your Word. Show me how the use of those words creates food, heals flesh, and brings change in a person. Amen."

Try this: Find a commandment of Jesus you have never acted on in the supernatural. For example, "You give them something to eat." Or "Heal the sick, raise the dead, cleanse the leper, cast out demons." Act on that commandment within the week.

Journal the experience:

_____

_____

_____

_____

_____

When we have faith to believe that what
He said is true, we are able to walk in our divine nature and speak
into any circumstance and see it change.

DAY 54 – BROKEN HEARTS – PETER

In most cases when addicts come to us to get clean and sober, life has beaten them up so badly, that massive amounts of healing must take place in their crushed souls. The abuse, trauma, and neglect is so pervasive and has gone on for so long it sometimes feels like this one cannot be mended. Although we have therapists on staff to work with our clients, it sometimes takes a miracle of huge proportion that only God can do to bind up those wounds and heal that broken heart.

In the book of Hebrews, the author talks about the Word as a living being, calling it "living and active, and sharper than any two-edged sword, and piercing as far as the soul and spirit." This is the tool of the Holy Spirit to heal such desperate cases. The word "active" in this verse is translated energy, or medical treatment. In other words, like a surgeon cutting away a cancerous tumor, the Word acts as a scalpel to cut away the disease in the soul.

We pray this living Word over a wounded soul, and it goes forth to accomplish what it was sent out to accomplish. The beautiful, wonderful new life begins in this little soul, and everything changes.

One such man came to the Mission utterly crushed. His alcoholism was acute. But the addiction was only the symptom to deeper older wounds. When he was a little boy, his father used to beat him for sport. He would drag the child to the basement and chain his wrists to an overhead pipe leaving his little legs to dangle in the air. He would then take a broom stick and beat the boy until he was tired. The father would leave the boy hanging while he went up to the kitchen for a glass of tea. Refreshed, he would return to the basement and go at the boy again. Needless to say, the physical wounds were lasting. The emotional wounds were even more so. To numb the horrible pain, he began to drink.

In the months that Peter was in the program to get clean and sober, we knew that forgiving his father for this atrocity would be the only way to heal this crushed soul. Peter refused to do that. He would never forgive the man. As the months rolled by, we went at the problem every way we could think of with no results. His time with us was almost over. His graduation day was coming, but this crucial piece to his healing was refused flatly.

One morning in Staff and Student Chapel, a pastor from the local Baptist church came to be our guest speaker. His message was on forgiveness. It was a very simple and straightforward talk on what Jesus said about forgiveness in the parable of the unforgiving slave. He delivered the message with kindness and grace.

The pastor then asked us to bow our heads and pray. Peter bowed his head and closed his eyes. As the pastor prayed, Peter felt a breeze blow by his face. Startled, he looked up to see what it was. Everyone else had their heads bowed and seemed undisturbed. He closed his eyes. The breeze came again but stronger. He did not look up, but let the breeze grow and wash over him. He began to notice a lightening of his burdens, his anger, and his resentments. It felt so odd not to have the weight of them. He gave way to these feelings.

The pastor said, "Amen," and Peter looked up a little stunned. What had just happened? He was not sure, but he knew that he felt better, lighter, different. He sat in Chapel a long time by himself, trying to work out what had changed. Then it came to him. He had forgiven his father. Still he sat in wonderment of the strange peace he felt. The Word had washed over his soul and healed his broken heart. His anger, resentment and depression all evaporated in an instant. He was a new man, set free from his own prison.

God sent a dear sweet pastor to speak softly and tenderly to Peter. In the Kingdom, any FedEx delivery guy will do.

Hebrews 4:12

Psalm 23:3

Psalm 41:4

Matthew 18:21-35

Kingdom Principle: When delivered by a tender heart, a hard truth can become so very easy and one is then able to be healed.

Prayer: "Lord, is there anything in my own soul that needs healing? Any wound, fissure, or unforgiveness that I need to deal with? If so, would You, in your kindness, show me what that is, and walk me through healing? Amen."

Initiation: Set aside a block of time to spend alone with the Lord. Ask Him if there is any woundedness that needs to be healed, any unforgiveness, or resentment, bitterness, or character flaw that needs to be addressed. Ask Holy Spirit to come and brood over you, speaking to your heart, and healing you.

Journal your experience:

_____

_____

_____

_____

_____

_____

_____

When delivered by a tender heart, a hard truth can become so very easy and one is then able to be healed.

DAY 55 – CONSEQUENCES – ALEX DIABETES

In most societies and in the Church, there is a general belief that we must pay for the consequences of our actions. Indeed, the book of Galatians warns us "whatever a man sows, this he will also reap." The idea is that we can get forgiveness, but we must pay the consequences of our actions. If we smoke 5 train cars full of cigarettes, we will pay with lung cancer or COPD. If we feast on quarter pounders and a large fry every day, we will be profoundly overweight. And don't we deserve it? If we drink ourselves to oblivion, we will destroy our liver.

Sadly, I too fell into this attitude of "just desserts." I smugly believed that the atonement did not cover the consequences of poor choices, especially in the area of obesity, until one day Jesus sat me down in the time out chair and set me straight.

"Jena, do you not believe that My grace, My unmerited favor saved you from death, hell, and the grave and wiped away your sin?"

"Yes, Lord" I replied.

"Am I not able to extend mercy to wipe away the consequences of your sin, too? Even the physical consequences in your body? My blood covered it all."

I had to embrace this new revelation. I believed it in theory, but not in reality, where the rubber meets the road. I struggled terribly.

In Isaiah, God makes a powerful statement, "So shall My Word be which goes forth from My mouth. It shall not return empty, without accomplishing what I desire, and without succeeding in the matter for which I sent it." That verse is extraordinary. It is His Word which brings about the healing, the miracle, and the deliverance.

Albert Einstein said, "Everything is energy and that's all there is to it. Match the frequency of the reality you want, and you cannot help but get that reality. It can be no other way. This is not philosophy. This is physics."

God created His universe to operate in a certain manner we call physics; laws that govern the physical realm. In the Kingdom, it could be said that the Word is the law that governs that realm. It is, however, the same principle. Jesus said, "Therefore I say to you, for all things for which you pray and ask, believe that you have received them, and they shall be granted to you."

To take the truth further, one need only go to John where it reads, "In the beginning was the Word. And the Word was with God; and the Word was God. He was in the beginning with God. All things came into being by Him, and apart from Him nothing came into being. In Him was life and the life was the light of men." The Word is a person, Jesus. He is the healer of our spirit, soul, and body.

David said, "He sent His Word and healed them, and saved them from their destruction." We deserve the consequences of our actions, but He saved us from those consequences, just as He saved us from our sins.

When one is involved with addiction, be it alcohol, drugs, food, shopping, money, television, fame, glory, or image, it all leads to the same place, destruction. When addicts come to us to get clean, they have every type of physical problem from their former lifestyle such as diseased bodies, cirrhosis, COPD, diabetes, terrible teeth, bad heart, or mental disabilities. Most cannot be healed medically.

Remember the story of Alex? He was miraculously and instantly healed of stage 4 cirrhosis of the liver and jaundice; against his will I might add. It was certified by his doctor. Alex had decimated his liver by drinking two gallons of vodka a day. And yet, God, in His mercy, healed Alex. There are dozens of stories of men and women healed from a disease caused by their excesses. He also suffered severe diabetes and had to take insulin shots every day.

One day in Chapel, I felt that God wanted to heal chronic illness. I asked all who had chronic illness to stand up. Eleven people stood to their feet. As I asked what they were struggling with, nine reported diabetes. That was shocking.

We gathered around them all and began to pray for healing. Alex was one who stood. Others gathered around the students and laid their hands on the area above the unhealthy pancreases. They prayed God's mercy on each one.

The next day, Alex reported that his blood sugar was normal. He stayed on his insulin but tried eating terrible things to see what would happen. It stayed normal. He decided to get off the insulin to see what would happen. Still, the blood sugar remained normal. For one week, Alex continued to eat sugar, carbs, and every bad food he could think of, and it stayed normal.

"Alex! I think you're healed, buddy! Stop with the testing!" I exclaimed.

In God's mercy, He wiped away every consequence of Alex's destructive lifestyle. Thank you, God!

Galatians 6:7

Isaiah 55:11-13

John 1:1-3

Mark 5:19

Psalm 107:20

Kingdom Principle: The revelation of God's mercy, saving one from the consequences of one's actions releases the Kingdom into our midst.

Prayer: "Papa Forgive me for my skewed thinking of Your grace and mercy. Forgive me for demanding consequences for myself and for others. Will You cleanse me of this unrighteousness? Amen."

Galvanization: In the days to come, make a note of your reaction to those around you, be it friends or strangers. Is there a prejudice against anyone else's flaws, habits, or shortcomings? Do people who are overweight offend you? How about those who are sexually promiscuous? Or smokers? Or those who drink too much, drug too much? Do you feel that they deserve the consequences of their actions? Now take a look at your own actions. Do you believe that you deserve in your body the consequences of your habits?

Did I step on your toes?

_____
_____
_____
_____
_____
_____
_____
_____
_____
_____
_____
_____

DAY 56 — FAITH — YOUTH GROUP

When it comes to the Kingdom of God, there is a great deal of emphasis put on faith, and rightly so. Some believe it is the gasoline to the engine that drives the Kingdom. Indeed, an entire movement arose in the western church, beginning in the 1950's, that produced great faith healers who traveled with enormous tents around America. Many were healed by the hands of these mighty men and women of God. Later, in the 1980's, there was another huge faith movement in the church, a sort of "name it and claim it" movement. Many leaders believed there was a grace on the church for faith to see revival as we had never seen it. Sadly, in America, much of that faith went toward BMW's and bigger houses, as opposed to signs and wonders.

The trouble is, the Kingdom does not act like an engine at all, but rather a living organism. It is fluid and gossamer in its workings. It is as delicate as a spider web but more powerful than a nuclear missile. Jesus addresses faith many times in His time on the earth.

There is a particularly telling story in the book of Matthew in which a Roman centurion, a Gentile, unbeliever, a "goya" came to Jesus in desperation on behalf of his servant, the housekeeper so to speak, who was paralyzed and in much pain. Jesus was willing to immediately go and heal him. The centurion's response was extraordinary.

"I am not worthy for You to come under my roof, but just say the word and my servant will be healed. For I, too am a man under authority, with soldiers under me; and I say to this one, 'Go!' and he goes, and to another, 'Come,' and he comes, and to my slave, 'Do this,' and he does it."

Jesus marveled at this man's understanding of the Kingdom. Just like a spider web with its levels radiating out from its center, the Kingdom radiates from the One. He had not found anyone in Israel who understood the Kingdom to such a degree.

He exclaimed, "Truly, I say to you, I have not found such great faith with anyone in Israel... go your way, let it be done to you as you have believed."

The word that Jesus uses in this dialogue is the Greek word *pisits*, meaning persuaded to such an extent to have confidence in certain divine truths, especially those of the Gospel as to produce good works, as opposed to a knowledge of the truth without good works, or false faith.

In other words, there is the state of no faith, "Healing is not for today." There is a neutral faith, "God will heal me if He wants to." And there is active faith, "These signs follow them that believe, they lay hands on the sick and they will be made whole."

During spring break, many youth groups from surrounding towns come to spend several days with us and volunteer at the Mission. They do everything from painting, to weeding, cleaning, or serving. One year, a youth group from another town in the Texas panhandle came to serve. They were in middle school and worked hard while they were there.

One day, they decided to sit in on Guest Chapel while I was preaching. After the message, there was a time for praying for the sick. The students wanted to be a part, so I invited them up. They laid hands on many people and prayed for them. One fellow rolled up in his wheelchair. His legs did not work at all. The muscles were deteriorating, and they could not support the man. The kids all laid hands on him and began to pray. They spoke to the mountain and commanded it to be cast into the sea. I stood back and watched. When they closed their prayers, one young girl commanded the man to get up and walk. A little nervous he stood. At their urging, he walked. The kids all hooped and clapped. They had seen a cripple walk! What a glorious day. Their young faith had healed this man.

Matthew 8:5-13

Matthew 17:20

Luke 17:6

Mark 11:23,24

Kingdom Principle: Childlike faith indeed launches the supernatural.

Prayer: "Jesus, please restore to me that childlike faith that moves mountains! Amen."

Activation: Go to a busy street and walk. Watch for someone who is obviously needing healing. Stop and visit a minute. Then point out their need for a miracle and ask to pray for them using childlike faith.

What happened?

_____

_____

_____

_____

_____

_____

_____

_____

_____

_____

Childlike faith indeed
launches the supernatural.

DAY 57 – WORKS – THE FOOTBALL GAME

There is an astonishing, but little read Scripture in the book of James discussing works and faith. We have determined that faith is belief to such a degree as to produce good works. What good works is he talking about? A cursory glance immediately discusses a brother or a sister without food or clothing. Pure faith would produce in us a need to do something about that for our brother or sister, to perform an act of kindness for them. Hence the faith-based outreach centers, homeless shelters, and pantries that see to these needs are everywhere.

Another clue given to help us direct our faith in action is the fruit of the Spirit. A good analogy might be that a healthy tree does not have a say in whether it will produce fruit or not. It cannot help itself. By its very nature, it will produce fruit after its kind. In like manner, the truly faith-filled cannot help but produce good fruit such as love, joy, peace, patience, kindness, goodness, faithfulness, gentleness, and self-control. It is not a discipline and cannot be accessed through self-discipline (ask me how I know). Self-discipline or behavior is under the law, and we know where the law got us. "Just behave yourself, don't smoke, don't chew, and don't go with the girls that do." If we could achieve that, Jesus would not have had to be made a sacrifice.

Paul's message is clear, "If you are led by the Spirit, you are not under the law." Walking by the Spirit is a personal, daily relationship with God. It is not a state of mind; it is a state of friendship. When Holy Spirit and I are close and have been abiding together in companionship and conversation, it's easy to produce the fruits and the works. When I slip back into "behave" mode, it ends in disaster.

Not long ago, the male staff took the students who are in our year-long discipleship program to a football game in town. Alex (you remember Alex, miraculously healed of cirrhosis of the liver and diabetes) who is now on staff had purchased the tickets prior to the game. As it turned out, he had extra tickets left over and decided he had miscounted. As everyone entered the stadium, Alex noticed a family of four sitting to the side of the ticket booth discussing something. His "fruit antenna" went up. Walking in the Spirit, he went over and asked if everything were alright. They explained that they did not realize the tickets were so high and could not afford to go to the game after all. Alex took out the envelope of extra tickets. Surprise, surprise, the remaining tickets were exactly the number the family needed to get into the game. He handed them over to the father and said, "Enjoy the game."

It was such a small act of kindness that cost Alex nothing but to be in the Spirit. Alex was thrilled he could help. After all, did Jesus not say that His joy would be in us and our joy would be made full when we bear much fruit? That joy is so exciting, and fun that many of the faith filled stay alert and look for these wonderful opportunities to bear much fruit. I actually know some who have a bank account with a debit card attached to it that is dedicated to good works only. Many acts of kindness go unnoticed and remain anonymous, known only to God, and He is the only one who matters. It truly is a thrilling adventure to walk in the Spirit and participate in the Kingdom of God this way.

James 2:14-24

Galatians 5:16-25

John 15:1-11

Kingdom Principle: Consciously looking for ways to bear fruit will give way to opportunities to see chances to do good works. That is when one's joy is made full.

Prayer: "Holy Spirit, today I choose to walk with You, abiding in Your love. Whisper in my ear when an opportunity to show Your love to another presents itself. I will be faithful to stop and work Your works. I will perform an act of kindness. I will show Your love to another today. Amen."

Initiation: Today, look for an opportunity to show an act of kindness to someone. Once you start consciously looking for the opportunities, you will find them everywhere. Now act on the situation that you see with an act of kindness.

What act of Kindness did you perform today?

Consciously looking for ways to bear fruit will give way to opportunities to see chances to do good works. That is when one's joy is made full.

DAY 58 – STAND – THE BABY

In this domain that Jesus requires us to operate, we are constantly told to do things that are not within our power to do. Upon His departure from the earth, He gives some alarming instructions to us. "And these signs will accompany them who believe. In My name they will cast out demons. They will speak with new tongues…they will lay hands on the sick and they shall recover." Any believer has access to these works because of the power that lies within us. At the Mission in Homeless Chapel, I tell the guests, "If you are a believer, you have healing in your hands. Lay your hands on those standing up for a miracle." Now they watch with wonder as the person that they are praying for is healed. Many believers hope to see it happen, but do not really expect it.

What further complicates the issue is that Jesus also commanded believers to heal the sick, raise the dead, and cleanse the lepers. Even after years of seeing people healed and delivered, raising the dead was a huge stretch for me. I simply could not wrap my head around that actually happening.

After a Guest Chapel service, a couple came up the aisle. The woman looked to be about 8 months pregnant.

"Oh! Look at you! You look like you are about ready to bingo."

"That's just it, we quit feeling the baby kick, so we went to the emergency room. The doctors said the baby was dead." Tears rolled down the man's cheeks; she was weeping as well. "We decided to come to Guest Chapel to get some peace. Will you pray for us?"

My heart broke for this couple. What a sense of loss they must have felt. I laid my hand on the woman's belly. Bill, our head of security, stood behind the couple and laid his hands on the shoulders of the couple.

As I began to pray for peace and healed hearts, something else came out of my mouth.

"In Jesus name I command this baby to live! I speak life over this baby…" I was shocked at my own gross lack of respect for this grieving couple. This was not appropriate. Hadn't they been through enough? I was embarrassed at my insensitivity.

I tried again to pray for peace in their grief, but I heard decrees and commands to the baby to live coming out of my mouth. To add to this debacle Bill was yelling in tongues. I knew Bill did not have a prayer language and had never spoken in tongues before. This was turning into a circus.

Suddenly, the baby kicked my hand! I jerked it away in shock.

"Did you feel that?"

"Yes!" The mother said in wonder.

I continued to pray over the baby and the couple. Holy Spirit filled the room. Our faith soared. The baby kicked two more times. We began to rejoice and praise God. That which was dead was alive again! We were stunned, and really did not know what to do at this point. The baby was alive. My God!

It was suggested the couple go to a different clinic and ask the doctors to confirm that the baby was alive. They left with our phone numbers.

A little stunned and a bit shell shocked, Bill and I could do nothing more than sit in Chapel in the presence of Holy Spirit.

"Bill, do you realize if the doctors confirm that the baby is alive, we just saw our first raising from the dead?" I exclaimed. Bill was speechless and was only able to nod.

The following day, the mother called us. Yes, the baby was alive. We went nuts at the Mission. Yes, we screamed, yelled, hooped, and praised God. And then I wept for joy.

What does that tell me about the Kingdom? God will use us despite our faltering. As the children's Sunday school song says, "We are weak, but He is strong." As I had often done in the past, I went on Facebook and told the story. It went viral.

The following day, the mommy called me again. "We haven't felt the baby kick since you prayed for us. We want to get another opinion. Will you help us?" Of course, I said yes. I arranged for one of our staff members to take the couple to yet another emergency room and stay with them to be their advocate, but also hear firsthand what was said. She took the couple and we waited. I went to Chapel and sat before the Lord. What had I done? I had put this story out on social media, and it may not even be true. My faith plummeted. I began to wallow in misery. Suddenly the Lord spoke to me very clearly.

"Jena! Are you going to stand for this baby's life or not? Stand up and stand for this baby!" The words hit me like a bucket of ice water. My faith had folded like a cheap tent. I jumped to my feet and began to pray and decree and declare, praying over that baby's future and the calling on his life. I walked, flailed my arms, shouted, and fell in a heap on the floor. Exhaustion took hold, and I had nothing left, so I did nothing.

At last the phone call came from our staff member. The baby was fine. The doctors did discover that the mommy would need daily shots, which cost $99.00 per day. They donated these to her, but other than that, all was well. My heart soared. Jesus taught me to stand and having done all still stand. Thank you, Jesus!

Papa, I am speechless at Your sovereign power at work through us. Thank you for allowing us to participate in the Kingdom. Thank you for teaching me to stand. Amen.

Mark 16:17

Matthew 10:8

I Corinthians 2:4-6

Ephesians 6:14-18

Kingdom Principle: When we choose to stand up and STAND for the miracle, and having done all, we still stand, the Kingdom of God is loosed.

Prayer: "Father, today I ask to be used in the Kingdom despite my faltering. Give me strength to stand, and having done all, still stand. Amen."

Activation: Today, make a commitment to stand firm on behalf of another. look for and act on that commitment.

Write what happened:

_____

_____

_____

_____

_____

_____

_____

_____

_____

_____

DAY 59 — HOPE — ERRON

Years ago, when I was in a hopeless situation trapped in a horrible life, I lost all hope. This was the way it was going to have to be. And besides, did I not make this bed of burning coals? I deserved every bit of the firestorm I now found myself in, including the bruises around my neck. I remember thinking often of the story of the Wizard of Oz. The wizard had a marvelous black bag of gifts and miracles. The Lion, the Tin Man, and the Scarecrow all received hope out of that bag. But it was Dorothy's words that haunted me, "I am sure there is nothing in that black bag for me." I quoted those words most days. There was no hope for me. My marriage was in shambles.

One day in my quiet time, I fell upon this verse. "Hope deferred maketh the heart sick, but when desire comes it is the tree of life." Could it be that there might be a tree of life at the end of this poverty and abuse? I found a 3X5 card and printed the verse on it. I hung it on my mirror so I could see it. There really could be a tree of life for me. Things still might change for us all. I held onto that verse with all my heart. Years went by and nothing changed, until one day I was forced to make a move. It was frightening and offensive to me. This was not the way it was supposed to end up. The marriage had demolished what was left of my life. Now it was a pile of ash. I was filled again with hopelessness. I moved to another city with my children to start over.

In my tiny new apartment, my thoughts were interrupted by the ring of the phone. The fellow on the other end of the line was calling to welcome me to town and the church I had visited the week before. He asked how I had come to be in this city. The flood of tears started again, and the story spilled out.

"You know what you need? You need to come to our weekly recovery class at church. You are a mess and you need to get well. It starts at 6:00. Be there."

Hence, the healing began. Slow for sure, but with God's help I got well. One day I found that 3X5 card about hope. I pinned it to my wall next to my bedside lamp. Hope had been deferred, but desire had come, and it was the tree of life.

That was 25 years ago. If I could have peered into the future and seen myself today, I would not have believed a word of it. I now have a family, children, and a husband who adores me. We share laughter, jokes, teasing, games, fishing, and picnics. We have a home with a garage and a garage door opener, a car with hubcaps, clothes from real stores, and a job that fills me with passion. Who knew? The Lord was faithful to my 3X5 card. There is now a tree brimming with life and beauty. He made me new.

By the time men and women come to us to join our year-long program for sobriety, they have lost everything and are so beat up, physically and mentally, their mental illness is in full bloom. They have been diagnosed at the city clinic as bipolar, paranoid schizophrenic, borderline personality disorder, or multiple personalities. Try as we might, sometimes we cannot keep them in the recovery program. At best, they can join the Missionite Program and live with us doing small chores and helping out here and there. There is no hope of helping them in their present mental state.

One such young man came to us to get clean and sober. Our intake manager told the team that he was too far gone in his mental illness to stay.

"What's wrong with him? Why do you say that?" I asked.

"The minute you see him, you will understand," was his reply.

We brought the young man in and instantly, I came to the same conclusion. His eyes were wide and wild, like an animal cornered, and they darted around the room in a panic. His comprehension of our questions was nominal at best. When he answered, only gibberish came out. I saw the problem. He had destroyed his brain function with meth.

We quickly ended the interview, and I asked if I could pray for him. He agreed. I laid my hands on his head. He bowed his head and we all began to pray. I do not remember the prayer, only that as a mama, my heart was breaking for this lost soul. When we said, "Amen," the boy looked up at me. This was not the same young man who had bowed his head moments before. His eyes were clear and normal. They were no longer darting around the room with that wild animal look. He smiled broadly.

"I've been prayed for before, but never like that! I feel so different!"

He was lucid, calm, and coherent. My Gosh! I had never seen anything like it. Before our very eyes, Jesus had healed this young man's brain and his self-confidence. He was wrecked. We were wrecked.

We continued to visit with him and found him to be capable of joining the program. A year later he graduated with the distinction of never having broken one rule. He went into our Culinary Arts Program and became a sous chef.

God restored hope to this boy in a single moment and gave him the tree of life. Thank you, Papa!

Proverbs 13:12

Luke 8:26-30

Isaiah 54:11-14

Kingdom Principle: There is always hope.

Prayer: "Thank you, Lord, for the revelation that there is always a way where there seems to be no way. Thank You for the joy of serving You. Amen."

Try this: Look up several verses on hope and write them down on 3X5 cards. Fix them to your mirror or dashboard and read them often. Memorize them. Craft a prayer of them for your family and loved ones.

Record a time when you hung onto hope when it looked hopeless and God answered your prayers.

DAY 60 — IDENTITY — CHILI'S

Previously, we talked about Blind Bartimaeus and his need to throw off his identity as a blind person in order to be healed. Over the years, I have seen many people wear their illness as some sort of badge of honor. In a sense, their actions and words indicated that they were in some way special because they had this disease or that illness. They have taken their illness on like a cloak of identity. When that happens, I never see a healing. Some join associations with others who have the same illness, which is a wonderful way to support one another. Nevertheless, when that "sisterhood," or "brotherhood" becomes their moniker, the illness has a legal right in the Kingdom to grow.

In my own health battles, I have chosen to tell only a few people who will turn their attention to the signs and wonders needed to heal this thing, not dwell on the seriousness of the disease and slap an "Oh, this is a tough one" sticker on my back.

By the same token as a healer, I have had to unload some other cloaks of identity that were foisted upon me as I was growing up. For example, in my family it was very important to be appropriate at all times. That meant one must strictly adhere to the social manners of the day. Social manners pronounced that it is inappropriate to bother strangers. "Hello, how are you?" or "Have a nice day" were acceptable exchanges, but nothing beyond that. My father constantly preached that we were not to impose on people, especially strangers. It was simply inappropriate.

I have since learned that in order to be obedient to the nudges of Holy Spirit and see people set free, I must throw off the cloak of my identity as a well-mannered and appropriate member of society. I must throw off the old family belief system.

If one wants to see the Kingdom, one might want to examine one's constraints and attitudes.

One day, I was at Chili's at a lunch meeting. After our meal, I went to the lady's room. As I walked in, I saw a walker under one of the stalls. I got that nudge. As I came out of my stall and washed my hands, the walker lady was washing her hands. God has told me over and over,

"Just strike up a conversation. Say something nice. It's not that hard."

I knew I needed to say something, so I complimented the woman's hair style.

"Gee, your hair looks pretty today." Not profound, but it broke the ice.

"Thank you! It's my birthday today, and I am 65 years old."

"Oh. Well, may I pray a birthday blessing over you today?"

"Yes, I would love that!" I began to pray a simple prayer that God would give her the desires of her heart for her birthday.

"Oh! I know what that is!" She pointed to a large bulge on her right side under her ribs. "See this? This is a hernia, and I have to have surgery. I am going to the surgeon today at 2:30."

"Do you want me to pray for God to heal your hernia?"

"Yes! That is what I want for my birthday!" I surmised she was a Roman Catholic by the crucifix around her neck (I love Roman Catholics. They are taught to believe in miracles). I laid my left palm on the large bulge on her right side and began to remind Jesus of what He told us to do - heal the sick, raise the dead, cleanse the lepers, and cast out demons. As I prayed, my left hand began to feel tiny electrical shocks. Suddenly the woman cried out.

"Hot! Hot! Caliente!" She threw my hand off of the bulge.

"What's wrong?" I asked.

"Your Hand! It is so hot! It burned me!" She reached out and touched my hand. "Your hand is cold!"

"Yes, Honey. It's not my hand. It is the Holy Spirit and He is healing your hernia right now. So, let me keep praying for you." I laid my palm on the bulge again and prayed some more.

When I said, "Amen," I asked her how she felt.

"I feel wonderful! It doesn't hurt anymore!" She began to praise God right there in the lady's room.

"Oh! Let's go tell my husband what God has done!"

I was unsure how that might go but agreed to come with her to her table. As we approached, she started telling him in Spanish what had just happened. He looked at me as if to say, "You're crazy, and she's crazy."

Suddenly, she began to cry out again. "The bulge! It just disappeared! I felt it disappear! It's gone!"

We all looked, and truly the bulge was gone.

"I wish I could be there when you show your doctor this afternoon what just happened." I commented with a smile.

Right there in the lady's room in Chili's, Jesus touched His daughter and made her whole just as he did when He walked on the earth. He just used a very small mailman to do it.

Matthew 10:8

Mark 10:46-52

Kingdom Principle: In order to step into the miraculous, we must throw off our cloak of identifying with our infirmity, our difficulty, or our inappropriate behavior.

Prayer: "Jesus, remove from me the cloaks of identity that would hinder the Kingdom from coming. Make me new. Make me different. Amen."

Assignment: Look over your own upbringing and see if there might be protocols are hindering your step into the Kingdom of God. Throw them off and start a new family legacy.

What did you discover?

DAY 61 – DISTANCE – TORI

Early one morning in my quiet time, I asked the Lord if He wanted to heal anyone that day in Chapel services. Instantly, I saw the midsection of a body. The skin was not visible, but I saw the muscles and ligaments. At the waistline, the ligaments were stretched apart, and large masses were pushing through the muscles. I know nothing about the human anatomy, but the vision was crystal clear.

As Chapel started, I got up and described the malady as I saw it, wondering if the masses might be hernias. In my limited knowledge, it was all I could think it could be. There was no response. I knew that I saw it, so I repeated the description of what I saw, verbalizing the hernia part. No one responded. I was certain of the sight that I saw so I asked the individual, whoever they were, to see me after Chapel. The Lord clearly wanted to heal them.

We worshipped the Lord, and I introduced the pastor from a local church who came to speak to us. He stood up and came forward, but as I turned to go back to my seat, he stopped me, and explained, "As we speak, my worship leader at my church is lying in bed in terrible pain from four hernias across her waistline. She was scheduled for surgery but the fires yesterday (prairie fires) shut down the medical center at the edge of town. I believe the Word is for her. Will you pray for her?"

Everyone rose to their feet and we all prayed for the woman. Her name was Tori. The Spirit of the Lord fell and we all got wrecked. We did not know if Tori was healed, but we all felt great!

There is a lovely story in the book of Matthew about a pagan woman who boldly came to Jesus shouting out of the crowd. Her daughter was demon possessed. Initially, Jesus refused, citing the fact that the woman was not of the house of Israel, therefore, was not entitled to the "children's bread." He even referred to her as a dog. Shocking! Personally, I think He was putting her to the test. She was determined, and graciously agreed with Jesus, but reminded Him that even the dogs feed from the crumbs that fall from their master's table. Impressed, Jesus declared that her faith was great and said, "Be it done to you as you wish." Her daughter was healed from a distance that very hour.

Tanya experienced the same miracle. At the very hour we stood and prayed for her, she realized that she felt so much better. Strength came to her, and she stood up. The pain was gone. She went to see about her children. They took one look at her and exclaimed, "Mom! You look great! Are you better?"

She was indeed better. So much better that she called the doctor and explained she would not be requiring surgery after all.

A few weeks later, I got to meet Tori, a stunningly beautiful woman. She was leading worship for a wedding out at the Mission Ranch. One of our previous program guys was getting married. It was a glorious day of healing and restoration. Visiting with her, I asked how she was feeling.

"I am a walking miracle. I have never felt better. Praise the Lord!"

Praise the Lord indeed! That morning in my quiet time, God had Tori on His mind. He wanted to heal His daughter. I have come to know that any willing FedEx guy who is determined to drive that day will do.

Matthew 15:21-28

Matthew 8:5-13

Kingdom Principle: If we will take a moment to seek out what the Father's agenda is for the day, we will be allowed to participate in the inexplicable.

Prayer: "Jesus, it is the greatest joy to serve You in the Kingdom. Increase my seeing. Show me who You want me to deliver to today. Amen."

Try this: In your quiet time set aside a period to ask the Lord who is on His mind, and what He wants to do today. Then go out and deliver the package.

Record what happened in the delivery.

If we will take a moment to seek out what the Father's agenda is for the day, we will be allowed to participate in the inexplicable.

DAY 62 – INVESTIGATION – TERRY

Of all the stories in the Gospels that record deliverance from demonic torment, the most troubling to me was the account of a boy whose father brought him to the disciples. He was mute, and often thrown to the ground foaming at the mouth and grinding his teeth. The disciples could not seem to cast out the demons. When they brought the boy to Jesus, he was thrown into another convulsion on the ground and foamed at the mouth once again.

Interestingly, Jesus conducts a bit of an investigation (as if He did not know already).

"How long has this been happening to him?"

"From childhood." In other words, a possible childhood trauma started the whole affair, opening the door to demonic access. The boy's father goes on to describe in detail what would often take place. He begged Jesus if He could do anything to take pity on the family and help. Jesus then gave the man the key.

"All things are possible to him who believes."

The desperate man cried out, "I do believe! Help me in my unbelief!"

As Jesus saw a large crowd begin to gather, He rebuked the unclean spirit and commanded it to come out. After one last convulsive attack, the demon came out, and the boy appeared to be dead. Jesus took the boy by the hand and raised him, and he got up.

Here at the Mission, Jesus does the same today. One day during noon Chapel, a security team member came to me and asked me to pray for a young man who was apparently ill in chapel. I peeked in the door and saw him sitting on the front row. He looked terrible leaning over as if at any moment he would be ill on the floor. I asked security to bring him out into the hall and provide a chair. As it turned out, he was here for community service ordered by a judge. He was very young, about 15 or 16, and addicted to the opioids, Hydrocodone and Oxycodone. Evidently, he was desperately in need of a fix. He looked so sick and was crying. I asked him to look at me, so I could see the demons in his eyes. His right pupil was the size of a pin prick. His left pupil nearly covered all of his iris; it was so dilated. I pointed this out to him.

"What does that mean?" he asked.

"It means you've got some demons we need to cast out. Then you will feel a lot better."

"I have demons?!?"

"Quite a few actually. We are going to get them out. But you must repent of what you have been doing or they have legal ground to stay. Have you been involved with witchcraft? Say for instance, Dungeons and Dragons, Ouija Board, the magic eight ball, or horoscopes? If so, this is going to take some time."

"No! I am a Christian! I have done a lot of things, but I knew better than to get into witchcraft!"

We took him through repentance and then began to cast out the demons, one by one. As we did, his pupils righted themselves and became the same size. He coughed, and his nose became runny, which are manifestations of a demon leaving. Finally, I asked him how he felt.

"Better!" he said. "I don't feel sick anymore, but I feel exhausted."

We knew that was common. When the demons that have been literally driving the person for years leave, the individual realizes he is physically worn out. We allowed him to sit in the lobby and rest.

Once again, Jesus set a captive free. He always comes to seek and save that which is lost. He just uses us now to do it.

Matthew 10:1

Mark 16:17

Mark 9:14-26

Kingdom Principle: A childhood trauma can open the door to demonic oppression in an individual, causing aberrant behavior. Jesus gave believers authority to cast these out.

Prayer: "Jesus, teach me how to investigate the troubles of the individual so that he can truly be set free. Show me the things that would hinder a healing or deliverance. Amen."

Try this: When praying for a healing or deliverance, ask Jesus to show you what might be blocking a healing. Conduct a forensic investigation. Wait on Him and do what He says.

Write down what you learned:

A childhood trauma can open the door to demonic oppression in an individual, causing aberrant behavior. Jesus gave believers authority to cast these out.

DAY 63 – PROTECTION – THE DUMPSTER

Over the years while working at the Mission, I have seen countless men and women who have come to get clean and sober. In the early years, the average age of those recovering was about sixty. Most were males who wanted to "quit the drink."

Today, 90 percent of our incoming addicts are 25 years old and this is their third try at getting clean from street drugs. As we dig into their past, we look for traumas that may have been the root or reason for picking up the drugs in the first place. An alarming number of stories center around unspeakable abuse experienced as children at the hands of their parents. Then, there are those who have suffered brutality in their older years. They are rendered as helpless as the children.

Arthur was just such a case. He was an older gentleman, slight of build, and living on the streets. He came to us to join the program. We noticed right off that he was frightened and nervous. He was afraid of everything and everyone. His story was horrific. He had been raped on the streets. His mental health was frayed. We hoped we could bring him a sense of safety and protection.

Over the course of several months with us, he had several psychotic breaks, even threatening suicide at times. This required contacting the Crisis Intervention Team, a squad of policemen that come to assess an individual while talking them off the ledge. Many times, they made the decision to take Arthur to the psychiatric Hospital for treatment.

His torment over being abused to that degree kept him from being able to focus on getting clean and sober. We all felt badly for him. No amount of prayer seemed to help. Eventually, he left the program and went back out on the streets.

One day recently, I walked into the lobby of the Mission, and there sat Arthur. He was thinner than before, if that was possible. He had scrapes and bruises all over. Alarmed I sat down beside him and asked what had happened to him.

"Mrs. Taylor, you won't believe what happened! I was on the street looking for a safe place to sleep when I found a brand-new dumpster. It was empty, so I climbed in and fell asleep. It became my home because no one ever dumped trash into it. Everything was great, until one day I woke up to find the dumpster was being lift off the ground! Before I knew it, I went flying through the air into the trash truck. Then the trash compactor began to crush the trash, and me! My knee and my head were getting crushed. I was so afraid! I cried out, 'God! Save me!' Then the Lord spoke to me and said, 'I am here with you, Arthur. I will protect you.' Right then I was not afraid. I heard His voice! So clear!"

"All of a sudden, the compactor stopped. The ambulance guys climbed in and took me out of there. They took me to the hospital."

Arthur bent his head forward. "See my head?"

Indeed, there was a circular abrasion about 4 inches in diameter on the top of his skull. Shocked, I asked what caused the compactor to stop.

"They said there was a guy in a wheelchair right there on the street and he saw me fly through the air! He had a cell phone and called 911."

"My gosh, Arthur! You are a miracle! You are like Jonah and the whale!"

"You know what else? I am not afraid anymore! God was with me! He saved me! He is right here now all the time." He pointed to his heart.

I was astounded by this incredible story. Of all the people who could have been in that dumpster, it was Arthur who found himself in a sudden life and death emergency. But something happened in that dumpster that utterly changed him. God profoundly spoke to him and saved him. He also changed him forever.

God reached down and rescued this frightened old man from the most horrific accident; now Arthur walks in confidence and peace like a river. And Papa reminds me how much He loves the little ones.

Psalm 41:2

Judges 6:23

Psalm 23:4

Matthew 10:28

Kingdom Principle: God is able and willing to protect His own, and we will not fear.

Prayer: "Lord, You are the Protector, the Shield, our shelter, and our high tower. We will not be afraid. Amen."

Try this: Examine your level of fear in your day to day life. Do you trust Him to see you through, to provide the miracle at precisely the right time? Think back to a time He did provide a miracle out of left field for you. Begin a miracle journal to chronicle all the wonderful things He has done for you over the years. When you begin to doubt Him in the present crisis, pull out your journal and read the miracles again.

What happened?

_____

_____

_____

_____

DAY 64 – BESEIGED – IGNACIO

In sickness or chronic conditions, I have, on occasion, noticed a sort of spiritual and emotional paralysis in the individual who is afflicted, as well as his loved ones. Everyone is weary. Sometimes, it seems to extend to the family and friends. It is as though they are besieged by the illness in much the same way an enemy will lay siege to a city. It is as though they have come to tolerate it, especially when the condition is not able to be healed medically.

There is an interesting story in the Old Testament about a similar situation where the city of Samaria was besieged by the King of Aram. The siege caused a great famine in the city to the point that cannibalism ensued. The people, as well as the king, were exhausted. All their frustration was aimed at the prophet Elisha. When confronted by the messenger of the king, he gives an extraordinary promise, that by the following day there would be plenty to eat. Still, the messenger of the king remained in unbelief. He was rebuked with the statement that he would see the prophecy come to pass, but not eat of the food.

The story goes on to reveal that there were four leprous men sitting outside the gate of the city sandwiched between the famine and the Aramean army. They were "between the devil and the deep blue sea," as they say. They reasoned together that, either way, they were likely to perish. Doing nothing was not an option. They decided that their only chance to live was to walk into the Aramean camp and surrender. They got up out of their malaise and pushed themselves forward.

When they arrived at the camp, it was completely abandoned. There was no one there. Apparently, the Arameans had heard the sound of pounding horse hooves and chariots coming toward the camp. In their fright, they all literally ran for their lives, leaving everything behind. The lepers ate their fill and took treasures of every sort. They were triumphant in their miracle.

Eventually, the four began to feel they ought to share the bounty with the city. Upon receiving the good news, the people rushed the gate to plunder the camp. As Elisha had prophesied, the messenger of the king was trampled to death in the rush and did not taste the bounty.

What is the moral of this story for us? In order to receive the Kingdom of God, we must believe in God's desire to give it to us in abundance. In addition, in a hopeless situation, we must not sit around "crying in our beer," as they say in Texas. We must get up off our backsides and take action.

Not long ago, a man and a friend of his had driven to the Mission from a little west Texas town about two hours away. They had heard somehow of the miracles taking place among the homeless and addicted here.

Ignacio suffered from acute pancreatitis. The pain was excruciating and extended just below his sternum to his back. He was literally crying from the pain. He asked us to help him.

We took him into our little Chapel and listened to his agony. I, myself, have experienced acute pancreatitis and the pain is intolerable. I was hospitalized for it. The head of security, formerly homeless with a fifteen-year meth addiction, laid his hands on Ignacio's back. I laid my hands on his front. Suddenly the Lord spoke to me. The man had a particular sin issue that needed to be dealt with first. Secret sin can block a healing. He instantly repented to the Lord. We cast out the offending demons and began to pray God's glorious healing verses over Ignacio.

Initially, I noticed that the area just below the sternum was concave. It felt empty under my hand.

The Lord whispered to me, "Do not pray for the diseased organ. Pray for a brand new one."

I began to pray for a creative miracle. Instantly the area under my hand kicked me, just as a baby kicks in the womb.

"Did you feel that?" I asked. The security guard responded to me.

"I felt it all the way back here!" Glory!

We continued to pray. To my amazement, the hollow under my hand filled out and area became convex! Ignacio's old shriveled up organ was replaced with a new, healthy one. It filled up my hand! Thank you, Jesus!

"How do you feel?" I asked. Ignacio jumped up moved all around. The pain was utterly gone. Ignacio was wondrously healed that day. He hugged us all. His friend wept and wept. She was completely undone by the goodness of the Lord toward His little one. We were too.

Like the lepers, Ignacio got up off his duff and drove to Amarillo to gain healing for his body. He took action. God met him there and gave him a new pancreas.

II Kings 6:24-7:20

II Kings 5:1-14

John 9:7

Kingdom Principle: In times of weariness and elongated sickness, taking action pierces through the heaviness to the miracle.

Prayer: "Father, in my weariness, show me what action to take that might break through into the Kingdom and produce the miracle I so desperately need. Amen."

Try this: Write down the miracle you desperately need. Ask the Spirit what action you might take that would prophetically shake open the gates of the Kingdom. Stay in that activation until you see the shift.

Write down what happened:

_____

_____

_____

JENA RAWLEY TAYLOR

DAY 65 – THE PLAN – ESTHER

When I was a little girl, starting around six years old, I would wake in the night hearing my name called. It was audible and I would initially assume it was my father coming to wake me up as he did every morning. But when I answered back, no one was there. The house was dark and still. It did not happen often but over the years I heard it several times. When I reached high school, I no longer heard it. It was a concern of mine. I never mentioned it to anyone, as I was already considered a bit odd.

One Sunday morning in Sunday School, dear old Mrs. Powell told us the story of Samuel as a boy being awakened in the night by a voice calling his name. I cannot tell you the relief I felt. I was not crazy after all. I continued to wonder, if God called Samuel and gave him a job and He called me, what was my job? I need not have been worried. God, in His timing, would reveal it to me.

Indeed, it appears God calls all of us at one time or another. He has plans for us all. In the book of Micah He says these words, "But they do not know the thoughts of the Lord, and they do not understand His purpose."

The Hebrew word here for thoughts is the same word that is often translated plans. It is a delicious word that rolls off the tongue. *Mahcashabah*. It means the plans, intentions, thoughts; or machine.

Thinking in terms of a machine, God has an enormous overreaching plan for all of mankind, and each of us would be seen as cogs, wheels, screws, and gears all fitted together to create a mechanism, by which His perfect will is accomplished. The astounding twist to this plot is that it all takes place in the confines of billions of free wills. That is fascinating to me.

Actually, just two verses below the scripture in Micah, God tells us about THE PLAN. It is the beautiful prophecy to Bethlehem, "too little to be among the clans of Judah," from which will come the expected One.

It is amazing to me that even the most hateful, addicted, and naughty individual has a calling and a purpose for his life. There is a cog with his name on it. His failure does not negate the call. It stands as a beacon throughout eternity of the plans and destiny for each of us.

In day 64, we learned about Ignacio who drove two hours to come to the Mission to be prayed for. We learned he was instantly healed. The following week, Ignacio brought his mother to the Mission to be prayed for. Esther suffered from Leukemia, which caused her lymph nodes to be grossly swollen under her jaw, as well as scoliosis. Her back was badly twisted from the disease, and she had a huge "hump" on her shoulder. She was in constant pain. In addition to all this, her pancreas was hurting and distended, causing her midriff to bulge grotesquely. She was in bad shape.

Alex, my assistant Danita, and I took her to the Chapel to pray for her. Alex stood behind her and laid his hands on her deformed back. I stood to the side and laid hands on her lymph node. My assistant laid hands on her other lymph node. We began to pray the Word of God concerning healing over her.

Suddenly, out of the corner of my eye, I saw movement on her shoulder like a ripple.

"Alex! What just happened?" I exclaimed.

"The hump just disappeared!"

I looked at the place where we had seen the large lump on her left shoulder. It was gone! Completely! We praised God and laughed and high-fived each other. We continued to focus on the lymph nodes. I laid my palm on her right jaw and my assistant laid her hand on her left. We prayed again. Suddenly, my assistant yelped. The lymph node under her hand instantly shrunk to normal. We rejoiced again. As we continued to pray, her right lymph node shrunk to half its size. We were having such a great time with the Lord! Esther was getting set free.

"Let's go after the pancreas now," I said. I laid my left palm on her distended midriff and prayed. My palm began to tingle wildly. Immediately the midriff shrunk.

We stepped back and asked her to try something she could not do before. She twisted her back this way and that. She raised her arms in the air. She turned her head from side to side, twisted at the waist and leaned back. She was completely pain free. God had reached down and touched her entire body and healed it, and He used three little people to do it. It was in the plans. Two five-feet tall grandmothers and an ex-addict accomplished what was medically impossible through Jesus. It was His *machashabah* all along.

What an adventure!

I Samuel 3

Micah 4:12

Romans 11:29

Ephesians 4:1

Kingdom Principle: God has a plan, and He is working the plan. All we have to do is cooperate with the plan to see the Kingdom unfold before our eyes.

Prayer: "Jesus, You are faithful to Your little ones, calling them just as you called Samuel. Thank you for the plan; thank you for letting me be a part of the plan. My prayer is that You nudge me by the Holy Spirit when I am walking into one of Your plans for me, so that on the day I stand before you, I will hear, 'Well done.' Amen."

Assignment: For the next seven days, each morning as you rise, ask the Holy Spirit to prod you when one of His plans for you begins to unfold before you. Be mindful of the urging, and act upon it. Write down what transpired.

What happened?

DAY 66 – RAISED FROM THE DEAD – ANEURYSM

When Jesus called forth Lazarus from the grave, He set a precedent for all time. The proof of power, Holy Spirit power, became a benchmark.

It is really quite extraordinary in Matthew 10; Jesus commanded the disciples to "raise the dead" while no such act had been recorded yet, except in I Kings when Elijah raised the widow's son. In verse one, He gives the twelve disciples authority over unclean spirits and power to heal every kind of disease and every kind of sickness. In verse eight, He commands the raising of the dead. Only recently have we heard reports from various parts of the world where the dead have been raised. In I Corinthians, Paul talks about not coming in persuasive words of wisdom, but in demonstration of the Spirit and of power. I thank God every day for that power.

One day, I was driving home from a particularly stressful day at the Mission when I felt a sharp pain at the base of my skull as though someone just whacked me with a baseball bat. Nausea rose, and I knew I had to get off the freeway. As I exited, I realized the pain in my head was increasing. I managed to get home and asked a friend to drive me to the clinic. I was diagnosed with a cluster headache and given a shot with assurances I would feel right as rain in a few minutes.

That was not the case, and by the following Monday, I was ready to take a gun to my head. The pain was unbearable. More tests were run. The baseball bat and the nausea happened again. I was sent to bed. One night, I got up to go to the bathroom when a strange feeling came over me. I began to assure myself that I was fine, talking myself off the ledge so to speak. Bam! Down I went, out cold.

My husband heard me hit the tile floor and raced into the bathroom. I was lying near the tub. He turned me over. I had no pulse, no breath, and a fixed stare. He gathered me up and yelled, "Jesus! I need You and I need you right now!"

He began to scream in tongues, commanding me to come back in Jesus name. Meanwhile, I was conscious of being in a tunnel approaching a bright light. A silhouette of a man appeared. He was waving at me to come. I felt no fear as I went toward him.

Suddenly, I was aware that I was in my husband's arms. He was talking to me, soothing me.

"What happened?" I asked.

"I think you had a stroke. I need to take you to the emergency room. Let me get you dressed."

At the time, we were not taking in the fact that Jesus raised me from the dead. Later, it would sink in.

"Okay but turn on the lights."

"Jena, the lights ARE on."

I was blind. I could not see. Jay dressed me quickly and bundled me into the car. I felt incredibly ill and I still could not see. As we drove, my peripheral sight began to clear a little, but I still could not make out much.

Tests were run, and CT scans were taken. The diagnosis was made. I had an aneurysm at the back of my head. It was bleeding into the brain, killing every cell it touched. "You will have to go to Dallas for brain surgery."

In Dallas, we met with a neurosurgeon who asked me to walk him through the whole sequence of events. When I finished my story, he said, "What you have told me alarms me greatly. In the case of a brain bleed, 80% of the victims die on the way to the hospital. Of the remaining 20%, half are severely impaired. You have had three brain bleeds, so we are going to surgery right now. He left the room to prepare and I quickly called the staff at the Mission to ask for prayer. I was prepped and wheeled to the operating room.

As they began the surgery, the aneurysm bled for the fourth time. Blood shot into the brain once more destroying brain cells. Then, the unspeakable happened. I had a stroke on the table. The surgeon quickly backed out of the brain and wheeled me to recovery, hoping for a miracle. From there, I was taken to Neurosurgical ICU. I stayed there for ten days. The surgeon told my husband that I must be living right to survive four brain bleeds and a stroke. His worry was the massive impairment I would be subjected to.

"The odds of your wife surviving would be 0.16%. In other words, imagine 625 people in a room and every single one falls down dead but your wife. The odds of no impairment are nonexistent." My husband knew that it was the prayers of the saints and his prayers that raised me from the dead and had gotten me this far. God would not abandon us now.

Every morning, the team of doctors would come into my room and make me go through a sequence of commands to see if I was coherent. Every day, they would ask questions such as, "What day is it? When is your birthday? Who is the President?" One day I answered that the President was John Saucier. They became alarmed. My husband laughed.

"That is the name of the President of her Board of Directors." They all sighed in relief. Finally, I was allowed to go home and recover there. It was a long three-month journey to recovery, fraught with extraordinary pain. The only thing that saved my sanity was the prayers of my friends and my husband. Still, I only had peripheral vision. I cried knowing I would never be able to paint a portrait again.

For three long months I sat at home grieving and trying to heal. A caregiver looked after me. When I was alone, friends would come by with flowers or a meal, and we would visit a bit. Many times, they would feign an excuse to go to the kitchen. I would hear them calling my husband concerned that I should not be left alone. My sorrow was acute. The pain was more acute. How I wished I had died.

I finally returned to work at the Mission, but the staff was secretly alarmed at my lack of mental clarity. They covertly covered for me and prayed that my mental capacity would miraculously return before the Board realized that I was no longer capable of running the Mission. In my heart, I knew I was no longer myself, and I mourned the loss. Those were very dark days. I wished I had stayed dead. Each week, my husband dressed me in a white Karate Gi and took me to his class with him. The instructor would put us through the steps, the holds, and the katas. It was grueling. I was unable to get my right side to do the steps properly.

I prayed for a miracle; my husband prayed for a miracle; my staff prayed for a miracle. The days stretched into weeks, and then months. Everyone played their part in the charade, each of us pretending I was okay. I was not okay.

Several months later, I was visiting about an upcoming Board meeting with the President. Suddenly he remarked, "You're back!"

"What?"

"You're back. You are yourself again. I can tell. Thank God!" Yes, thank God! The faithful prayers of the saints had been answered. God had healed my brain.

In the book of Romans, Paul assures us if the Spirit of Him who raised Jesus from the dead dwells in us, He who raised Christ Jesus will also give life to our mortal bodies. My husband believed that and raised me from the dead. I am so grateful. I look back at the things God has allowed me to do and see since that fateful night - salvations, miracles, healings, food multiplied, and even raising of the dead. Not to mention seeing my children happily wed with babies of their own. I have partaken in Christmases, Easters have been celebrated, and my birthdays have been glorious. There are many other things I have been privy to, such as holding my grandchildren, baking cheesecakes, fly-fishing on the Pecos River. I am able to breathe in and breathe out, to see the redbud tree bloom once again, and the tulips pop up. Snowy days with a fire in the fireplace are a blessing. Every minute of every day a priceless treasure. Oh, by the way, my eyesight was restored, and I've painted hundreds and hundreds of portraits and abstract paintings since my aneurysm. Thank you, Papa, for allowing me to stay here on the earth and finish a good race.

Matthew 10:7,8

Luke 7:22

John 12:17

Romans 8:11

Kingdom Principle: In prayer, a believer is able to affect the Kingdom to such a degree that they are able to raise the dead.

Prayer: "Papa, teach me how to walk in this power that Paul talks about. Make me brave enough to risk laying hands on the sick and the dying, even the dead. Show me Your glory here on earth, that I may preach that the Kingdom of Heaven is at hand. Amen."

Exercise: Look up every Scripture that speaks of healing, deliverance, or being raised. Write them down on 3X5 cards and post them on your mirror, in your car, or on the refrigerator. Recite them out loud until you know them by heart.

What did you learn?

In prayer, a believer is able to affect the Kingdom to such a degree that they
are able to raise the dead.

DAY 67 – FRUIT – THE WALKING DEAD

Recently, I was asked to travel to another state to a Mission wanting to know about signs and wonders. The director had heard me speak at a national conference catering to Gospel Rescue Missions the prior year.

"When I walked into the room where you were speaking, I felt the change in the atmosphere," he said. "I could feel the Spirit already there. When you began to tell the stories of people saved, healed, and delivered, I knew that is what we needed at our Mission."

When I stepped on the property of their Mission, I felt the oppressive spirit hovering over everything. There were hundreds of people milling around. What struck me was their demeanor. Their faces were dark and dull as though they were carved out of stone. There was no light in their eyes. They really did look like the walking dead. I felt such a burden for them, but it really felt hopeless.

In the book of Matthew, it describes this very scene and Jesus's reaction to it. "And seeing the multitudes He felt compassion for them for they were distressed and downcast." His response was to his disciples.

"The harvest is plentiful, but the workers are few. Therefore, beseech the Lord of the harvest to send out workers into the field." In the very next verse, Jesus sent out the disciples to heal the sick and cast out demons. Today, He sends us out to do the same. We were never meant to stay in the four walls of the church and critique the sermon each week. We are called out to the multitudes.

The following day, I was asked to preach in Guest Chapel at their Mission. Afterward, I invited anyone who wanted prayer to come forward. The people lined up along the wall and waited their turn. The line was long. I was reminded of what Jesus said, "The devil comes but to kill, steal, and destroy, but I have come to bring life and bring it abundantly." Each of these little sheep needed that abundant life.

One by one, they came up with that terrible sense of hopelessness. Many were ill and asked for divine healing. Some were healed on the spot. Some came to receive more of the Holy Spirit. I laid hands on their head and prayed for the baptism of the Holy Spirit. They received it with the evidence of speaking with new tongues. Most wanted to be delivered from addiction. As we began to pray for them and cast out the demons that tormented them, their faces would change before our eyes. A light seemed to glow beneath their skin. They would begin to smile; a spark would return to their eyes. It truly was extraordinary to watch. Others wanted to get their children back from CPS, which meant getting their lives back on track. After prayer, they were up to joining the recovery program at the Mission.

In most every case, Jesus answered their prayers. It was a remarkable day. I was filled with joy to see so many set free, to see life come back into their eyes.

In the gospel of Matthew, Jesus talks about that very joy that we would feel when we did His bidding.

He said, "Well done, good and faithful slave; You were faithful with a few things, so I will put you in charge of many things. Enter into the joy of your Master."

It is so true; I have never known such joy as seeing the downtrodden set free to such an extent their faces physically begin to glow. What a privilege to participate in the Kingdom in such a way.

Matthew 25:21

Matthew 9:37-38

John 10:10

Kingdom Principle: When one is faithful to do His bidding, one is rewarded with the supernatural joy of the Kingdom.

Prayer: "Jesus, thank You for allowing us to participate in Your Kingdom in such a way we see people set free from the devil and encounter You to the extent that they are physically changed before our eyes. Thank You for letting us experience that joy. Amen."

Activation: Volunteer at a homeless shelter each week for one month. Extend God's love to each guest. Speak to them personally and ask their names. Ask to pray with them.

How did it go?

_____

_____

_____

_____

_____

_____

_____

_____

_____

_____

When one is faithful to do His bidding,
one is rewarded with the
supernatural joy of the Kingdom.

DAY 68 – WOMAN AT THE WELL – THE PANHANDLER

There are some extraordinary stories in the Gospels that record Jesus seeking out and targeting specific people to speak the Kingdom to. They are rare jewels deposited into the Bible that speak to the particularly troubled. One such story is about His traveling through a district of pagans, half breeds who are not even to be spoken to. Samaria was an area settled by the Babylonians long ago, resulting in a great deal of interracial marriages between Jews and foreigners.

Typically, no one would be coming to the city's well at the noon hour. Nevertheless, Jesus sat by the well alone and waited. A Samaritan woman approached the well with her water pot. There has been a great deal of conjecture as to why this woman came at such an odd hour. Many believe her reputation would require her to wait to come alone, so as not to be taunted and ridiculed for her many sins. In any event, Jesus was ready to engage with her in order to heal her shattered heart.

He began with a simple request, a drink of water. She was shocked that He would even speak to her, as Jews have no dealings with this people group. The conversation ensued and after avoiding a theological debate, He cut to the heart of her hurt. He told her everything she ever did, including being married to five husbands and now living with a lover. He healed her heart and she became Samaria's first evangelist, telling everyone about this Jesus. In fact, the impact of her testimony was so great that the next time He traveled through that way, the villagers brought all those who were sick and laid them at His feet to heal.

It has been my experience that most citizens feel about the homeless the same way the Jews felt about the Samaritans. They have no dealings with them. Part of it has to do with the fear factor. What we do not know, we fear. We also fear the con job, being duped into kindness, only to discover that we've been had.

One day while running an errand on my lunch hour, a homeless panhandler approached my car at a stop light. I recognized him from the Mission. He often went to eat or get fresh socks. I rolled down my window.

"Hi, Mrs. Taylor. I got a job moving pallets at a warehouse. I am on my lunch break. Say, do you have some cash? I was going to that Toot-n-Totum gas station to grab a sandwich."

I dug in my wallet and found a twenty. I handed it over and wished him the best. As I waited on the light, I watched him walk to the next intersection and turn left to the store. When I arrived at that intersection, I caught the red light. As I waited, I glanced to my left at the convenience store, and caught my homeless friend walking out with a 40-ounce beer. The dirty dog had conned me! I vowed never to give cash to a panhandler again.

That Christmas season, the Lord mentioned the "panhandler question" to me. "Do I give? Do I not give?"

I complained about the con, and my sense of injustice, "Lord, they are just swindlers."

"It is true," said the Lord. "Some are cons, some are not. It doesn't really matter. Your job is to love them, regardless of their character." I hung my head. I was ashamed of my attitude. I knew I was to love them. I just forgot that it had to be unconditional.

He went on with instructions in detail of the Christmas bags I was to personally assemble and place in my backseat at the ready. In a large gallon baggy, I was to put a can of Vienna Sausage, a fruit cup, a bag of nuts, a small water, crackers, candy bar, a red plastic spoon with a Christmas napkin, and two five dollar bills in a Christmas card which was to read, "Merry Christmas, pass one of these fives forward." There were ten in all. The rule was, I was to stop, approach, engage, give the bag, and pray with them.

Over the next few weeks prior to Christmas, I stopped, visited, gave the bag, and asked if they needed prayer for anything. Every one of them wanted prayer, most for their families, especially for their kids. The last guy standing by an abandoned building took the bag and wanted prayer for a job, a good job. He had been a waiter in the restaurant business in the past but had "fallen on hard times" and lost everything, including his family, home, and job. We held hands and prayed for a Christmas miracle.

That night, a local restaurant opened their doors to the homeless and fed over 250 meals to the special guests. The place was packed. They had a wonderful party in a clean warm eatery with mountains of food. It really was Christmas. My friend from the abandoned building came as well. He accidentally bumped into a stranger while refilling his plate. They got to talking and, as it turned out, the stranger was the owner of the restaurant. They continued to visit, and, out of the blue, the gentleman hired my friend to wait tables. Out of all the guests at that crowded party, my friend bumped into the owner…and his Christmas miracle came to him.

God is still the God of miracles. It is my very great pleasure to get to see such astonishing things happen on the earth.

John 4:7-30

Luke 15:1-6

Luke 15:11–32

Kingdom Principle: When we serve the stranger or the needy, regardless of their intentions, the Lord is pleased, and the extraordinary happens.

Prayer: "Jesus, thank You for loving the misfits, rebels, and swindlers. Teach me that kind of love. Spread abroad in my heart Your love for these lost ones. Amen."

Activation: Go to the Lord and ask Him to show you a way to reach people who are in dark places. Listen to His instructions. Then act on them.

What happened?

DAY 69 – PRESENCE – HOLY SPIRIT

One of the most beautiful chapters in the Bible is in the Gospel of John. Jesus was explaining to the disciples that He must go away. Alarmed at the news, the group had questions.

"Why? When? Where are you going?" Like children, they had so many reservations about him abandoning them. He comforted them with these words.

"If anyone loves Me, he will keep My word and My Father will love him, and we will come to him and make our abode with him." Jesus assured them that He will send them another Helper, the Spirit of Truth.

"He will teach you all things and bring you to remembrance all that I said to you. Let not your hearts be troubled." Like a tender older brother, He assured them all that the Comforter would be with them always.

In the days following His departure into Heaven, the disciples could not feel less assured. Hiding from the authorities along with many other followers, they wondered what the future held for them. Crammed into an upper room, they waited and prayed.

Then there was one of God's famous "suddenlies." On the feast day of Pentecost, a violent and rushing noise like wind tore through the upper room. Flames of fire appeared to settle on each person. Jesus's promise came to pass. The Helper filled the room, causing each of them to speak in a new language and in many different tongues. When people in the neighborhood heard the sound, they rushed to the streets to see what had happened. Everything was chaos.

Many were amazed at the phenomenon. Others, seeing this odd behavior, claimed that they were drunk.

The results of the incident were astonishing, for thus the Church was born on that day with Peter's first sermon. Three thousand people gave their hearts to Jesus and were saved.

Down through the ages since that day, the Comforter has come upon those who wish His friendship. Like that day on Pentecost so long ago, crazy miraculous things have happened. I have found that to be true in my own life. He has been with me. As I turn my affection to Him throughout the day, I have felt Him turn His affection to me with His comfort, refreshment, and peace. His companionship is my greatest treasure.

What I have recently discovered is that others feel His presence around me also, even unbelievers; it profoundly affects them.

After my brother's death several years ago, his wife, an intellectual unbeliever, called to visit. She had a question about the night my husband and I flew up to their home at her request. My brother was in the final throes of death. He was extremely agitated, and the rest of the family gathered around the bed were struggling with their own grief. As we walked in the room, I could feel the death pall. A heaviness blanketed the area.

Knowing he could hear us, my husband and I greeted my brother. He continued to thrash about almost violently. I had the thought to read Psalm 91 to him. As I began, he became very still and held on to my hand tightly. I turned to Revelation and read all about Heaven and everything he was about to see and experience. My sister suddenly exclaimed, "Look at his face."

I looked up from the Bible and was astounded to see a brilliant glow shining from his face, as though a candle was lit within a frosted glass. We were spellbound. As we looked on, the glow dimmed and went out leaving darkness. My brother was gone.

My sister-in-law had questions about that night.

"You know that I am an unbeliever," she started. I was aware that her academic mind could not grasp the things of the Kingdom. They were children's fairy tales to her.

"But I cannot deny that when you both walked into the room, the atmosphere changed, and a peace came over us. The heavy gloom left. What was that? How did it all change so suddenly?"

I explained about the Comforter and His love for her, that He was our dearest friend. He had come with us into the room. His presence always brings peace and a sense of wellness.

"I just don't understand how that could be. But I cannot deny what I felt that night. I will have to think about that."

Even an unbeliever can feel His presence when we carry His glory. Jesus said that the fields are ripe for the harvest. Jesus has given each of us a field and we are the laborers in that field. All we have to do is carry the Glory.

John 14:16

Acts 1:8

Acts 2:1-13

Acts 2:37-41

Kingdom Principle: When one is intimate with the presence, unbelievers are affected, and incredible things happen.

Prayer: "Holy Spirit, thank You for being my constant companion and comforter. Will You allow me to carry Your glory to my field? Will You have the same effect on those I am assigned to as You had on me? Pour out Your glory! Amen."

Initiation: Set aside 15 to 30 minutes a day getting to know Holy Spirit. Look up every Scripture that mentions Him or describes Him. Invite Him into your inner room. Sit before Him and wait on Him. Get to know Him as companion. Practice this habit for one month.

Write down your experience:

DAY 70 – I HEARD – DOUG

It is a regular occurrence at the Mission for people to come from near and far, saying, "We heard you are kind to the poor," or "I heard you will help us find jobs here," or "We heard that people are being miraculously healed here." Some have come from as far away as Washington state and Las Vegas, even California, to get help. How does the word get out that far away? It is unclear, but the CIA could take some pointers from the non-electronic communication system among the homeless.

Evidently, this same system was used in Jesus's day in Israel and the surrounding pagan countries. After a stunning creative miracle involving a withered hand at the synagogue in Capernaum, Jesus withdrew to the sea. "And a great multitude followed from Galilee and Judea, also from Jerusalem, Idumea, and even Tyre and Sidon. They had heard of all that He was doing and came to Him. For He healed many with the result that all those who had afflictions pressed about Him in order to touch Him."

Even an unbelieving pagan nation, Samaria, when they heard what Jesus had accomplished in one outcast woman's life, came to believe in Him and asked Him to stay. After two days in His presence, they were saying to the woman, "It is no longer because of what you said that we believe, for we have heard for ourselves and know that this One is indeed the Savior of the world."

Everywhere He went, the news would spread of blind eyes opening, the dead raised, and demons fleeing through Jews and pagans alike.

One evening at the Mission, a Jiujitsu class was in full swing. The security team was learning defense maneuvers and body throws in order to protect our students, staff, and guests from any unsavory types that sometimes come in high and become violent. As the instructor taught the team how to roll (the beginning stage of learning to take a fall), one security team member, Doug, rolled improperly and injured his shoulder. He could not lift his arm at all and could not rotate his shoulder. He was in a great deal of pain and was taken to the clinic to be examined. He was given a brace to wear, but the pain was excruciating.

The following evening a guest pastor came to preach the evening service and said, "I heard that signs and wonders are happening here at the Mission. Is that true?"

The students assured him that they were happening on a weekly basis.

"Well, I want to lay hands on someone and pray for them to be healed."

The security team looked at each other and knew the perfect subject, Doug. One of the guys went to retrieve him and bring him to the Chapel.

"Here you go, injured shoulder. Have a go at it."

The pastor laid hands on Doug's shoulder and prayed for a miraculous healing. He stepped back and asked Doug to try something he could not do before. Doug began to lift his arm and rotate his shoulder. The pain was gone, and he had complete mobility again. Everyone rejoiced, especially the guest pastor.

For reasons known but to God, He has allowed a tiny little homeless shelter to participate in the Kingdom with signs, wonders, and miracles of every sort. He has always favored the least and the littlest, thanking His heavenly Father that, "Thou didst hide these things from the wise and intelligent, and revealed them to babes." Indeed, we are babes.

Mark 3:7-11

John 4:39-42

John 12:17-19

Luke 10:17-21

Kingdom Principle: There is supernatural power in the stories of miracles and healings that releases the power to even more miracles and healings.

Prayer: "Jesus, bring revival to our city with the evidence of miracles and healings. Use whomever You wish to bring revival. Use me! Amen."

Activation: Go to the places that you have heard are experiencing signs and wonders. Watch and observe what is happening.

What did you see? What did you experience?

_____

_____

_____

_____

_____

_____

_____

_____

_____

There is supernatural power in the stories of miracles and healings that releases the power to even more miracles and healings.

DAY 71 – THE POWER OF PRAYER – ROBERT & STEFANIE

Early on in Jesus's ministry, He went about in a small district on the east coast of the sea of Galilee, teaching and proclaiming the Gospel and healing every kind of disease and every kind of sickness among the people. That little district could be likened to an out of the way region as the Texas Panhandle, a little backward and "countrified." The news of the astonishing miracles reached all the way to a pagan country to the north named Syria, about sixty miles away. In that day, sixty miles was a long way. They loaded up all who were ill and brought them to Jesus. Everyone one with pains, diseases, epileptics, and paralytics; He healed them all. The Bible records that great crowds followed Him from Galilee, Decapolis, Jerusalem, and Judea, and even from beyond the Jordan, which would be pagan. The people were desperate. He healed them all.

The book of Matthew records story after story of synagogue officials, leprous men, paralytics, even women who were not supposed to be in public with their condition coming to Jesus because they had heard the news of the miracles He was performing. The multitude marveled and said, "Nothing like this was ever seen in Israel!"

It is the same at the Mission. The homeless come for prayer, as well as addicts. People in the community bring their loved ones to be prayed for. One evening, I was leaving the Mission after a very long and arduous day. The guests were lining up outside to go to Dinner Chapel, when I spotted a man sitting in his trunk with the lid up. He had on some Hawaiian swimming trunks and no shirt. The trunk, along with the inside of the sedan, was completely full of belongings, all randomly thrown in. He looked to be about 70, but it was hard to tell because he was so shriveled. He appeared as though he may have started smoking at the age of 6. His complexion was gray and pasty. He was gasping for breath and trying to make his inhaler work. He had the panic-stricken look of a man who cannot get any air.

I stopped in front of the trunk. "Sir are you alright?"

Wheezing he explained his predicament. He and his wife had driven from Las Vegas, Nevada heading to West Virginia. They were both very ill.

"They told us to go to Faith City Mission for help."

I do not know who "they" were, but I went and got another staff member to come pray with me out at the trunk. As we laid hands on him and prayed, his complexion turned pink. He drew in a huge breath for the first time and began to cry.

"I can breathe! I can breathe!" He wept and wept. He explained that when they started out from Las Vegas, he had prayed that God would send them to a church along the way that could pray for his wife and for him. He prayed that God would heal them.

"Oh, please pray for my wife!" He called her over and introduced a young woman who was about 30 years old. She had a confused look on her face. She clearly was not in her right mind. The man explained that she had epilepsy, and several mental disorders. We began to pray for her, casting out many demons.

When we said, "Amen," she looked up at me and smiled. The confused look was gone. The man began to cry again, thanking God for answering his prayer.

We gave them a meal, showers, and a room to stay in for the night. They were so grateful. Who told them about our Mission? How did these unknowns hear about us? We will probably never know. God did answer the man's prayer and sent them to us. He healed them and set them free. Thank you, God!

Matthew 4:23-25

Matthew 9:18-33

Mark 1:21-34

Kingdom Principle: Hearing the stories of the miraculous and praying for a miracle gives passage into the supernatural.

Prayer: "Papa, thank You for the opportunity to labor in Your fields and see miracles happen before our eyes. Please let us participate with You wherever we go. Amen."

Launch: Search for churches and ministries that are seeing signs and wonders today. Find a mentor who is working the works of God and learn everything you can about the Kingdom of Heaven here on earth.

Write down what happened:

Hearing the stories of the miraculous and praying for a miracle gives passage into the supernatural.

DAY 72 – WHOEVER SAYS – JERRY

The very first miracle documented at the Mission is an extraordinary story. The history of signs and wonders actually began with the healing team from a local church. They were coming in the evening to pray for anyone who was sick. My husband, Jay, was a part of the team. Each week, he would go to the Lord and ask for a Scripture that God wanted to impart to one of the sick. One night, he was directed to a real gem in the book of Mark. Jesus instructed, "Whoever says to the mountain, 'Be taken up and cast into the sea,' and does not doubt in his heart but believes that what he says is going to happen, it shall be granted him."

One evening, as people gathered in the Chapel for healing prayer, a man hobbled in on crutches, and sat on the front row. One foot was bare, with no shoe or sock. It was hugely swollen and very purple. The toes looked like sausages and splayed out grotesquely. My husband thought, "Woah, that one is going to be a tough one."

After a brief sermon on healing, the leader asked anyone who needed prayer to come forward. As they made their way to the front, every team member had someone in front of them, except Jay. The guy with the crutches stared intently at him. Finally, having no choice, he walked over to the fellow.

"I guess it's you and me, buddy. Do you want me to pray for your foot?"

The fellow had no teeth but looked at my husband with disdain and waved at his foot as though to say, "Of course I want you to pray for my foot."

Evidently, the foot was diseased, causing extreme pain if anything touched it. Even a sheet over it would cause pain. He had been on crutches and had worn no shoe or sock on that foot for six months. He had sores under his arms from the crutches.

"Anything else you need prayer for?"

"Yes, I am blind as a bat. I can't read the Bible anymore. That makes me sad."

Jay shared the Scripture in Mark 11 about the mountain. He read it to the fellow.

"I think you are supposed to speak to your disease, and command it to be cast into the sea."

The man did point to his foot and commanded the disease to go in Jesus name. As they looked at the offending foot, it began to lose its purple hue; before their very eyes, the swelling went down. They stared in wonderment as the foot turned pink and toes became normal. They were both in shock. The foot looked perfectly normal.

Suddenly the man jumped to his feet and yelled, "I'm healed! I'm healed!" He began to stomp his foot to see if it hurt.

Alarmed, Jay cautioned him to be careful, but the man began running around the Chapel yelling, "I am healed!"

He ran out the Chapel door and into the dining room to show his friends, yelling at the top of his lungs. Everyone froze. They had not seen Jerry without crutches for six months. Jay stopped him and asked if he saw any change in his eyesight. The man walked to the pulpit where a Bible laid open and began to read. He could see perfectly. He began to cry again.

That night, my husband was so quiet when he came in; I wondered what had happened. Bewildered, he related the story about Jerry, his foot, and his eyes. God had reached down to an old worn out homeless man and given him a new life, without crutches, without pain, and with new eyes.

For months afterward, no one could get within 50 feet of him without him saying, "Say, did you know God healed my foot and my eyes?" And off to the races he went telling the story of the mountain and the sea and what God had done.

This was the very first miraculous healing we had seen at the Mission. The story was told over and over. Since that time, hundreds of people have come to be prayed for and hundreds have been supernaturally healed. Hallelujah!

Mark 11:23,24

Matthew 17:20

Matthew 21:21

Kingdom Principle: When one rises up and speaks to the mountain in one's life and does not doubt, the Kingdom is revealed and the remarkable happens.

Prayer: "Jesus, give me the faith, I pray, to boldly command the mountain to be taken up and cast into the sea; that I may command blind eyes open, the lame to walk, the food to multiply. Help me to believe without doubting. Amen."

Galvanization: Think of a mountain in your life that needs a miracle. It could be finances, children, addiction, spouses, or illness. Hold out your palms and place that difficulty in your hands. Thank God for His wonder-making power. Now speak to the mountain in Jesus name and cast it into the sea. Now, turn your palms down and let the mountain fall into the sea.

Record the results:

_____

_____

_____

_____

When one rises up and speaks to the mountain in one's life and does not doubt, the Kingdom is revealed and the remarkable happens.

DAY 73 – CONFIDENCE – CONFERENCE

In the Scriptures, there are many instances in which people came to Jesus asking him to heal them. In one such instance, Jesus had just raised a little girl from the dead in the home of a synagogue official. As Jesus passed on from there, two blind men sought Him out. They cried out saying, "Have mercy on us, Son of David!" Evidently, Jesus kept walking, but when He came to the house, the blind men came up to Him. Jesus asked a simple question, "Do you believe that I am able to do this?" They replied, "Yes, Lord."

He then touched their eyes and said, "Be it done according to your faith." And their eyes opened.

I was asked to speak at a conference in the area and tell stories of healings taking place at the Mission. As I gave account after account of God's incredible interventions in these little lambs, the audience was visibly growing with excitement. I could literally feel their faith levels rise to believe. The air was electric with Holy Spirit.

Throughout the rest of the afternoon, people approached me to come pray for their spouses, their children, or friends.

Anna had a twisted pelvis which caused a great deal of constant pain. Added to that, one leg was shorter than the other. I had her girlfriend lay her hand on the thigh of the offending leg just below the groin. I lifted her feet up and held them together. One leg was indeed about ¾ of an inch shorter than the other. As I prayed, the girlfriend cried out. She could feel the ligaments growing out under her hand! I checked the heels still in my hands. They were the same length. Anna rose to her feet and walked around. The pain was gone. She was healed.

Ellen and her husband came up to me and asked for healing. Her left ear was filled with buzzing and she could no longer hear at all. It was so annoying, and there was no escape. I laid my hand over her ear and prayed. Nothing happened, but I told her to hang on to the seed of faith. The following week, she and her husband came to the mission to report that she was completely healed and could hear perfectly.

In the evening, a husband came to me on behalf of his wife. She was diagnosed with MS and was having trouble with her legs. They had driven from Colorado to come to the conference. I grabbed my husband to come outside with us where it was quieter. We all four sat down.

She was young, beautiful, and smart. Nevertheless, I felt hurt and bitterness from her. When I asked her about it, she became agitated and angry. Tears began to fall. She had been deeply hurt by the leadership in her church. She vowed that she could not forgive them. I knew from personal experience that she must, or she would be stopped in her tracks.

I pulled out the big guns to shock her into reality.

"If you do not forgive them you are going to die of MS." My words had the effect I had hoped for. She looked at me as if I had slapped her.

She grew quiet and lowered her head. The struggle in her inmost being was palpable. Mournfully, she looked up at me. The words would not come. We all waited.

As tears rolled silently down her cheeks she said softly, "Alright I will try to forgive." I walked her through the whole "wanting to want to" forgive, and the scale from 1 to 100, and the supernatural power of God to take her from step 1 - "wanting to want to," all the way to step 100 - total forgiveness.

As she repented for her unforgiveness and asked God to rescue her from her torment, she wept. It was a struggle of epic proportion, but eventually she released it into His capable hands.

Suddenly, she fell back in her chair exhausted. Relief flooded her face. She looked at me and grinned. She was free at last.

My husband stood and walked around behind her and laid his hands as an elder upon her head. As he prayed, her scalp began to ripple under his touch. He described it to us as it continued to move this way and that under his hands. He continued to pray, and it continued to ripple. I was certain she was healed.

The following day, the couple came to the Mission for a tour. They felt that God was calling them to open a similar shelter in their town. She looked like a new person, with new joy and new energy. I knew she was healed in two ways the night before. Both were equally dramatic. Both were equally needed.

Matthew 9:27-29

Mark 5:25-34

Luke 5:17-20

Kingdom Principle: Simple faith activates the supernatural healing.

Prayer: "Jesus, please strengthen my faith to believe for my own healing and for others. Amen."

Try this: Set a goal to lay hands on and pray for ten people this week who need a healing. Find the Scriptures that document healing. Speak these over the individual as you pray.

What happened?

_____

_____

DAY 74 – SET FREE – THE DEMONIAC

One of the most colossal Scriptures in the Bible is found in the book of Isaiah. It is actually cited as a prophecy of the coming Messiah, but also a herald for all believers who follow Him. It speaks of the Lord anointing us all to preach the good tidings to the poor, to bind up the brokenhearted, and to bring liberty to the captive and freedom to the prisoners. It is a call to arms, so to speak, for our marching orders. Throughout His days on earth, He instructed as well as demonstrated to His followers what they were to do in this new Kingdom of His. They, in turn, instructed others. We all have been given Holy Spirit to empower us with supernatural gifts to carry out our orders so that we could set the captives free.

Jesus sent seventy disciples out by twos with instructions to heal the sick, cast out demons, and preach the Kingdom of God. When they returned, they were filled with joy saying, "Lord! Even the demons are subject to us in Your name." At the news, Jesus "rejoiced greatly" which translated from the original Greek to mean to rejoice excessively, jumping up and spinning around as well as skipping fervently. In other words, He was thrilled that the seventy demonstrated the Kingdom on their own. In turn, we too are to demonstrate the Kingdom everywhere we go.

One day, I was preaching in Chapel to our guests off the streets. They were unusually attentive, asking questions, and sharing their stories of what God had done for them. Seven individuals accepted the gift that Jesus presented to them which was salvation. Afterward, several people came forward needing prayer.

One gentleman in particular came forward with tears in his eyes, his face twisted in torment. He told us of the torment he was going through because of his inability to stay out of an exceedingly perverted lifestyle of drugs, phone sex, and porn. He grieved his life and his poor choices. He was literally trapped and held prisoner by every sort of demonic entity. He had been a Christian for years, went to church, and watched Christian television to stay on the right path, but no matter what he tried, he always got sucked back into the lifestyle. He begged for help.

After a few questions, it was determined that, as a child, he was violated in every way by the adults around him. He, in turn, violated other children, which is quite common. Clearly, there was a legal ground for the demons to stay and torment him. His expression was that of a frightened child lost in the dark.

We walked through repentance with him and began to break the curses that held him tight. Once the demons no longer had legal ground to stay attached to the curse in his life, we were able to cast them out. His torment turned to anger toward the demons, and he began to fling them off one by one. The expression of terror and anguish left his face and his eyes began to clear. They began to brighten.

"How do you feel?" I asked.

"I feel different! I feel better, and sort of blank." That blank feeling after deliverance is common. When the demons are cast out of an individual after years of being oppressed by them, they describe a feeling of "lighter" or "blank" or "emptier."

We praised God for His kindness toward us, and His faithfulness to set this captive free. The young man looked up at me and smiled brightly. A look of utter relief came over his face.

"I do have a question though. I was told that if you were baptized in the Holy Spirit you could not have any demons. I am baptized in the Spirit so how could I have demons?"

I am no expert, but it has been my observation that the baptism of the Holy Spirit does not preclude demonic activity. They know their legal rights. We as Christians are not possessed by them. Few of us have "invited them in." Nevertheless, we can be oppressed by them because of the open doors caused in childhood or generational curses passed down. In addition, when we practice sin and make it a habit, there can be an open door.

Picture this in your mind. You are at home. Outside you notice a gang of thugs watching your house. They begin to circle the house, obviously looking for an unlocked door or open window by which to gain entrance. In practicing sin, you are virtually opening the front door and shouting,

"Come on in, boys!"

Demons do hit below the belt. By that, I mean they are assigned to bring your downfall by luring you into a situation for which you are not prepared. Many are the individuals who have said to themselves in the morning, "What was I thinking?"

The stinkers sneak back in by luring us once again into an old habit. Left unattended, it can wreak havoc in our lives.

A good habit is to regularly go to the Lord for a checkup. For instance, every three or four months, ask the Lord if some attitudes, habits, or lusts have snuck back in. Listen to His answer, repent, and cast the thing out.

Several years ago, the Lord mentioned to me that I might need to do some housekeeping. I agreed. He gently suggested we take one item per morning and deal with it. Every morning in my sacred place, I would ask what we would be dealing with today. He would tell me. I would write it down, adding to the growing list.

Critical Spirit

Anger

Confusion

Covetousness

Etc. Etc.

I would repent, come out of agreement with it, then cast it out.

The good news is, that in the Kingdom, we have the power and authority to cast them out of ourselves and others. Thank You Jesus!

Isaiah 61:1-3

Luke 10:1,2,9, 17-21

Psalm 37:40

Kingdom Principle: Simple repentance is so powerful in the Kingdom. It breaks the legal rights of the demonic.

Prayer: "Jesus, thank You for setting the captives free. Thank You for setting me free. Give me the courage to set others free. Amen."

Activation: On a regular basis, choose a period of time yearly to sit down with the Lord and do a "spiritual overhaul." During this period, ask Him each morning to reveal any demon that may have snuck back into your life. As He speaks, write it down. Repent of allowing the attitude, behavior, and the thought life back in. Ask Him to cleanse you of all unrighteousness. Then cast the sucker out. Typically, he will manifest with a yawn, burp, runny nose, even gagging. Sometimes, you might even throw up, or race to the bathroom. Don't be alarmed. It means the stinker came out. Thank the Lord! Now seal yourself with the Holy Spirit.

Write down what you experienced:

_____

_____

_____

_____

_____

_____

DAY 75 – BREAKTHROUGH – THE RANCH

There are times in each of our lives when we desperately need a breakthrough in any given situation - our job, finances, spouse, offspring, health, or addiction. We then fix our eyes on an expected solution.

"If only they could find a cure for cancer."

"If only my husband would change."

"If I could just win the lottery."

"If only I could get a better job."

Throughout the Bible, there were nations and individuals who needed a colossal miracle. Abraham needed a miracle to have a child at 99 years of age. King Saul needed a miracle with Goliath. Esther needed a miracle before the King.

For four hundred years, the Jewish nation needed a miracle to be freed from its oppressors. Their prophets told of a Messiah who would come and kick some backsides, expel the oppressors, and restore the glory of Israel. They had some very specific expectations of Messiah and how this would all play out. John the Baptist was no exception. He knew all of some 3,000 prophecies of the Expected One, and he knew that his cousin, Jesus, was the One. He "knew" Jesus would vanquish the enemy and set up a new political regime. He would win the day for Israel.

However, things did not go according to plans. John was arrested and thrown into jail. To add insult to injury, his cousin was doing nothing to alleviate his confinement. Further, John's disciples were reporting all the extraordinary miracles Jesus was performing, including raising up a widow's only son and fulfilling the Old Testament prophecy that the Messiah would raise the dead and restore sons to their mothers. But like many of us, John was disappointed. Despite the Old Testament prophecies being fulfilled, things were not going as he thought they should.

Frustrated, John sent a group of his followers to Jesus to confront Him with some highly charged words that held the bite of insult.

"Are you the Expected One, or do we look for someone else?"

Jesus's response was epic. "Go report to John what you have seen and heard." He then proceeded to quote Old Testament prophecies Himself: "THE BLIND RECEIVE SIGHT, THE LAME WALK, THE LEPERS ARE CLEANSED, AND THE DEAF HEAR. THE DEAD ARE RAISED, AND THE POOR HAVE THE GOSPEL PREACHED TO THEM. And blessed is he who keeps from stumbling over Me."

We have all "stumbled" over disappointments when things did not turn out as we had prayed or hoped.

There was a time when we at the Mission realized that our cranky old building was too small to meet the needs of so many guests. We had to turn some little ones away, including mommies with toddlers. Those who remained were lined up like cordwood along the floor. It was time to find another place. We had just received a sum of $700,000.00 from an estate of a man whom we did not know. He was from an oil town in the panhandle of Texas, but He had never been a giver of record. These miraculous funds from God would help with a down payment on a larger facility. We searched high and low for something suitable but could find nothing except an old abandoned hospital that was big, but surely not habitable. It would take millions of dollars to abate it, tear it down, haul off the debris, then build a new building. Still, we began proceedings to make the purchase.

One day while in the accounting office located in the basement of our present building, I noticed that our accountant had a deep and troubling cough. Indeed, it had been a chronic cough for several months. I began to think of that unspeakable problem inherent to old buildings - black mold. Worried, we contacted a company to come run tests. The results were stupefying. The stuff was reported to be everywhere. We were instructed to move out of the facility so that walls could be knocked down and the mold eradicated at the sum of $350,000.00. We were in shock.

"Move out?!? We can't move out! There are two hundred people staying here! Where would we go? And where are we to feed them? Or even cook the four hundred meals a day?"

Our disappointment was profound. This was not how we saw this playing out. What were we to do? Where could we go? The nearest hotel was out of the question, as was any restaurant. It was cost prohibitive. I pictured us all out in a field somewhere with a huge campfire and cauldron. It looked completely hopeless. Like John, I was bitterly disappointed. So much so that I did not go to the Lord for help. Nevertheless, we needed a miracle.

On my way home one day, I pondered the question for the hundredth time. I had to find a place to move the guests. Suddenly in one of those moments of crystal-clear clarity, a thought dropped out of Heaven. The Episcopal Church Camp outside of town was a huge campus of trees, hills, and creeks and most importantly, dormitories and a dining room with a kitchen. It even had a Chapel and a pool. The camp had been in operation for sixty-six years; two of my sons had attended.

Just six miles north of us, the summer camps would be over, and we could possibly rent the place for the duration of the repair to our building. I rushed home and called the camp. The number was disconnected. I found that odd. I looked online and found the website, which appeared to be in order. I messaged from the website with no reply. Finally, I decided to drive out and approach the camp manager in person. I grabbed our Director of Operations and jumped in the car. When we arrived, the gate was closed and chained with a sign which read, "For more information call…" What in the world? In wonderment we drove back to the Mission. As we drove, we recalled that our accountant was an Episcopalian and might know something.

"Oh sure, the camp is going on the market. The Bishop decided it was too old and too costly to run."

"Do you know whose number that is on the gate?"

"That is our senior warden."

"Do you think we could go look at it?"

The next thing I knew, she had whipped out her cell phone and punched in speed dial. We were informed that the property was not ready for showing and not on the market yet. My dear accountant bullied the man into submission. That afternoon as we had finished the tour of the 228-acre property, I stood on a grassy knoll and looked at the blue sky, the clouds, and the trees. I listened to the absolute quiet, except the twitter of birdsong. I knew that I knew that this was our new home. It was meant for us. Never have I felt so sure of anything in my life. This was our miracle. I burst into tears.

I broached the obvious question - the price. It suddenly occurred to me that we could not possibly afford such acreage so close to town.

The gentleman had a kind smile and silver hair. I had met him before and knew him to be a good man.

"I talked to the Bishop this afternoon about your interest in the property," he said. "The Bishop loves what you all do at the Mission and would be willing to let you have it for a fraction of the asking price."

I was dumbfounded. "We'll take it!"

"Don't you need to talk to your Board of Directors?"

"Oh! Yes, of course."

Within the week, the Board had made an offer on the property. It was promptly accepted. We were still shy by a couple of hundred thousand to have the total in order to pay cash for the land. The day of closing was bearing down on us and we needed another miracle to obtain the rest of the cash needed in time.

One day just before Christmas, there was a call from an anonymous man instructing me to come to the pastor's office at First Baptist Church the following morning. I asked what this was regarding. The man simply said, "Be there at 9:00 am." Because it was Dr. Batson's office, I felt fairly safe.

The following morning, I was ushered into the beautiful office to find two gentlemen in business suits seated side by side with a large pile of papers in each lap. Dr. Batson greeted me warmly and we all sat down.

"We have called this meeting to discuss an estate that was settled recently. Both of your entities were named as recipients. You each are to receive one half of the estate of…in the sum of…"

When the amount of the estate was mentioned, and I realized what our half was, I nearly yelped. It was within a hair's breadth of equaling what the balance was on the acreage. God had supernaturally given us what we could not even imagine. It did not play out as we had expected, it was galactically bigger than we could even dream.

Looking back, I realized that God had to take us on a route of deep disappointment to even begin to see the property for sale, or His plan for us to have it all along. What a good Father we have.

Post Note: As far as the black mold issue, I contacted another person to run tests in our building. I wanted a second opinion. He came by with his instruments and ran a test. He assured us the only spot that had black mold was in the wall outside the accounting office. It was dealt with quickly.

Genesis 17:16-21

I Samuel 17:1-51

Esther 2:12-23, 3:1-15, 4:1-14

Luke 7:16-23

Kingdom Principle: When things look utterly impossible and at their worst, it is fertile ground for a miracle.

Prayer: "Father, You are the kindest person I know. Your ways are incomprehensible to us. Thank You for Your patience with our disappointments and misguided expectations. Help us learn to put our hope in You and You alone. Amen."

Activation: Name the miracle that you need in your life or your loved one's life. Make a decision to trust the Father's process in this need. Read the accounts of miracles from the Scriptures. Recount a time when the Father brought you a miracle out of a hopeless situation.

Write down those accounts as a testimony:

_____

_____

_____

_____

_____

_____

_____

_____

_____

_____

_____

_____

_____

DAY 76 — TERRITORY — BLIND EYES

Have you ever come onto a piece of property that immediately made you feel uneasy? Have you walked into a house and the hairs on your neck stood up? Or a certain street felt dark and foreboding? It is not discussed much what the phenomenon is, but your gut knows this is not a safe place.

Years ago, my husband and I were looking to buy our first house. We found a possibility in the country, an old home place of a farm the children chose not to keep. As we drove up, I saw a wonderful Spanish Mission style house with creamy stucco walls and red tile roof. It looked like it needed a lot of work, but the bones of the house were good. However, the minute I stepped across the threshold, the hackle went up on the back of my neck and I was gripped with fear. The longer we stayed in the house, the worse I got. Later my husband expressed an interest in buying the place. I flatly refused to discuss it. We were NOT buying that house. What was the phenomena? What caused me to be gripped with fear?

The Bible talks about ruling demons over a territory or country that govern what can and cannot happen in this domain. The book of Daniel talks about the angel Gabriel battling the "Prince of Persia" for twenty-one days in order to get to Daniel to answer his prayer.

Isaiah speaks of a land where the people sit in darkness. Ezekiel tells of a wicked prince over the land of Rosh, Meshech, and Tubal. Who are these ruling entities that can cause such great darkness?

There is a story depicted in the Bible where Jesus teaches in the synagogue in His hometown of Nazareth. The people there were greatly offended by Him. The Word records that He could do no miracles except lay hands on a few and heal them. A spirit of offense ruled them.

In Jesus's travels, He condemned cities who did not repent when they saw the mighty miracles that happened in their midst. Bethsaida was one of these cities. It was a serious matter as He described judgement day to them. It was so serious that when He came to Bethsaida and they brought Him a blind man to heal, He took him by the hand and led him out of the city before He began to minister to him. Bethsaida had a ruling demon of defiance and rebellion to the point that the town would not repent, even though they saw the signs and wonders. Still, it took a few tries to accomplish the healing. Before departing, Jesus said the strangest thing to the man, "Do not even enter the village." Why? Because their rebellion gave power and authority to the demonic entity, and the devil had a legal right to be there. Further, he had the legal right not only to hinder the works of the Holy Spirit, but to steal the healing if the man returned to the village.

I have seen the very same legal ground in cities and organizations. Whether the ruler is offense, defiance, or religious in nature, it blocks the miracles and works of God.

At the Mission, we carefully guard the premises against any demon who tries to make its way in to rule. The guests off the street bring in every type known to man, but it is the mindset of those in authority that invites the rulers of darkness. That is why the Board of Directors and the staff must be very careful. In the past, ruling entities have snuck in via naughtiness in the staff, disunity, or offense and all heck broke loose. Together we have worked to keep the Chapel a sacred place of residence for Holy Spirit so that He reigns supreme there.

Long ago a young man was led to Guest Chapel by his girlfriend. His eyes were bandaged, and he had a stick to help navigate what was before him. Anger pulsed off of him as he sat in the back on the aisle seat. As I walked up and down the aisle preaching, the sullen look on his face hardened to a bitterness. I longed to know his story.

After the service was over, the girlfriend led the young man up to the front. He had been shot in the eyes with a shotgun and had lost the sight in both his eyes. She asked for prayer. Bill and I laid our hands on his sightless eyes and prayed for healing for them just as Jesus had done long ago. We saw no improvement, so we prayed again. Still nothing. Finally, they went off to lunch. Bill and I felt deflated. It was heartbreaking, and I could see how bitterness could seep in.

Months later in Guest Chapel, I was praying again for the sick when Bill led a young man up to me. He looked pale and pasty, but happy.

"Do you recognize him?" Bill asked. I did not.

"He has been in jail for nine months, that is why he looks so pale, but nine months ago we prayed for him. He had been shot in the eyes with a shotgun and lost his sight. He went to jail after that."

The youth took over the story. "I was so freaked out about my blindness they had to send me to the Pavilion (the mental health hospital in Amarillo) to get counseling. They tried to help me adjust to the fact I was blind and would be for the rest of my life. One morning in the jail cell, I woke up and could see out of my left eye. It looked like trees walking around, but I could see! As the day went on, my sight got clearer and clearer. God healed me! I just got out of jail this morning, and I came straight here so you could pray for my other eye."

I was trying to take in the fact God healed this young man in JAIL! We celebrated and praised God. What an extraordinary miracle! Thank you, Papa for being a good, good Father to this boy! We laid hands on the other eye and prayed. Holy Spirit hit us all. We saw no change in the right eye, but I was unmoved. I knew that I knew God would heal that too.

"You come see me when the other eye is healed." We all hugged and enjoyed the euphoria of the miracle of sight. Holy Spirit tabernacles in our little Chapel, our little Mission. He heals the sick, the broken hearted, the lame, the halt, and the blind. Thank You, Jesus!

Isaiah 9:1,2

Daniel 10:10-14

Mark 8:22-26

Kingdom Principle: Ruling demons can block a healing in a geographic place. Keeping a geographic place sacred and holy invites the Holy Spirit to abide there whereby the Kingdom is already accessible.

Prayer: "Jesus, You taught us so much in Your short time on earth. Thank You for continuing to teach us about the Kingdom, its laws, and our part to play in it. Thank You for healing this young man's eye. Thank You that you will heal the other one. Amen."

Try this: Look up every reference in the Bible where there seemed to be a hindrance to miracles. See if you can glean the reason.

What did you discover?

_____

_____

_____

_____

_____

_____

_____

_____

_____

DAY 77 – INSTRUCTIONS – A LITTLE BETTER

There is an interesting observation made when looking back over the many divine healings we have seen over the years. No two are the same. Some are healed instantly. Some come back weeks later telling of being healed over time. Some experience almost unbearable heat. Some feel ice cold. Some do not see the healing until they try to do something they could not do before.

There is an interesting story in the book of II Kings about a commander of the king's army in a neighboring country, one who had sent raiding parties to Israel many times. The commander, Naaman, was a leper. A small slave girl who had been captured in one of the raids saw her master's disease and commented on the ease of being healed by a prophet in her land if the commander were in Israel. Political arrangements had to be made, but soon Naaman and his troops made their way to Israel.

Upon arriving at the prophet's house, Naaman was treated with what might be called "diplomatic contempt." The prophet did not want the gifts of gold and jewels brought to his door. To add insult to injury, the prophet did not receive the commander but sent instructions for him to go wash in the Jordan River seven times. Naaman was infuriated and deeply offended by this treatment. His servants tried to smooth over the diplomatic mess by suggesting he just try it. He finally relented and went to the offending river and dipped himself seven times. As he did dip seven times, his flesh was restored like the flesh of a child. Some healings happen a little at a time.

A few years ago, my daughter-in-law received an alarming phone call from across the country that her father was dying in the hospital. She threw some clothes in the car. As she traveled east, she picked up her siblings and they made their way to the east coast to his bedside.

When they arrived, things looked grim. Organs were shutting down. The prognosis was not good. They sat by his bed grieving what was to come. Families back home were sending up prayers, including three little grandsons. Each night, their father knelt them down in a row by the bed. They folded their palms together and prayed for their grandfather, "Papa," and that their mom would come home soon.

One night, Erin's father rallied, and things looked hopeful. The siblings wearily packed up and started home. Two days later, their father made a turn for the worse again. This time it looked fatal. Understandably, Erin was very distraught.

One morning as she was dressing the boys for school, her oldest, who was just five years old, said, "Mom, Papa just needs to get a little better every day. If he gets a little better every day, soon he will be well. He put his little thumb and forefinger close together to show her what "a little better" meant. The family agreed that this would be their new prayer.

Within a week, Papa walked out of the hospital. The faith and wisdom of a five-year-old boy raised a half dead man out of his hospital bed and brought him from the brink of death. Since that time, I have adopted that prayer many times for those who cannot make the psychological leap of an instant healing but could believe that they can get a little better every day. I have seen the Father honor that prayer. Thank you, Papa!

II Kings 5:3-14

Acts 10:1-14

Matthew 17:20

Kingdom Principle: God sometimes speaks to a child to point the way to open the Kingdom.

Prayer: "Father, You know our weaknesses and our fragile hearts. Thank You for answering our "just a little better every day" prayers. Amen."

Activation: If you are struggling with doubts about supernatural instant healing, declare every day that you are getting a little better. Every day find a new Scripture about healing to speak over yourself. Every morning, look in the mirror and say out loud, "I am better today in Jesus name."

What happened?

God sometimes speaks to a child to point the way to open the Kingdom.

DAY 78 — MERCY — BACKPACK

One of the most confounding passages in the Bible to me is Jesus's extraordinary tongue lashing at the scribes and Pharisees, a high-ranking group of scholars well versed in the writings of Moses. They knew the law inside and out, but Jesus hurled these accusations at the group of legalists, "Woe to you scribes and Pharisees, hypocrites! For you tithe the mint, the dill, and the cumin, but have neglected the weightier provisions of the law, justice, mercy, and faithfulness. These are the things you should have done without neglecting the other." He was clearly frustrated with their attitudes to say the least.

The religious leaders of the day were so careful to follow the law that they even gave ten percent of their garden vegetables to the temple to fulfill the law of the tithe. The trouble lay in them neglecting the more important commands of the law - justice, mercy, and faithfulness. They were judgmental and condemning to the "lower orders." He was so angry with them that He flung insulting names at them, "Hypocrites!" And yet, in just a little while He would face torture and death on their behalf to save them from themselves.

At one time, I did a word study in the Bible looking up every verse having to do with the "poor" and "needy." The search was exhaustive. There were 142 references to the "poor," most having to do with orders to treat them well. There were 52 references to the "needy" and 130 verses about the "stranger." Being kind and merciful to the less fortunate is not a suggestion. It is a command, with serious consequences if disobeyed. It seems He is quite fond of the poor, the needy, and the stranger.

Long ago when I first began to volunteer at the Mission, the Lord said these words to me, "It is an honor to be chosen to serve the poor and the least in the Kingdom of God. I don't let just anyone serve them." I may have stumbled onto part of the reason that He is so particularly fond of them. In the book of Philippians Paul makes a profound statement.

"…that I may know Him, and the power of His resurrection and the fellowship of His sufferings, being conformed to His death."

The poor and the homeless are in the mess they're in primarily because of the childhood neglect, abuse, cruelty, and other unspeakable things they suffered at the hands of the adults around them. I will never know the kind of suffering that they have shared with Jesus. That might be why they are His favorites. In a way, they have known better than anyone the fellowship of His suffering. They are the innocents.

At the Mission, the staff is reminded to treat our guests and poor with the utmost respect and hospitality. For their regard, volunteers serve them their meals just as though they were at Chili's, not through a cafeteria line. The meals are not goulash, but Chicken Cacciatore, Lasagna, Pork chops, Cobb Salad, Roasted Chicken Quarters, Button Mushrooms and Wild Rice. Green vegetables are served with every meal. The Mission is kept clean and freshly painted with nice furniture, fixtures, paintings on the walls, matching end tables, and lamps. Guest preachers are admonished to speak of God's reckless love and mercy, without condemnation. The guests have been fully apprised of their misdoings already. They need to know that He loves them dearly. For the Scripture says,

"It is His kindness that leads us to repentance."

One day in Chapel, I was walking up and down the aisle praying for all the guests as they bowed their heads. I saw a young woman who was brand new to the streets. She was clearly having a tough time with this new lifestyle. I felt compassion for her, and without thinking, I laid my hand on her back to comfort her.

That afternoon, she came to my office door. "May I ask you a question?" she asked. I nodded, and she stepped into the room.

"What did you do to me in Chapel?" Alarmed that I may have offended her I went to her and had her sit down.

"I don't know what you mean. Tell me."

"I am new to the street. My backpack is so heavy, and I broke a rib. Now every step hurts. My shoulders are killing me. In Chapel, I felt so hopeless and afraid. Then you laid your hand on my back, and all the pain disappeared. Since lunch, I have tested my broken rib twisting around. It's fine now. How did that happen?"

All I knew to do was to tell her of the powerful love of God for her. We both cried. I prayed for her again.

We saw each other often. She eventually found a job and got off the streets. Thank you, Papa, for Your kindness to the poor!

Matthew 23:23-28

Exodus 12:42

Psalm 94:1-7

Philippians 3:10

Romans 2:4

Kingdom Principle: Mercy is a key that unlocks the extraordinary in the Kingdom.

Prayer: "Jesus, I am so grateful to You for allowing me to serve Your favorites. I have learned so much about the Kingdom through them. Please point them out to me on the streets so I may serve You by serving them. Amen."

Try this: Find a non-profit organization that serves the helpless and the poor. Make a commitment to volunteer once a week to serve them. Now go do it.

What did you discover?

JENA RAWLEY TAYLOR

DAY 79 — THE LIMP — DAVE

The Old Testament prophets predicted many things that would happen when the Expected One, the Messiah, came. One prophecy in Malachi is dear. It was that, "The Sun of righteousness will rise up with healing in its wings; and you will go forth and skip about like calves in the stall." He was to make the lame walk. It is recorded many times in the Gospel He accomplished that miracle. In Matthew 10, He commanded the disciples to go out and do the same. I am one of His disciples and it seems to me I run into a lot of wheelchairs, walkers, and canes. In Dillard's, on the street, Walmart, and at the Mission.

One day as I walked down the hall in the Mission, I noticed one of our new students, a tall fellow in his fifties, walking with a significant limp favoring one side. I stopped him and asked about the limp.

"When I was sixteen, I was working on a construction site. I was standing under a scaffolding when suddenly a sledgehammer fell from above and landed right on the arch of my foot. It crushed the bone, and never properly healed."

"Is it painful?"

"It aches a lot and hurts at night. I have learned to live with it."

I asked him if I could pray for his foot and he agreed. We went to my office so he could sit down. I laid my hands on the arch of his foot and began to pray. The pain disappeared. He stood up, walked around, looked at me, and smiled.

"The pain is gone! I'm not limping!" God healed Dave right there in my office. For the rest of his days with us, he never limped again. For forty years he had chronic pain in his arch and could only limp in an exaggerated rolling gait. In an instant, God healed him. That is an example of, "Thy Kingdom come, Thy will be done on earth as it is in Heaven." Believers get to take part in it. That never becomes commonplace to me. It is a source of joy and wonderment every time I see someone set free from their pain or sickness.

One day in Guest Chapel, I saw a tall slender woman hobble in with a cane. After the sermon, when the guests went to lunch, the woman limped up to me with her cane. She had been in a terrible automobile accident that had left her in constant back pain. She was unable to walk without a cane, stand up from a chair unaided, or get out of bed by herself. She regularly received a disability check each month for her injuries. She could not work.

She had heard about miracles happening at Faith City Mission and came for prayer. A security guard stood behind her and laid his hand on her shoulders while I stood in front to pray for her hips and legs. We prayed for her entire body to be mended. Then we asked her to do something she could not do before.

The first thing she noticed was the back pain was gone after so many years of chronic discomfort. I then took the cane from her and asked her to walk unaided. She panicked and looked longingly at her cane. It had been her best friend for so many years; she was frightened to be without it. The guard walked with her but did not touch her as she tentatively took a few steps. She became bolder and walked faster. Then she began to circle the Chapel again and again, gaining momentum with every step. She walked to us smiling and crying. It had been so long since she could do that. I asked her to sit down and stand up unaided. I held her cane. She eyed it wistfully.

"Just try," I said. She rocked forward and stood up. She sat down and tried it again. This time she popped up like a jack-in-the-box.

"Well! I haven't been able to do that in years!" We cried and hugged. Suddenly her eyes widened.

"I can work again! I can get a job!"

"What did you do?"

"I was a counselor before the accident. I would love to go back to that, to help people."

I knew she meant business when she sent me her resume. We had no openings, but I knew she was putting her life back together. That moved me as much as the healing. The Father was able to accomplish what concerned her and work all things together for her good. Extraordinary!

Malachi 4:2

Matthew 15:3

Psalm 138:8

Philippians 1:6

Kingdom Principle: When one turns their focus to the power of God instead of injury and pain, the miraculous explodes.

Prayer: "Father, thank You for allowing us to explore Your Kingdom freely and participate in all its wonders. Make me brave enough to at least try to pray for those around me who are in pain. Amen."

Initiation: Be conscious of those strangers around you using a walker, a wheelchair, or a cane. Summon the courage to strike up a conversation with the individual and ask him if you might pray for him. Be sure to ask him to do something he could not do before.

What happened?

DAY 80 – PROVISION – FIVE DOLLAR BILL

For many of us who pursue the Kingdom ardently, provision for our needs and even our wants is the trickiest thing to trust the Father with. And yet, over and over again there are stories in the Scriptures that prove His faithfulness. The children of Israel had no choice but to trust Yahweh for everything during their forty-year trek across the wilderness. And He provided it all. The water out of the rock, the manna from Heaven, even a night light in the desert.

Jesus admonished His disciples to stop fretting about their needs by citing the lilies of the field and birds of the air. He even obtained a shekel out of the mouth of a fish with which to pay His taxes. He multiplied the food and created wine from water.

And yet today, we wring our hands and worry over the bills, the medical expenses, the car lasting one more year. By its very nature, a Mission implies poverty and lack. Everyone who comes to us is struggling to keep their heads above water. Many have lost everything but the clothes on their backs. The commitment here is to provide everything we can, such as meals, clothing, a warm bed with clean sheets, toothbrushes, soap, furniture, dishes, and appliances. In order to do all of that, we in turn must trust that Papa will bring us the provisions needed. Every effort is made to be frugal and careful with the funds that come in, but sometimes in the summer months, it is tight.

One day, the staff was meeting to discuss our funding issues; actually, the lack thereof. The accountant had a bill of $20,000.00 due that very afternoon. The Mission did not remotely have the funds to pay it. We all joined hands at the table and asked our heavenly Father to provide for us so we could provide for His little ones. At the moment we said "Amen," the door opened and in walked the receptionist from the front desk. I told him that we were in a meeting and…

"I could not wait. A gentleman just walked in the front door and handed this to me." He thrust a check into my hand. I looked at the amount. Yes, it was $20,000.00! We cried, we hooped and yelled. We celebrated. The name on the check was unfamiliar to me. No one recognized it. We searched the donor records. Apparently, he had never given to us before.

Years later, the very same thing happened again. It was a rough year for cattle, oil, and gas which are the basis for the economy in this west Texas community. All the nonprofits were struggling. Unfortunately for us, we were also in a large Capital Campaign to refurbish an old hospice facility to give us more room for our growing population of homeless, addicted, disabled, and poor. A payment was due that very afternoon to the bank for $100,000.00 (no, I am not exaggerating, and yes, we had cut the budget to the bone).

I went to Chapel to sit before the Lord. I confessed my fears and worries, but called up my favorite picture in my mind, God on His throne NOT wringing His hands over our dilemma. It is always a reassuring picture for me. I knew He was not worried; I knew to trust Him yet again.

That afternoon a vice president from a bank in town walked into my office with an end of year check for, yes again, $100,000.00.

Many times, the provision from God comes to our guests and students. One day in Chapel, I was visiting with a couple who regularly came to eat lunch with us. Their electricity was turned off because they could not pay the bill.

"Why don't we ask God for a miracle?" I suggested. They looked dubious but agreed. We all held hands and began to pray that somehow, some way, the electricity would inexplicably be turned back on. The couple stayed for Chapel service and lunch then went home.

Later that afternoon I walked out to the lobby for something and there sat my little couple.

"Well, hello! What are you all doing here? Is everything okay?"

The husband took the lead.

"We wanted to come back and tell you what happened. When we came home after lunch a guy from the electric company was doing something to our meter box. We asked him what he was up to and he said, "I'm turning your electricity on." When questioned why and how, he simply replied that he just does what he's told. He did not know the details."

Extraordinary! I have seen a lot of miracles, but this was the first one having to do with one's utilities. This much I have learned. God is God and we are not. He can do anything He wishes to do. Apparently, His favorite thing to do is to extend grace and mercy, even when you do not pay your electric bill.

A year or so ago, there was a visiting ministry from another state speaking at a local church. Tickets to the weekend-long gathering were made available to our students living at the Mission. We loaded up the students and drove to the church. It was a real treat.

They were taking up an offering for the ministry, so I dug around in my wallet and found some cash. Not thinking, I handed a five-dollar bill to the girl next to me so that she could give as well. In addition, someone behind her handed her two twenties. She handed one of the twenties to one of the other girls who had nothing to give. When the offering was taken to the front the preacher prayed for a thousand-fold return for all who gave. Frankly, I never truly grasped that concept. I had complete faith in the lame walking, the blind eyes opened, and diabetes healed. Again, God is God and he can to whatever He wishes. He has proven Himself to me over and over in the arena of finance, but I still struggled with the 1,000-fold return principle in the Kingdom.

One day, the girl to whom I had given the five dollars to ran up to me while I was waiting for my turn with the chiropractor who volunteers weekly at the Mission (that truly is a gift from God). She asked me if I remembered the money I had given her for the offering that weekend. I did. She recounted the five and twenty she had put into the plate, as well as the prayer for a thousand-fold return.

"Well! This week the court settled on a case I was involved in. They awarded me $25,000.00, exactly one thousand-fold of the money I put into the offering plate that night!" We yelled and hugged and thanked our heavenly Father for His goodness to us. He loves to give good things to His children. He has done it over and over throughout history.

Genesis 22:1-17

Matthew 6:25-7:12

Matthew 17:25

Luke 6:38

Malachi 3:10–12

Kingdom Principle: Monetarily giving to the Kingdom opens the coffers of Heaven so blessings may be received here on the earth.

Prayer: "Lord, Your assurances are true. Teach me to trust You with provision for me. Teach me the laws and principles of the Kingdom of God on provision.

Exercise: Look up Scriptures that have to do with "provision," "provide," and "given." Write down the verses. Study the principles of finance in scripture. If you have never tithed before, begin to give tithes and offerings to your local church or favorite charity. What happened?

Write it down:

_____

_____

Monetarily giving to the Kingdom opens the coffers of Heaven so blessings may be received here on the earth.

DAY 81 — AMAZED — PAULA

There is a word in Scripture that is seen repeatedly expressing wonder, excitement, and astonishment. When the people saw Jesus accomplish things with a word that no man had ever done before, they were amazed. Healing the sick, casting out demons, calming the storm, Jesus caused quite a stir wherever He went. And everywhere He went, people were downtrodden with their blind eyes, deaf ears, issues of blood, and withered limbs. The people had no emergency room or urgent care. They simply lived with their injuries, illnesses, and infirmities. But the Word says that He healed them all, which means He never turned anyone away "so that they could learn to build strength of character in themselves."

In today's western civilized world, there are urgent care clinics and hospitals and modern medical science for our injuries and ailments, even insurance to pay for it all. Still, there are diseases and conditions that cannot be healed, like Parkinson's or uneven leg lengths. Even today, we tend to just live with it. And yet, God has made a way for healing all of our diseases and injuries. Isaiah 53 tells of the wonderful things Jesus accomplished on our behalf. "But He was pierced through for our transgressions, He was crushed for our iniquities; the chastening of our well-being fell upon Him; and by His scourging we are healed." That one verse sums up the extraordinary work He achieved for all humanity. He took it all, so we do not have to. We do not just have to live with it.

One day, I commented to my assistant about the beginning of arthritis in my hands, and how they were taking on the knurled look in the knuckles of my grandmother's hands. She held up her own smooth hands and related her story to me. Arthritic tumors on the knuckles ran in her family and her dad's hands were crippled with them, as was his mother's. Her cousin commented at how her hands were taking on the family trait of severe arthritis. Right then, she objected.

"NO! I refuse to take on that family curse. I choose not to receive arthritis in my hands, in Jesus name!" Her knuckles shrunk and she no longer had the hands so common in her family.

It dawned on me that I had just accepted something from my family that Jesus took a cat of nine tails to relieve me of. I had, by default, chosen to live with it. Now I have decided to take a stand.

Just recently in Staff and Student Chapel, a woman came for prayer. Parkinson's disease ran rampant in her family. Her father, uncles, and brother all had it. She had begun to experience the telltale signs of the disease, such as shaking, tremors, stiffness, hunched shoulders, and the appearance of a "masked face" (the face appears frozen with no expression). Fear had begun to well up in her. She had come to the Mission a few years ago to be prayed for because of her severe scoliosis. She had been instantly healed which was certified by her doctor. She hoped that God would also heal the Parkinson's. The first thing we did was break every generational curse of the disease passed down in her family. We then began to cast the demons out, but a spirit of fear was blocking their exit. It showed in her eyes. We led her through repentance and told her to come out of agreement with the demon. She did. Now we could go after the other entities, Parkinson's, tremors, stiffness, and so on. The tremors stopped; she looked up at me. She was literally glowing and smiled radiantly. The masked look was gone. We continued to command the Parkinson's to come out. Suddenly she yelped.

"I felt something leave out of my head! Right here!" She touched her skull at the top left.

"It's gone! I felt it go!" And right there she was healed. The tremors stopped, and her balance was sure. We marveled at the symptoms leaving one by one; but for me, the change in the radiance of her face was astounding!

Our Board President who joined us weekly for Staff and Student Chapel watched the whole episode.

"Wait! I inherited a condition from my dad as well. My left leg is shorter than my right. It makes my pelvis bone out of alignment causing severe back pain. I went to the doctor once and he x-rayed it. He showed me the problem. Will you pray for me as well?"

I asked her to come sit down in a chair and scoot her hips all the way to the back. I knelt before her and asked her to raise her feet straight up. I took hold of both heels and held them together. Yes, indeed, one boot heel was ¾ inch longer than the other. I had seen this done before but did not believe the validity of this exercise because there were too many ways to mimic the leg growing out. I carefully held the heels still and watched to see if the woman shifted her hip. A staff member placed her hand on the right hip and prayed. I held the heels and prayed. The staff member yelped.

"Your hip is wiggling, buzzing, quivering! I don't know what! But it is moving!"

I looked down at her heels. The left heel was now only a half inch shorter. Oh, my goodness! I knew I had not moved her leg and she had not moved her hip, and yet the discrepancy between the heels had diminished by half. We continued to pray. The hip continued to shake, quiver, and quake. The two heels were only 1/16th of an inch apart.

"Almost there!" My excitement grew. We prayed more. Suddenly they were perfectly even. I was astonished and amazed. So was our Board President. It was a good day in Chapel.

Isaiah 35:3–6

Isaiah 53:3–5

Acts 3:1–10

Matthew 8:14–17

Matthew 12: 8–21

Kingdom Principle: We do not need to just accept our chronic illness or the generational curses. When we break those curses, the windows of Heaven are opened and the supernatural tumbles down into our laps.

Prayer: "Jesus, You bore every sin and every sickness for us, so that we did not have to just live with it. Thank You for making a way for us to be freed and healed and delivered. Holy Spirit, whisper in our ear when we forget that. Amen."

Suggestion: Make a conscious decision to quit accepting aches and ailments that you have been, heretofore, just living with. Choose every day to take a stand against these and trust wholeheartedly in His will for you to be supernaturally healed. When symptoms occur, recite a memorized healing scripture. Thank Jesus for what He did for you.

What happened?

DAY 82 – OPPRESSION – CARL

There are times when there is no physical ailment, or even mental illness; but there is a chronic sense of oppression that hovers over a person for an extended period of time. It sometimes has to do with a spouse, an incident, and sometimes there is just no apparent reason for the malaise. Regardless of the reason, some people become trapped under a blanket of heaviness and despair. Some have lived with it for so long they do not realize they are suffering with it. Like a well-worn sweatshirt, it becomes an old friend.

One day a young man came to the Mission to get clean and sober. In the interview, we could not help but notice the extensive tattooing that covered every square inch of his body visible to us. There was clearly an occultic and violent theme with pentagrams, demons, and goat heads.

He was raised in a normal Christian home, played football in high school, and loved Jesus. He was as normal as apple pie. In one of his games, he was injured with a torn ligament in his thigh. It had been a source of constant pain since the night of the injury. One night he complained of the pain to his mother. She went to the medicine cabinet and retrieved a half of a pink pill and gave it to him. He experienced relief at last.

Thus, started his insatiable craving for opioids. He begged, bought, and stole whatever he could get his hands on. He spiraled down into the dark abyss of addiction. He became involved with the occult. One night he put his beloved dog out of his room, turned out the lights, and invited the demons into himself. From that night, he slid into the darkness of hell itself. By the time he showed up on our doorstep, he was a physical, mental, and emotional wreck. I asked him if I could pray for him. He said yes, so we placed our hands upon him, as one staff member held his hands. The storm of tears and wailing came. The devil was not going to give him back to us so easily. We knew we had authority over the enemy, so we kept at it. His torment was unbearable.

Finally, the sobbing and wailing subsided. The storm had passed. At last he raised his head and smiled. It was as though the dark clouds parted and the sun had come out. He felt extraordinary relief. The dark blanket of demonic oppression had lifted. After he left the room, the staff member who was holding his hands rubbed his own. "He nearly broke my hands!" He was accepted into the program and worked hard to live a new lifestyle. The Son had set him free, and he was free at last.

It was women's shopping day at the Mission, which means women and their children come to Chapel services, eat lunch, then go to our free store to pick up whatever they wish. We do not sell the donations. We give it all away. Louisa and her daughter had come to shop but came to Chapel first for prayer. Louisa asked me if I could pray for her daughter's knee. She had had a terrible bicycle accident when she was ten and the ligaments in her left knee were torn. She was never treated. Now at eighteen, it caused a great deal of difficulty for her and was very painful. We prayed together for healing, and I asked her to do something she could not do before. She got up, walked around then began to jump up and down. Not only could she now perform the tasks, but there was no more pain. God healed her instantly. He is so very kind to His little ones.

Louisa then asked me to pray for her as well. She and her daughter had found Jesus and she was clean and sober. Life was good until her husband got out of prison and came home. She began to cry as she divulged the truth of things. His addiction was to meth. He was furious that the family had become believers and would not let them read their Bibles. He taunted them about their new-found faith. He would become angry and shout at them about it. Louisa was afraid that her resolve to stay sober was slipping. The oppression lay over them like a heavy blanket. We prayed for a miracle for this man, that he would find Jesus. We prayed that the joy that they had known would return and Holy Spirit would never leave them. They both felt much better, and I reminded them of the women's shelter at the Mission should it ever come to that. We hugged and off they went to our free store.

On the same day, a very young woman approached me. She was pale, with dark circles under her eyes. Her face was mottled. Her lips looked like chewed pencil erasers. She had clearly been on the street for a while and in need of a shower. A sour smell clung to her, which sometimes occurs when demonic entities have taken up residence in someone. She looked to be maybe sixteen.

"Do you recognize me?" She asked. I did not. She went on, "I am the girl who was abducted from my home two years ago and sold into sex trafficking. Later I was recaptured and brought home, but they had to send me to the Pavilion Mental Hospital for psychiatric care. They put me on every known tranquilizer including Ativan. "

"Are you okay?" I questioned.

"I'm okay. I'm better," she commented, unconvincingly.

"What can I pray for you?"

I want to have peace without all the drugs, especially Ativan. How do I do that?"

Right then, my heart broke for this young girl whose life was destroyed by the evil one. In the aftermath, the oppression clung to her. She desperately needed peace.

"Jesus said He would give us this peace. It is a peace that the world cannot understand. Let's pray for His peace that defies our circumstances." I laid my hand on her back and began to pray, asking Holy Spirit to come and brood over her, to bring new life to her. Suddenly, she doubled over and sobbed. I knew Holy Spirit was lancing the wound in her heart. I just kept my hand on her back while He worked. She wept and wept, but I could feel His presence over her. She did not need me right then. She needed Holy Spirit.

Finally, she straightened and smiled at me. Her face was clear, even radiant, as though she had had a spa day. The splotches were gone. Her eyes were clear, and the spirit of oppression was not upon her. Even the sour smell was gone.

"I feel better," she exclaimed, a bit mystified. Holy Spirit had washed the horrid aftermath of trauma away for this girl and set her free. God, You really are so gentle with Your little ones.

Isaiah 55:11-17

Psalm 51:10-12

John 8:31-32

John 8:36

John 14:27

Kingdom Principle: When we take our authority over the demonic and cast them out, then ask Holy Spirit to brood over His little one, the heavy blanket of oppression is flung off and the little lamb is set free.

Prayer: "Holy Spirit, thank You for coming and healing our wounds, and our hurts. You do not leave us in our mess. Come and heal my wounds today. Amen."

Try this: Do a study on the word "peace" and its definition in the Old and New Testaments. Look up references to peace.

What did you discover?

_____

_____

_____

_____

_____

_____

_____

DAY 83 – THE IMPOSSIBLE – THE CANE

All of us have had times in our lives, believers and unbelievers alike, when we need an answer to a prayer. Some situations seem desperate, others seem absolutely impossible, and nothing short of a miracle can resolve the problem. We fret, stew, and worry ourselves sick. We feel completely powerless; hence, the sudden interest in a deity.

Jesus addressed this issue with His disciples with a very short sentence, "With God all things are possible." We know that in our head but find it difficult to "know in our knower," as one little nun once put it.

Early in my new-found faith, I had a desperate situation arise. I went to my mentor, an older woman who was much further down the road in her faith. She was a veteran believer. After I explained this terrible circumstance to her, she said these words, "God is not up there sitting on His throne wringing His hands over your problem. It is not a surprise to Him. At this very moment He is completely at peace over the situation, and already knows how it will play out."

With God, all things are possible. Another way to say it might be, "In the presence of God, all things are possible." I have since saved in my mind that ridiculous picture of God wringing His hands over the situation. It reminds me how foolish I am being.

Jesus gave an entire discourse on worrying in the book of Matthew. He reminds us how futile worrying is. He goes on to say that our heavenly Father knows that we need things like food, clothing, and a long life. He even gives us the answer to our dilemmas, and it is so extraordinarily easy.

"But seek first His kingdom and His righteousness and all these things will be added to you."

There is a story of a man who brought his son to the disciples to heal. He was desperate, for the boy was mute and dashed himself on the ground often, foaming at the mouth and grinding his teeth and becoming stiff. He was so hopeless that when Jesus appeared, the man actually said, "If You can do anything, take pity on us." Jesus replied, "If you can! All things are possible to him who believes." The father cried out, "I do believe; help me in my unbelief." Jesus then rebuked the deaf and dumb spirit. The boy convulsed, and the spirit went out.

One day the phone rang and a good friend who is a big supporter of the Mission asked me to meet him at a specific address he wanted to show me. As I arrived, I realized that the address was the beloved hospice that had helped my parents and my former husband die with dignity. Oddly, they all three occupied the same room at their appointed times.

The Director of the Hospice program and my friend met me and explained their intentions. They wanted to give the beautiful building to the Mission. The building was in pristine condition. It had courtyards for each guest as well as green grass and trees. Each room had its own ADA approved bathroom. Upstairs were twelve offices, a conference room, and a kitchen. This was beyond my wildest dreams. The trouble was the neighborhood. It had become dangerous, filled with homeless men breaking into the abandoned hospital to the north for shelter. These were my peeps. I had no qualms about the neighborhood. I accepted their proposition immediately with permission from our Board of Directors. God had surprised us with a wonderful piece of property at no cost.

While the property was wonderful, it would need a bit of renovation. It had no kitchen, the Chapel was tiny, and a dining room would need to be added. This became the sticky part. We were already in a Capital Campaign for the Ranch. How could we add this on top of the needed funds to renovate the buildings at the Ranch? I became overwhelmed at the scope of expense. It was turning into a huge project, and we were just a very small homeless shelter. Our faith began to waver.

We decided to focus primarily on funding the old hospice building first. We were going to have to eat this elephant one bite at a time. We encouraged each other with the promises God had made in the Bible concerning provision. Our main verse was, "With God all things are possible." We set about giving tours of the two locations and calling on major donors to help with the projects financially. Funds were coming in slowly. After a year and a half, we only lacked five hundred thousand.

An event was planned to hopefully fully fund the hospice building renovations. In the fundraising world, it was really not possible to raise that much money in one evening, especially for a small shelter in a small town. To make matters worse, half of the invitations sent out were never received. Difficulties were cropping up left and right. Technical mistakes tangled up so many things. We were very discouraged.

One day, I was at the mall walking toward a department store when I noticed an older gentleman walking in the opposite direction toward the smaller stores. He was limping badly and had a cane. I felt the nudge to go pray for him, so I crossed the large expanse and approached him. As I approached, I noticed some nasty bruising on his arm. Other places were bandaged.

"Excuse me, sir; I could not help but notice your limp and your bandages. Did you have an accident?"

He turned his gaze to me, and I noticed the bluest eyes I had ever seen. He explained he had fallen, and it looked worse than it really was. He had polio as a child and had to wear a brace on his leg, so he was a bit unstable in walking; hence, the cane. I asked if I could pray for him. He was delighted. I laid my hands on his wounds gently and prayed for healing, especially his leg. When I said, "Amen," and looked up at him, he smiled and thanked me for the prayer.

"I have something for you," he said. He dug into his side pant pocket and fished out a coin. On the front was a silver cross on a blue background. I turned it over and read, "With God. All things are possible." Mark 10:27.

"Oh! This is our verse! To believe God for a miracle!"

He pointed his finger at me and said, "Don't forget that."

I looked more closely at the elderly man and realized not only did he have the bluest eyes, but his complexion was smooth. His hair was silver, but shiny. He looked a great deal like an older guy who approached me for gas in the Walmart parking lot. The bluest eyes, shining hair, and smooth complexion. I could not figure out how they appeared old at first glance, but upon closer scrutiny, they appeared to be angelic. I suspected that they were both angels sent on assignment to encourage me. I felt encouraged. I felt as though the heavy burden of the event was lifted from me.

In the weeks leading up to the event, I found myself actually having fun in the preparations. I was enjoying myself. I had never "enjoyed myself" in prior event preparations.

I shared my mall experience with the Board of Directors. They, too, felt that the man was an angel I had approached unaware. We were all encouraged.

The night of the event arrived. There were the typical snags with technical difficulties, but the most alarming thing was the poor attendance. Only about half of the seats were taken. We could not possibly meet our financial goal.

During the evening, a gentleman whom I was slightly acquainted with approached me and asked what our goal was to fully fund the renovations at the old hospice building. I told him $450,000.00. He smiled at me.

"Whatever you make tonight, I will provide the rest to fully fund the project."

I nearly fell over and I know I looked ridiculous opening and closing my mouth like a fish out of water. I was dumbfounded at his offer, and speechless. The stipulation was that he remain absolutely anonymous. I promised I would tell no one.

That night as I lay in bed, I pondered the evening and how, despite our bumbling and fumbling, God had provided a way where there seemed to be no way. I thanked the Lord for the miracle. With Him all things were truly possible. What is more exciting is, that because of all the snags and missteps, dropped balls, and technical difficulties, only God could get the credit. Wow!

A few days later, I sat in the gentleman's office in order to give him the results of the net profit raised on the night of the event. He promised the difference of the full amount left within a week. He then began to tell me how he came to the decision to give that night.

"My wife and I were driving to your event and I really was not thinking of the Mission or the Capital Campaign, when suddenly the Holy Spirit whispered in my ear reminding me that I had not yet given my large end of year gift to a non-profit yet, as was my habit to do. He nudged me to give it to the Mission's Capital Campaign. By the time we had arrived at the event, I knew that was what I would do."

I thanked him profusely, again, and left. As I drove back to the Mission, the Lord whispered in my ear, "I told you that all things were possible with Me. You can trust Me." Yes indeed. He had sent me an angel to deliver the message. Then He sent me a donor to provide the needed funds. I am learning to trust Him. My coin sits beside the lamp in my sacred space so that every morning I remember, no matter what happens today, with God all things are possible.

Matthew 6:25-34

Matthew 19:26

Mark 9:23

Luke 18:27

Kingdom Principle: When I put my trust in God, I have nothing to fear. With Him all things are possible.

Prayer: "Jesus, I do not know why I doubt You. You have never failed me or deserted me. Thank You for teaching me to trust You, that there is always a way when there seems to be no way. Amen."

Activation: Write down your needs and wants and desperate desires on a card. Now, find a Scripture where God promises to meet your needs. Find a Scripture that promises to give you the desires of your heart. Write it down. Everyday read your cards and thank God for His promises fulfilled. When the prayer is answered, write down the story.

What Happened?

DAY 84 – TORMENTED – THE DEMONIC

On many occasions, people have come to the Mission for help with getting free of the demonic. They know full well the onslaught of tormenting demons. Many cultures mix their faith with occultic practices such as tarot cards, seances, palm reading, horoscopes, and even sacrifices. Those that find themselves engaged in witchcraft are particularly plagued by spirits. Heavy drug use exacerbates the problem.

The law of Moses strictly forbade these practices for that very reason. They opened the door in the spirit realm and to every sort of mischief.

One day, a young heavy-set man came to the Mission in a terrible state, begging us to cast out these tormentors. He was beside himself with dread. I was called to the lobby to help. As I entered the lobby, the stench was overwhelming. It was not the usual smell of unwashed bodies and dirty hair. It was vile smelling. I knew it was demonic. His face was dark and dull. His eyes looked dead like pebbles.

I sat down next to the man and asked what had happened. He said his sister had put a curse on him, and the demons had tortured him day and night. His involvement in witchcraft gave them legal rights in the spirit realm. I asked what part he might play in witchcraft. Evidently, the whole family was involved in it.

We knew he could be set free. Jesus came to set us free. But the young man had to change his thinking about witchcraft. He repented for dabbling in it and asked forgiveness. Tears started trickling down his cheeks. He regretted ever getting mixed up in it. We broke the curses spoken over him. As a believer he was "redeemed from the curse, Christ being made a curse for him, for cursed is every man that hangs on a tree." We thanked God for that gift alone. Now we were able to cast out every demon attached to the curse. They no longer had legal ground to be there.

Finally, the man was set free. He smiled at me. His face was glowing, and the sparkle was back in his eyes. Better yet, the stench was gone. Thank you, Jesus, for making a way for this little lost sheep to find his road back to You.

Not long ago a woman from the community called and begged us to pray for her. We set an appointment for her to come to the Mission. Upon arrival and greetings, we took her to the Chapel. She was meticulously dressed and coiffed. She was shaky, however, and clearly at the end of her rope. We sat down and asked her to explain her predicament.

Her physical illnesses were many, as well as her losses. As she told her story, we realized her many physical problems were brought on by her reactions to the mishaps. Much anger, resentment, bitterness, and unforgiveness had snuck in and stripped her of her health, especially in the area of digestion. Satan had robbed her of her joy and her physical health. She wept and wept.

Although a devoted Christian, she did not realize to what degree demonic oppression had taken over her life. While she would not dream of hurting anyone, fudging on her tithe, or cheating on her husband, she had been subject to what some call "good Christian sins." Good Christians try very hard to live a life of good behavior but have a tough time with their emotions ("I don't lie, and I don't spit, but I do like to throw a fit").

Fear, worry, depression, jealousy, and self-pity all go unnoticed as demon driven. Even if, at some point we do get them out, the little rascals sneak back in.

We asked the woman to stand while we laid hands on the diseased areas and asked the Father what was causing the physical ailments. Instantly, He revealed one demon after another. As each one was revealed, she was able to relate the incident that caused it. We walked her through forgiveness and release for that incident and proceeded to cast out the offending entity. Demons are very legalistic and territorial. They know exactly what they can and cannot do. They know when they have to go. Air began to be released up her throat over and over again. She was being set free. There was a particularly stubborn spirit in the digestive system.

As she forgave the offending party, the demon released, and her stomach began to literally shrink under my hand.

"How are you feeling?" we asked.

"I feel so much better!" As we talked, her abdomen kept shrinking like a balloon with a small leak. It was amazing to watch. She looked so happy.

She was puzzled at the extent of demonic occupation. We told her about our habit of a quarterly cleansing. Every three months or so, we ask the Lord to show us anything that we may have allowed back into our lives. He is so kind to reveal an attitude or emotion that has carried us back into a dark area. Usually, He reveals one or two per day. Each day as He uncovers an unsavory matter, repentance is first. Next, one must come out of agreement with the attitude or emotion. Finally, one must cast out the aberrant spirit firmly. Spirits are breath, so they usually come out with a cough or burp, or yawn. Some manifest with gagging or actually throwing up. Some require a powder room. But they must obey once they no longer have legal ground to stay.

Thank you, Jesus, for teaching us Your ways so that we can help others become free.

Matthew 9:32

John 8:36

Luke 9:1

I Corinthians 10: 20-21

Galatians 3:13

Kingdom Principle: Demons have no legal power unless we give it to them. If we take our blood bought authority over them, they must leave.

Prayer: "Jesus, You truly overcame the devil for our sake. Thank You for showing us the way out of the dark and into the light. Amen."

Try this: Ask the Lord what negative attitudes and emotions may have worked their way back into your life, and what demons are attached to them. Write it down and find the scriptures that address that attitude. Repent, ask God to cleanse you of all unrighteousness, thank Jesus for forgiveness, come out of agreement with the attached demon, and cast it out in Jesus name out loud. Make note of any bodily manifestation that may occur.

What happened?

DAY 85 – JUST BELIEVE – STAGE FOUR CANCER

There is a Chiropractor in our town who is a radical believer in Jesus and is a member of our Board of Directors. He loves to come to the Mission to volunteer his skills. Once a week, he adjusts every student and every staff member. His energy is boundless, and his enthusiasm for life is contagious. It is such a pleasure to see him set up his mobile clinic in the boardroom all the while laughing and cutting up with each "patient" as it comes their time to lie down on the table and get worked on. A bigger pleasure is to see him pray with each person.

Dr. Hand (yes, that is his real name) has observed that ailments and injuries seem to heal much faster at the Mission than the expected time for the average patient at his office. He vows and declares the number of salvations each month at the Mission are in direct proportion to the number of chiropractic adjustments he gives out here at the Mission. Every board meeting when we look at our stats sheet for the prior month, those two numbers are neck and neck. He is an exceptional man.

One dark and cold evening in December, Dr. Hand got a call from a woman who begged him to come immediately to the hospital to pray for her daughter. The girl was in stage four with cancer and had been ill for a long time. The doctors had told her the choice now was hospice or home. They could do nothing more for her.

There is a story in the Bible about a very similar case. "A woman who had been ill for twelve years with a hemorrhage had suffered much at the hands of the doctors. She had spent all that she had and was not helped at all, but rather had grown worse." She had obviously heard about the extraordinary power of Jesus and thought if she could just touch the hem of His garment, she would be healed. As she did, the hemorrhage dried up, and she felt in her body that she was healed.

Jesus immediately felt the power go out of Him and turned around in the crowd and said, "Who touched My garment?" He continued to look around to find the woman who had touched Him. Trembling with fear but knowing she had been healed, she came forward and fell at His feet and told Him everything. He said to her, "Daughter, your faith has made you well. Go in peace and be healed of your affliction."

Dr. Hand was cold and tired but knew he must go to the hospital and pray for the girl. He did not recognize her with all the tumors distorting her once beautiful face. He taught her that believing God would heal her, just as the woman with the issue of blood believed. He taught her to say, "I believe God has healed me." She repeated the words with him. He laid hands on every tumor and prayed. Nothing happened. Dr. Hand reminded her to continue to say the words out loud over and over.

The following morning, the doctors came in to learn her decision about hospice or home. Either way, she would be released from their care. Sitting up in bed, she confidently spoke the words that Dr. Hand had taught her, "I believe God has healed me, so I am not going to hospice. I am going home." The doctors shook their heads and left to do the paperwork.

The trip home had exhausted her; for several days she felt miserable and could not get out of bed, but she continued to say the words out loud. The following week, the girl's mother was shocked when she found the girl walking in the yard. The girl was feeling better. Each day, she would say the words and each day she got better, until a month later she walked into Dr. Hand's office. He did not recognize her because, this time, all the tumors were gone. God had healed this beautiful girl.

Mark 5:25-34

Matthew 9:28

Mark 5:21-23, 35-42

Mark 11:24

Kingdom Principle: When one holds to the truth of the Word and claims its promise over and over despite the medical evidence, the Kingdom unfolds and the exceptional happens.

Prayer: "Jesus, forgive me for my doubt and unbelief. I choose to believe. I choose to have faith. Will You send the Holy Spirit to help me with my faith to believe in signs and wonders? Amen."

Initiate: Look back over the times in your own life when crisis struck, and you did not believe God would work a miracle. Repent before Him for your doubt and unbelief in these situations. Cast out a spirit of doubt and unbelief. Now, select an area in your life or the life of your family where you need a miracle or a healing. Declare your belief in the miracle over and over.

What happened?

When one holds to the truth of the Word and claims its promise over and over despite the medical evidence, the Kingdom unfolds and the exceptional happens.

DAY 86 — GIVING IT AWAY — LUNG CANCER

There is a truck stop just over the state line in New Mexico that has been donating to the Mission for years. The donations each month are always odd amounts, so we decided to go meet the owners and learn more about the establishment.

As we arrived, we were amazed at the place. It could hardly be called a truck stop and looked more like a 1950's diner with shiny red booths and bar stools. Fifties music was playing over the loudspeaker, and everything was squeaky clean. Huge windows flooded the diner with light. The ladies room had fresh cut flowers on the counter. We met the wife who owned the charming place, a beautiful blonde who fit right into the décor. We had a wonderful visit and learned a great deal more about their business. They had been called to tend to the various needs of truckers on the I-40 corridor. There were spotless showers and locker rooms, a special lounge for drivers, as well as a small Chapel complete with stained glass windows. Every Sunday morning, a preacher would come and speak encouraging words to this very unusual congregation. In addition, the couple produced and supplied free of charge, CD's of sermons that the haulers could listen to on the road. It was all so remarkable. We were astonished.

The woman then led us to a spacious room off of the convenience store part of the place. It was a museum of sorts, with about 30 vintage cars in pristine condition. The rest of the space was packed with memorabilia from the 30's, 40's, and 50's. We were mesmerized by the cars, especially a bubble gum pink Thunderbird convertible with white leather interior.

Most extraordinary of all was a large bucket by the entrance to the museum above which hung a sign. Essentially, it said that the museum was free of charge, but one could make a donation to the bucket. All of the proceeds of the bucket were sent to two Missions that tended to the needs of the homeless. Our Mission was one of those; the other was in New Mexico. The sign also had a blank where each month the total number of meals served to the homeless over the years of giving would be updated. The number that day read 275,000 meals.

What a brilliant idea. The couple not only supported their own outreach to truckers but funded two shelters over several years with this income stream. What an inspired idea. There is a verse in Isaiah about the nobleman and his noble plans. It is a law of the Kingdom of God. Those who give to the poor are blessed by the Lord, and He pays with interest.

Suddenly, and without warning, the husband of this couple was diagnosed with lung cancer, and the disease had already spread. There were twelve tumors up and down his digestive system. One in particular hidden behind the pancreas was the size of a grapefruit. The doctor was as kind as he could be, but the fact was that the owner of this incredible truck stop which reached out to so many had stage four cancer.

When the couple asked how long he had, the doctor responded, "Two to four months."

"Go home and do what you want. Eat what you want. Enjoy your days."

"Wait a minute!" the wife exclaimed. "Blessed is he who gives to the poor! My husband and I give to the poor! God **will** heal him!"

The couple told the doctor that they believed God would heal this dear man. It was the right of anyone who knew Jesus, especially those who were good to the poor. The doctor gently said that he would pray for them.

"If you are still alive in two years, call me." That was December 14, 2016.

They did not shake their fist at God and ask, "Why?" They did not go home, shut the drapes and cry. They believed what the Word said about those who gave to the poor. They believed what the Word said about healing, and that is what they stood on. They knew what John 10:10 said.

"The devil comes but to kill, steal, and destroy, but I have come to bring you life and bring it abundantly."

That was two years ago and today, the man is cancer free. His truck stop is still reaching out to everyone who stops there. And he and his dear wife still feed the homeless. Last month, they went back to show the doctor that he was healed.

Mark 9:41,42

Luke 8:50

John 10:10

Proverbs 22:9

Kingdom Principle: Kindness to the poor and needy releases the blessings of the Kingdom.

Prayer: "Jesus, teach me how to serve the poor and needy here in my town. Teach me how to love them. Amen."

Launch: Become involved with the non-profit organizations and churches in your area that serve the poor and homeless. Give support and serve as a volunteer on a regular basis.

What happened?

_____

_____

_____

_____

_____

Kindness to the poor and needy releases the blessings of the Kingdom.

DAY 87 – LOST AND FOUND – HOLLY

So many times, I hear a heart-breaking story of someone whose life growing up was so horrific it is hard to imagine recovery. Yet, I have learned Jesus always leaves the ninety-nine and goes after the one who is caught in the clutches of the evil one.

Several of His parables refer to Father planning a large wedding feast for His Son. When all is ready, He sends His servants out to invite the guests. Excuses are made, and His intended guests refuse the invitation. The Father eventually goes to the highways and hedgerows to find anyone at all to fill the hall. If one pauses to think about it, highways and hedgerows are populated by the homeless. And they become the honored wedding guests.

One very hot summer day our street Chaplain came to my office.

"Do you have time to talk to this girl? I found her on the street, and she is a mess right now. She can't stop crying."

I asked him to bring her to my office and to get her a glass of ice water from the dining room. Sobbing, she walked in. I got her settled and handed her the glass. She was tense and afraid, nerves stretched taut. After introductions, I gently asked what the problem was.

Her story unfolded with a lot of starts and stops, but it was one of the worst that I had heard. Holly had just gotten out of a drug and alcohol rehab facility. She had nowhere to go and, left in the streets, she knew that she would eventually succumb to the heroin again. If that happened, she would not be able to get her boys back. CPS would hand them over to her father and she could not let that happen. She described him as a very wicked man. I assured her that CPS would seek out their father first. He would have first rights.

"My father IS their father!"

Stunned, I could not speak. I knew I was in way over my head. I had no grid for such wickedness. This poor lost lamb was subject to unspeakable things, and yet was valiantly trying to do the right thing.

What she needed more than anything was the love of the Good Shepherd to bind up her broken heart and heal her wounds. I asked if she had ever asked Jesus to come in to her heart.

"I never even heard of Jesus until yesterday in lunch Chapel service when you talked about Him."

Again, I was stunned. How was it possible not to know about Jesus in west Texas? We are the buckle of the Bible belt, for heaven's sake. I asked if she would like to invite Him into her heart.

"I would like to get to know Him first."

Okay. That was fair. I shot a quick prayer up to the heavens, "A little help here, guys!"

I asked her to start at the beginning and tell me her story. She was born into an occult family. Her parents were pretty far up in the local organization. By the time she was three, she was taken to attend the rituals. By the time she was ten, she was shot up with heroin and forced to participate in the rituals. As she matured, she became pregnant in the rituals many times. Abortions were performed each time. But with the twins, her father decided to let them live. Her life was a nightmare. Raped over and over again, she finally ran away and hid the children from her family. Sadly, she was physically, emotionally, and mentally addicted to heroin. The results were CPS getting involved and taking her children to her father. She had just gotten out of a program to get clean and sober but had nowhere to go. She knew she could not stay clean on the streets.

I assured her that she could join our women's program for sobriety. She readily agreed. Over the weeks, she began to relax, even smile occasionally. She began to blossom as the other girls made her feel welcome, but she never lost that wounded animal appearance.

Healing from such a terrible childhood takes time, and a lot of unconditional love. That is why the program here is twelve months long. It took a lifetime to get into the mess she was in and it would take time to heal from that lifetime. But she was slowly getting better.

One day, one of our more difficult girls came up to me in Chapel. She was a mess too.

"Guess what?! Holly just asked Jesus into her heart." She pointed over her shoulder toward the back of Chapel. Holly grinned at me and nodded her head. God can use anyone to rescue His little ones. His love is that reckless.

Holly became a woman on fire for Jesus. Over the rest of her stay, she became a radiant demonstration of what God will do with anyone who will come to Him.

Actually, Holly is a perfect example of the wedding banquet. God sent one of His servants into the highways and byways and brought a lost little one to the party. It is one of the most extraordinary testimonies of what He will do to wrestle one of His little ones away from the devil. It is a true miracle.

Today, Holly is married, has a career, and most importantly, she has her children. Jesus said on more than one occasion that He had come to seek and save that which was lost. He did just that for Holly.

Matthew 22:1-14

Luke 15:4-7

Luke 15:8-10

Matthew 18:11

Kingdom Principle: The power of God's reckless love for the least and the lost saves, heals, and delivers them from their own destruction.

Prayer: "Papa, open my eyes to the lives of others who have been so wounded by the devil. Show me how to show Your love to them. Amen."

Activation: Make a concerted effort to be aware of the wounds of those around you, be it a co-worker, friend, neighbor, or family member. Ask the Father how to give comfort and help to them. Act upon that.

How did it go? How did it make you feel?

DAY 88 – THE CHRISTMAS STORY – OXYGEN

One of the greatest joys each year is to read the entire Christmas story in each of the Gospels, as well as the prominent Old Testament passages that not only prophesied the exact nature of the birth of Christ, but all of the circumstances surrounding that birth. After 35 years of this tradition, it is still a stunningly beautiful story.

The recorded lineage alone is a goldmine of God's love for us. In the book of Matthew, one discovers that the Son of God's earthly lineage has some pretty naughty relatives in it.

Tamar, for instance, tricked her father-in-law into having relations with her so that she might bare children. Rahab was a prostitute in Jericho who married one of the spies. She was also a pagan. Bathsheba committed adultery with King David. Yet, God gave each of them the honor of being the ancestor of Jesus.

The wisemen's story is also quite remarkable along with the star, the shepherds, and the angels. Nevertheless, it is a complicated story spreading across the pages of the Bible in sometimes mysterious ways.

One Christmas season, the Mission was in full throttle preparing enough turkey, dressing, sweet potatoes, and all the desserts to feed approximately 400 people. Backpacks were being filled like stockings with every essential for the homeless to face the weather, as well as treats and toys for the children. The halls were "decked" as they say, and the Christmas service was being planned. People would be lining the walls standing through the entire service. We would be packed out.

Michael, one of the staff members here, was to speak to the guests at the service. I asked him about his topic, knowing that keeping that many men, women, children and crying babies still and quiet can be a trick.

"I am going to read the entire Christmas story from the Bible." I did not think that was a good idea at all.

"Michael, you will lose their attention; they will become restless and children will not be interested. That is a bad idea. What if you told a colorful version of the story for the children? Have them come up and sit on the floor with you."

"I asked the Lord what I was to do, and He told me to read the story from the Bible. That is what I am going to do."

Oh dear, this was going to be bad, and restless, and noisy. However, I respected the speaker's right to do whatever he or she felt the Lord wanted. We would just have to see it to the end.

The day of the festivities came, and we were ready. The Chapel Christmas tree was lit and beautifully decorated with a large manger scene below complete with wisemen, cattle, sheep, angels and the Holy family. The mood was festive as the guests filed in.

Each was given a candle with a cardboard circle around the middle to protect fingers. We would lower the lights at the end of the service, light the candles, and all sing "Silent Night" together.

The room was full to the brim. Michael walked in with his crisp white shirt and red tie. After greetings and Christmas salutations, I introduced Michael. He sat on a high stool and began to read out loud the age-old story.

"Now, the birth of Jesus was as follows…" His voice was clear and tenor as he delivered the story. A young girl, pregnant, and the man who loved her but would need to put her away discreetly. An angel in the night, the long ride to Bethlehem. On and on the story unfolded.

I stood against the wall and looked out over the crowd. To my utter surprise the congregation went silent…utterly silent. I watched their faces. Every man, woman, and child were held in rapt attention to the reading.

Honestly, I felt I was seeing a Christmas miracle. No crying babies or wiggling toddlers; no one was even whispering to his neighbor. The room was still. The atmosphere took on a sacred feeling, as though we were in a cathedral. Michael continued to read all about the stable, the manger, and the shepherds coming in awe. Still no one moved. I knew I would remember this moment for the rest of my life. My heart swelled with love and affection for my Savior and for these beautiful people that He had put in my charge. I was having a Christmas moment.

Almost too soon, the story was over. Michael had obeyed the Lord, even against my objections. In all the years of all the Christmas Eve services I had attended; this one touched the Throne of Heaven and moved my heart more than any other. It was truly astonishing.

The lights were dimmed. I lit my candle and went to the center aisle to light other candles, that lit others, and the light spread through the room. If possible, the atmosphere became more holy. There was a hush and the music softly played as we lifted our voices in "Silent Night." At the end of the song, we all sort of paused as if we did not want it to end.

The lights then went up and everyone greeted one another with good wishes and hugs. Guests filed into the dining hall as we lined up across the front to pray for people.

While waiting for their turn to eat, the guests came forward. A woman stepped up to me. She had oxygen tubes in her nostrils and wheeled an oxygen tank.

"I have had COPD for years. I always have to take all kinds of medication and have my oxygen on at all times. I just want to be able to breathe again. Will you pray for me?"

I began by telling her of the story of seeing a woman with COPD healed instantly at a church nearby not long ago. The story built her faith, so I took her hands into mine and began to pray.

Holy Spirit was definitely still in the room. I laid my hand on her chest and prayed for healing. As we said, "Amen," it was her group's turn to go to dinner. She melted into the crowd as I began to pray for the next individual.

Several months later, I received a note in the mail from the woman. She had not taken her meds or had to use her oxygen in a very long time. God had healed her gradually until she was completely free and healthy. She thanked me for the gift of lungs, healthy and strong.

A few months ago, a woman walked up to me after Chapel service and asked if I recognized her. I did not. She grinned and identified herself as the woman with COPD last Christmas. I was shocked. She looked so healthy and pink. We hugged, and we visited. Once again, God had changed a human life in a moment's time. This woman received a true Christmas miracle.

Matthew 1:1–17

Matthew 1:18–25

Matthew 2:1–23

Kingdom Principle: Obedience to the Father's instructions pulls back the veil of this world and reveals the other world of miracles, beauty, and sacredness.

Prayer: "Father, You are the kindest person I have ever known. Thank You for giving us Your only Son, to save us in our humanity and heal us of our diseases and deliver us from our own naughtiness. Teach us to do the same for those around us this Christmas. Amen."

Activation: This Christmas season, reach out in some way to those around you, especially the stranger. Make a point to look for an opportunity to do an act of kindness for someone you do not know.

What happened?

_____

_____

_____

_____

Obedience to the Father's instructions pulls back the veil of this world and reveals the other world of miracles, beauty, and sacredness.

DAY 89 — RHEMA — BUCK

There was a man who lived under the bushes in a local park for many years. He was addicted to meth and had lost every semblance of normalcy and civility. He lived more like an animal. He panhandled for food, until one day he heard about a place that served hot meals three times a day, the Mission. He decided to give it a try and walked across downtown to reach its doors in time for lunch. He sat in Chapel, not listening to a word the guest speaker was saying. He had to admit that he was glad to be warm and the place was clean and bright. After the service, he filed into the dining room and sat down to an admittedly delicious meal of lasagna. Friendly volunteers served him seconds on the food and tea. It really was rather nice.

That night as he climbed up under his bush, he could see the moon rising in the sky. As he looked at the moon the thought struck him, "I can't do this anymore." He was not sure how to go about change, but a good start was to go back to the Mission to eat. As he sat in Chapel, the guy speaking was telling his story of addiction to meth and homelessness, and how God saved his "sorry backside" through a free program to get off the drugs and reach sobriety. Buck sat up straight in his seat. This guy's story was a lot like his own. After Chapel, he decided to approach the speaker and ask a few questions.

Bill told him all about the program at the Mission (free of charge) to get clean and sober, to get healthy, and to actually be happy again.

"I won't lie to you. It is hard, and some days you will just want to leave and go use. But I thank God every day I am free from addiction, and at peace."

Peace. That was something Buck had not felt in years. The thought of a warm bed with clean sheets and meals as well as a sense of safety was tempting. He decided to apply to the Hope for Men Program.

As Buck settled into the program, he noticed what he called "the evidence of God." He had never been a religious man for he had grown up with not even the mention of a deity of any sort. He had developed a somewhat rudimentary theology. If there were a God, He was too big to worry about individuals and their problems. Still, he noticed things happening at the Mission which could only take place through a divine being. Take for instance the miracles. The food multiplying, the healings, and mental illness gone from some really disturbed people. All the same, he was unsure of most everything at that point.

He heard others talk about hearing God's voice speaking to them personally. Even one of the instructors spoke of "hearing God." It seemed completely out of the realm of possibility. Why would God take time to listen to a homeless addict, let alone reply to his questions? Yet, there were countless examples in Scripture where God was doing just that.

Moses heard God's voice out of a burning bush. It was a lengthy conversation between the two. Indeed, throughout the Exodus experience, Moses had lots of questions for God. The Lord answered them all. In fact, on the long trip there was a specified place outside of camp called the tent of meeting where one could go meet with the Lord and hear His voice. There was a particular passage that was quite profound, "Thus it was that the Lord used to speak to Moses face to face just as a man speaks to His friend."

There were times when Moses would leave the camp of the Israelites and go up on a mountain and stay a month in His presence. It has always been God's desire to visit with us. It is in "the tent" that we hear the words He speaks.

The Greek word in the New Testament for God speaking to us personally is *rhema*, the word uttered by a living voice; a pouring forth. We have noticed that when a student at the Mission learns to listen for the voice of the Lord, and hear clearly what the Lord is saying, a shift takes place. They have finally found what they have been longing for all their lives. They just did not know it.

One year, a local church offered to let our male students in the program come to a men's retreat at a lodge in Colorado for the weekend. The guys piled into our vans and took off for the mountains with strict instructions to behave themselves and mind their manners. Lastly, they were reminded they would all be drug tested when they returned.

That evening, they arrived at the center. It looked more like a summer camp for rich kids. The students were led to their bunk house to store their belongings before the evening meal. Buck was nervous. This was altogether a new experience. But when he was served a steak dinner, he decided this weekend might turn out alright. Later in the evening, the first session began in the Chapel with singing. As Buck listened to three hundred men lift their voices together with "Bless the Lord Oh My Soul," he was amazed. It was the most beautiful sound he had ever heard. Something came over him, a feeling, a "something" he had never felt before.

The following day, Buck hiked alone up to a mountain top just as Moses had. He sat down on a rock and looked down on the lodge. He had a question and thought he would try this prayer stuff.

"God, did You make me an addict?"

The Lord answered, "Buck, I made you to love Me, to crave Me. It breaks My heart that it turned into a fifteen-year addiction."

Buck sat stunned. For the first time in his life he heard God's voice. God had met Buck on the mountain top. In that moment, Buck became a believer. Pure joy came over him. He sat and looked out over the vista and was at peace.

Buck went on to finish the program and graduate. He opted for the college plan at the Mission where he could go to college on Pell Grants, but live free at the Mission for up to two more years. He got a part time job and joined campus clubs and fraternities. He worked hard and studied hard. He found an apartment he could afford, and finally graduated with a four-year degree.

The *rhema* voice of God utterly changed this lost soul. Once sleeping under a bush, now successful and at peace.

Exodus 33:7-11

Exodus 33:17-19

Matthew 4:4

Luke 1:38

Kingdom Principle: In the Kingdom, the Father will go to any length to save a lost lamb and bring him home.

Prayer: "Lord, it is my great wish for You to speak to me face to face as a man speaks to his friend. Will You be my friend, and speak Your *rhema* word to me? Amen."

Activation: For 30 days, make it your intention to meet with God at the same time and place every day. Ask Him questions. Listen for answers.

What happened?

_____

_____

_____

_____

_____

_____

_____

DAY 90 – FASTING – THE TUMOR

If one is a Christian for any length of time, one is made aware of the power of the fast. Fasting is refraining from eating in order to see a breakthrough in a loved one, or in one's own difficulties. It also is a catalyst to cleansing oneself of offensive habits. Here is another head scratcher; how can my not eating change the circumstances? It is a mystery indeed.

I grew up in a denomination that required its communicants to eat no meat on Friday and give up an addiction during Lent, like chocolate, or rolls in the school lunchroom. My parents always gave up their evening cocktail. I was led to believe this was a "discipline." It was simply "the right thing to do."

But later on in my walk when I actually read the Bible, I discovered that there is a supernatural power in refraining from a habit or food. It actually brings favor to the participant. In many instances during a fast, the "tables are turned" as they say; the prodigal comes home, the finances get better, or the illness is miraculously healed.

There is another type of fast described in Isaiah 58 that is altogether different from the abstinence fast. If one desires to break the bonds of wickedness (possibly having to do with a generational curse or habitual calamity), undo the bands of the yoke (which could pertain to an addiction), or release the oppressed (an illness or condition), one is offered a list of actions that miraculously affect a breakthrough. Instead of refraining from something that is desirous, one takes on a new action that is possibly distasteful.

The list of actions is found in verse 6 and 7 of Isaiah 58. "Is this not the fast that I choose? To loose the bonds of wickedness, to undo the bands of the yoke? And to let the oppressed go free? And break every yoke? Is it not to divide your bread with the hungry; and bring the homeless poor into the house? When you see the naked, cover him, and not hide yourself from your own flesh (translated in the original Hebrew as "mankind"). Years later I would blunder into this habit inadvertently at the Mission.

For eleven years, it was my daily pursuit to do what Isaiah 58 directed. It was my consuming passion to feed the hungry, cloth the naked, and shelter the homeless. It would later save my life. Thank God!

It was time for me to return to M.D. Anderson, the cancer hospital in Houston, for a checkup. The type of tumor that had been removed from my pancreas had a tendency to grow back; hence, the checkups each year. The first day was filled with tests and CAT scans. The second day was filled with consultations and directives. It usually did not reveal anything out of the ordinary. We were not concerned.

On this visit, the scan revealed a mass on the pancreas again. I would be required to get a needle biopsy first by an endoscopy, then back to surgery again to remove the tumor. We were heartsick. We had dodged a bullet with the last pathology report, but what would happen this time? I did not know if I could go through it all again.

As I lay on the gurney and waited my turn to be wheeled into the operating room for the biopsy, my husband stood up and laid his hand on my pancreas and prayed for healing once again. We both cried. The nurse appeared and drew back the curtain. It was time to go.

Back in my cubicle, I woke to find my husband beside me. It was over. We just had to wait for the results of the biopsy. Eventually, the doctor drew back the curtain and stepped in.

"Well, this was a head scratcher for sure. When I looked at your scan, the mass was very apparent, but when I went in, there was no mass; nothing to biopsy. I called in a colleague to take a look at the scan and the site of the mass.

We clearly saw the mass on the scan, but there was absolutely no mass there when we went in. There was not even any tissue that might be questionable. The tumor was gone."

God had been true to His word in Isaiah 58. "Then your light will break out like the dawn, and your recovery will speedily spring forth; and your righteousness will go before you and the glory of the Lord will be your rearguard. Then you will call, and the Lord will answer; you will cry, and He will say, 'Here am I.'"

That day at M.D. Anderson, God was my rearguard. His promise saved me, and I was extraordinarily healed. Thank you, God!

Isaiah 58:6-9

Proverbs 22:9

Psalm 41:1

Isaiah 58:10-12

Kingdom Principle: The Isaiah 58 fast unbolts the door to the Kingdom.

Prayer: "Papa, thank you for the blessings in serving the poor and homeless. Teach me to better serve them and give me a love in my heart for these little ones You love. Amen."

Initiation: Go to the Lord and ask Him how He might have you serve the poor. Sit before Him and wait for His answer. Once you have received instruction as to what to do, do it within the week.

What happened?

___

___

___

___

___

JENA RAWLEY TAYLOR

DAY 91 – THE ORPHAN – COLE

There is a particularly vulnerable group of people who end up at the Mission, because there is nowhere else for them to go. These are the young men and women who age out of foster care at 18 years old and find themselves utterly alone on the earth. At 18, these poor kids have a long history of rejection and pain. Some are addicts already or are pregnant. It is almost impossible to help them, because they are so young and have suffered so much; they refuse to trust anyone. Too, the younger ones still think they are bulletproof. They stay just long enough to meet someone who promises the moon to them and off they go down into the underbelly of society, only to resurface more addicted or pregnant again. Each time they return, the girls have had another child who has been taken by CPS. Some have had as many as six children by different fathers. Our job is to love them and make them feel safe. We try to teach them as much as we can before they head out the door or jump the fence again.

The Scriptures are very clear when it comes to the stranger and the orphan. We are instructed to bring them into the family and care for them. "For you were once strangers in a strange land."

Jesus could not spell it out more clearly than He did in the book of Matthew. "Come, you who are blessed of My Father, inherit the Kingdom prepared for you before the foundation of the world. For I was hungry, and you gave me something to eat; I was thirsty, and you gave me drink; I was a stranger and you invited me in, naked and you clothed Me. I was sick and you visited Me. I was in prison and you came to Me.

"Then the righteous will answer Him saying, 'Lord, when did we see you hungry and feed You; or thirsty and give You drink? And when did we see You a stranger and invite You in, or naked and clothe You? And when did we see You sick or in prison and come to You?'

"And the King will answer and say to them, 'Truly I say to you to the extent that you did it to one of these brothers of Mine, even the least of them, you did it to Me.'"

One such young man came to us out of foster care already addicted to meth. He had so many behavioral problems, we were not sure that we could keep him. His mother was a heroin addict and he was born addicted. They called him a heroin baby, and he cried incessantly, his tiny body craving the drug. He was taken away immediately and passed from one foster home to another, never staying long enough in any one family to bond.

Cole carried an orphan spirit and was rejected at every turn. When he arrived on our doorstep having just aged out, he was as lost a lamb as I had ever seen. He had no life skills or self-worth. There was only depression and oceans of anger.

One day in class, we were talking about home. The question was, "What does the word HOME mean to you?" Cole spoke up.

"What are you even talking about? I have no idea what HOME means. I have never had a home or a family."

My heart broke for him. Recovery and a sense of worth would take a long time to find.

Another student called out, "Hey Cole, it's okay, man. We're your family now. And right now, this Mission is our home."

I was struck once again by the love and acceptance the students had for one another. One would think putting that many addicts under one roof would be a disaster. There are the occasional upsets, but not nearly what one would expect. The Scripture in Psalms came to mind, "God sets the solitary into families."

Other students chimed in in agreement. The guy sitting next to Cole put his arm around his shoulder.

"Hey, man, we are all in this together; you will never be alone again. That guy's name was Johnny, a renewed Jew who was also trying to get clean. Cole and Johnny became fast friends that day. The two continued to be each other's family. Cole settled into a quiet confidence that he was safe now; he was warm and accepted by his brothers and his Savior. He was going to be okay. We even saw a humorous side to him. He was able to get clean and sober and came to know the love of Jesus personally.

As time went on, it became evident that Cole was extremely bright. After graduation from the program, he was encouraged to stay on for the college program. His grades were amazing, and he began to work in the accounting office at the Mission.

He eventually moved away, but he and Johnny stayed in touch over the years. Johnny stayed at the Mission as head of the fleet of cars that had been donated. His job was to keep them running.

One day, Johnny received a phone call from the Captain of Police in North Carolina. He had been given Johnny's name as a reference for Cole. He had just graduated from the police academy there and scored highest marks, not only academically, but also in marksmanship and take down. He was going to be a police officer.

We all rejoiced for Cole. God had brought this lost lamb to us to love into the Kingdom, to teach him how to be normal, feel normal, and act normal. Cole was set free from his terrible childhood and placed into a family. Our family.

Exodus 22:21

Psalm 68:6

James 1:27

Matthew 25:34-40

Kingdom Principle: Unmerited love is a powerful force in the Kingdom of God.

Prayer: "Jesus, Your mighty hand has saved so many lost lambs from destruction. Open my eyes to the lambs assigned to me. Show me how to care for them and bring them home to you. Amen."

Motivation: Look around your church, school, or workplace and intentionally look for someone who appears to be friendless, lonely, or perhaps a bit awkward and strike up a friendship with them. Show kindness as though you were doing it for Jesus.

What happened?

DAY 92 – GENERATIONAL CURSE – BELIEF SYSTEMS

There are times when a particular illness or condition is passed down from generation to generation in families. We might call it a genetic anomaly on the DNA strand inherited from our parents. Research shows that many illnesses are linked to inheritance, such as heart disease, diabetes, cancer, Parkinson's, arthritis, and so on. There are some biblical references to this generational inheritance, sometimes referred to as a generational curse.

God Himself discussed it with Moses when He hid him in the cleft of the rock so that Moses could see the Glory. God, by no means, would leave the guilty unpunished, but in His mercy would visit the iniquity of the fathers to the children and grandchildren to the third and fourth generation.

Joshua cursed an entire nation to slavery, announcing that they, as a nation, would never cease being slaves because of their treachery to Israel.

David spoke of his own iniquity in the Psalms which clearly was passed down to his son Solomon. The word "iniquity" in the original Hebrew carries with it the connotation of being passed down from generation to generation, from father to children.

We all know of entire families who die of heart attacks, alcoholism, or diabetes. We may all have bad backs, or daughters inherit their mothers' female problems. In our family, most every child experiences anxiety disorder onset at age thirteen.

Fortunately for us, Christ redeemed us from the curse of the law having been made a curse for us, "for cursed is every man who hangs on a tree." Jesus gave us full authority to break every curse off of those who are ill or inherited a family disease or condition. That is why we can boldly proclaim that "by His stripes we are healed."

A woman with Parkinson's disease had come to be prayed for. Several people in her family had the illness. We broke the generational curse in Jesus name and laid hands on her. She was instantly healed, and all of the symptoms disappeared. We rejoiced!

There is another type of generational curse that can be passed down from generation to generation in a family. It is a prevailing belief system, whether it be about another race, gender, salesmen, or those less intelligent. It could be the old adages, "You get what you pay for," "You reap what you sow," or "Nothing is more important than money."

There was a man who came to me on behalf of his wife. She had suffered from horrific migraines since she was thirteen. They were debilitating. She also had an auto immune illness, as well as a myriad of other conditions. She was quite pale, and she was angry and bitter at having had to suffer for so many years. At that moment, she was in the throes of the beginning of a migraine, pain pulsing up her neck.

In her family, the belief system was that intelligence and research were the most important things. As a little girl, she received far less love and affection than intellectual training. Her mother told her over and over that the brain was the most important thing. Emotions were childish.

The woman had to quit her job because of the diseases. Every day, she got up in the morning and spent the entire day researching her maladies. After all, "knowledge is power."

A lot of things had to be broken off of this girl. We began with the generational curses, breaking off their power. We then went after the word curses and belief systems. She had to repent of making her diseases her identity, as well as her anger.

Tears rolled down her cheeks as the Lord began to hover over this precious person. We knew to let Holy Spirit do what He does best.

Finally, she looked up at me and smiled. Color had flooded her cheeks and even her eyes looked bluer. The pulsing was gone. We hugged and rejoiced.

"Does this mean that I should throw away all my research on my diseases?"

"Definitely!!"

The next week she came to see me at the Mission and told me of all the other symptoms that had inexplicably disappeared. She was a new woman. Thank you, God!

Exodus 34:7

Joshua 9:22-27

Psalm 51:5

Galatians 3:13

Kingdom Principle: Breaking generational curses removes the spiritual block that may hinder a healing.

Prayer: "Jesus, thank You for redeeming us from the curse of the law. Thank You for breaking every chain off of us. Amen."

Initiation: Take a moment to look back through your own family tree and make a note of any generational curses passed down that repeated themselves in the children. Repent of any sin causing the curse and break it in Jesus name. Thank God for redeeming you and making a way to healing. Now, command every demon attached to the curse to go to the dry places in Jesus name. When you feel that they are gone, thank the Lord and worship Him.

What happened?

DAY 93 – INTERVENTION – CHRISTMAS

If one reads the Christmas story in the Bible through, one might be shocked at the amount of supernatural intervention that takes place. In order to get the Messiah safely into this world and keep Him alive long enough to grow up and save the world, countless angels were sent to intervene since the bumbling's of the humans were involved.

In the book of Luke, the bumbling began. Gabriel, the messenger angel was dispatched to Zacharia, the priest. A righteous man, he and his wife were childless, and their biological clocks had stopped long ago. Nevertheless, Gabriel appeared to Zacharia in the temple where, by the cast of the lot, he was chosen to go in and burn incense. There stood Gabriel.

"Do not be afraid, Zacharia, for your petition has been heard, and your wife Elizabeth will bear you a son, and you will give him the name of John. And it is he who will go as a forerunner before Him in the spirit and power of Elijah to turn the hearts of the fathers back to the children, and the disobedient to the attitude of righteousness; so as to make ready a people prepared for the Lord."

Zacharia was more than a little doubtful. He was very old, and his wife was half dead. He questioned Gabriel on the improbability of the plan. Gabriel appeared to be a little miffed at Zacharia's doubt and instantly struck him mute. That was a profound intervention. Some say that Zacharia had to be struck dumb so his negative words could not bumble the whole plan of redemption.

Later on, Gabriel appeared to Mary, a young Jewish girl from Nazareth. Again, he announces the coming birth of a child who will change the history of the world. He goes on to explain there will be no human man involved.

"For nothing will be impossible with God." That is a powerful statement. In fact, it is the bedrock of the Kingdom of God. Nothing is impossible with God.

Mary had a few questions on the finer points of this plan but did not doubt the angel. She simply believed it to be true, and said to Gabriel, "Behold, a bond slave of the Lord. Be it done to me according to your Word."

As the story unfolded, more angels were dispatched; to Joseph so that he did not put Mary away, to the shepherds in the field, to the wisemen warning of Herod's treachery, and to Joseph again in order to rescue the Christ child from the brutal clutches of a jealous king. There was even a star or stars that told the Magi of the impending birth.

All of this was planned before the beginning of time; God would intervene with human history and make possible that which was not possible.

It is profound and mystifying. And, like Mary, all we have to do is believe that all things are possible with God.

One Christmas at the Mission, it was time to select a speaker for the big Christmas service. I had just returned from surgery at M.D. Anderson and hoped I would at least be able to be present but was in no way able to do more than sit and watch the service. A young man nicknamed Thor was chosen. He was a great bear of a man with long blonde hair. He volunteered often, and the guests loved him for his kindness to them.

As the day arrived, a chair was placed in front of the Chapel beside the Christmas Tree for me to be out of the way, and safe from any inadvertent elbows. I looked out over the huge crowd and saw several new faces, including a whole group of women I can only describe as "ladies of the evening." Thor got up to speak. He had reams of notes. He was more than a little nervous, and he could not follow his remarks. Try as he might, the message became more and more confused. Fifteen minutes into it, I was squirming. This was our biggest event of the year and it was unraveling quickly. We needed an intervention. I longed to get up and turn the sermon into an "interview" to see if we could salvage any modicum of the message. I wanted to somehow make the altar call, but I was too weak to do anything to save the day.

Finally, Thor threw his notes up in the air in frustration. "Oh, forget it. If you want Jesus just come up here!"

Oh dear! What a mess! And the worst altar call ever. We waited. Nothing. We waited some more. Nothing. Finally, a young boy came forward from the back of the room.

"I want Jesus." The whole room froze. There was a change in the atmosphere. Suddenly, as in unison, people stood and flooded the front, including the ladies of the night. They were all crying as Thor prayed for them. They were all hugging and crying. I was shocked. I had never seen anything like it. Almost thirty people got saved that day. It was a record and could only be termed a supernatural intervention. It was indeed a Christmas miracle.

Looking back, I have wondered if in order to bring these little ones to want Jesus, God sent an angel to intervene with me and keep me in my chair, so I did not bumble the miracle. I have come to accept His mysterious ways in the Kingdom.

Luke 1:5-25

Luke 1:26-45

Luke 2:8-20

Matthew 2:1-12

Matthew 2:16

Kingdom Principle: God can turn any disaster dealt to Him into a glorious miracle. He does not need my help.

Prayer: "Father, thank You for Your divine intervention into our lives. Thank You for not leaving us in our mess but bringing Your possibilities into our lives. Amen."

Motivation: Read the Christmas story through and count how many miracles took place in order to insert the Messiah into humankind.

What did you learn?

DAY 94 – HEARING HIS VOICE – JULIE

When men and women come to join one of our long-term programs, they are required to go to classes at the Mission to improve their life skills. For instance, they are taught about parenting, budgeting, boundaries, as well as faith. In their faith class, they learn all about the love of the Father as revealed in the Bible, how to have a quiet time, and that which is supremely important, how to hear His voice.

Jesus told us that His sheep hear His voice and He calls His own sheep by name and leads them out. When He puts forth all His own, he goes before them and the sheep follow Him because they know His voice.

"I am the Good Shepherd; I know My own, and My own know Me."

This "hearing" will go with each of our students when they graduate and leave to start new lives. They will be able to hear His voice and discern what to do.

At a homeless shelter, even as clean as we keep ours, a tiny flu bug can be carried into Chapel by one of the guests and, like the plague, race through the Mission like wildfire. This last season, a particularly vicious virus made itself known on campus. No one was impervious. Stringent cleaning methods with lots of bleach and antiseptic did not help much. The whole city was struggling with it. The clinics were full. The symptoms read like the side of a Coricidin box - fever, chills, body aches, headache, cough, runny nose, sneezing, and sore throats.

One of the women in the REZ program was particularly ill. She had come to the Mission to get clean and sober and start a new life. She fell madly in love with her Redeemer, and through the classes at the Mission, knew how to have a relationship with Him, deep and abiding. She knew how to hear His voice. When she became ill with all the wretched symptoms of the bug going around, she turned to Jesus to be made well. For her, the obvious thing to do was go to her quiet time. In that secret place, she wrote in her journal to Jesus and asked for a supernatural healing. She had been taught how to wait on Him and to hear His voice, so she did just that.

In a bit, she heard the Savior say, "Touch the hem of My garment."

That became her prayer, "I am touching the hem of Your garment."

He continued to speak to her, "Today you will touch someone's garment and you will be made well." She thought of the story of Paul and his aprons and handkerchiefs healing those who touched them. Like a child, she accepted these words and wondered who she should touch.

That day was the gigantic Thanksgiving outreach at the Mission. In preparation for about 300 people coming for dinner, the front hall was rearranged, furniture cleared out, and stations manned. Feeling miserable, Julie manned the volunteer table. Soon, she was busy registering volunteers and handing out name tags. She soon forgot about touching someone's garment. The whole Mission was teeming with guests and volunteers. The mood was festive.

I arrived at the Mission thinking only of what our theme was this year and what I would tell the news stations when they brought their cameras and microphones. "Home for the holidays? A place at the table?" As I hurried through the crowd, I was formulating the speech in order to inspire others watching the news cast to want to do something to help the poor. As I passed the volunteer table, the girls greeted me. We hugged and one of the women commented on my jacket, a chestnut colored crushed velvet number (I do love a beautiful frock).

"Ooh! I love the feel of your coat. So soft." It was Julie. She was a bit of a clothing aficionado and loved a well-cut frock as well. I continued on my way to make ready for the day, the Chapel service, the guests, the festivities. It was going to be a great party.

Several days later, Julie caught me in the dining hall. She told me of her illness and how wretched she had felt on the day of the Thanksgiving outreach, that is until about noon, when she realized all her symptoms were gone. She went to the lady's room to check the mirror. The red nose, bleary eyes, and swollen sinuses were all gone. She was perfectly healed. The Lord then spoke to her heart.

"Did I not tell you that you would touch someone's garment today and be healed?"

She had forgotten all about His words in the crush of people and duties. She had touched, hugged, and patted so many people, she did not know who it could have been.

Instantly, she thought of me and the crushed velvet jacket.

"It was your coat. I touched your coat." Maybe; maybe not. The point is, God told her she would be healed by touching someone's garment.

Regardless of whose garment had the healing properties, Jesus used it to heal her. It was reminiscent of the story of Paul and his handkerchiefs and aprons that were carried from his body to the sick. "The diseases left them, and the evil spirits went out."

Oh, the wondrous mysteries of the Kingdom, where believers accept very odd instructions with faith and clothes carry power. Where signs and wonders follow those who believe and mankind is better for it.

Matthew 6:6

Isaiah 30:21

John 10:3-5

Matthew 13:23

Kingdom Principle: The touch of a garment is a powerful tool to pierce the division between the Kingdoms.

Prayer: "Jesus, Thank You for teaching us the mysteries of the Kingdom. Thank You for teaching us to hear Your voice. Amen."

Institution: Practice presence in your daily quiet time. Listen to His promptings, and His words. Write down what He says. Be sure to be obedient to any instruction He may give you.

What happened?

_____

_____

_____

_____

_____

_____

_____

_____

_____

_____

_____

_____

DAY 95 – HIS WILL – ELAINE

As far as head scratchers go in the sayings of Jesus, the most concerning is the verse in the book of Matthew that says these words, "Not everyone who says to Me 'Lord, Lord,' will enter the Kingdom of Heaven, but he who does the will of My Father who is in Heaven."

This part of the verse was announced every Sunday in church right before the ushers marched up the aisle with silver plates in their hands to collect the offering. The ushers would hand the plate to the person seated in the aisle seat so that he could lay his money in the tray, then pass it to the fellow beside him, and so on down the aisle. The inference was that one must "put their money where their mouth was," literally, and for all to see.

But Jesus said so much more. The verse goes on to declare something alarming, "Many will say to Me on that day, 'Lord, Lord, did we not prophesy in Your name, and in Your name cast out demons, and in Your name perform many miracles?'

"And then I will declare to them, 'I never knew you, depart from Me you who practice lawlessness.'"

As a student of the Kingdom, I find this verse alarming. Much of what we do is prophecy. We cast out demons and work miracles. What else is required to enter the Kingdom of Heaven? What is the missing piece to the puzzle?

The key might be in the statement, "I never **knew** you; depart from Me you who practice lawlessness." Now we have been told that God knows all of us and knows all about us. The word Jesus used here for "know" can mean to know intimately as a man knows his wife.

"I do not know you; we are not friends. We do not have a relationship. You do not come daily to the secret place to visit with Me or walk in the cool of the evening in the garden with me. Therefore, you practice lawlessness."

The first commandment of the ten is to love the Lord your God with all your heart and with all your mind and with all your soul. Therefore, those who say "Lord, Lord" and do not **know** Him or seek a constant abiding with Him are ingenuine. They do not love the Lord. Indeed, they practice lawlessness.

From the beginning, the Lord has wanted a relationship with us. It is for Him first and foremost. Anyone who practices the Kingdom without the friendship is practicing lawlessness. Heidi Baker puts it this way, "The glory is in the secret place." I have found that to be true. When one becomes distracted and preoccupied with other things, maybe starts to miss the sacred time set apart for relationship with Him, the friendship can grow stale. The signs and wonders start to take precedent. There can even develop a "thrill seeking" from the miracles.

One Christmas, I was particularly distracted with all the preparations of the season, both at work and at home. There was so much to be done and so little time. My sacred times became musty and flat. I did not feel His presence or hear much. I was so distracted.

Every year starting after Thanksgiving I read the Bible story of Jesus's birth in its entirety. Starting with the major prophecies in the Old Testament that predicted the various aspects of the events, moving to the genealogy of Jesus, and into to all the miraculous divine interventions that took place. Usually, I am caught up in the sheer beauty of the accounts, but this year it was tepid at best.

One morning before Christmas, I struck out yet again to wind-up last-minute errands. I began to feel conviction about missing out on the sacredness of the season. I knew it all had to do with the many preparations and distractions that precede the big day. I began to repent and ask for forgiveness for missing the point of the season. I asked Him not to let me miss any more of this sacred time.

I arrived at the store to select the final materials to finish the last project on the list. As I pushed my cart to the car, a tall woman stepped out. She was very young, had no coat, and wore only a sleeveless midriff top. She was clearly embarrassed, and it was obvious that she was miserably cold.

"Excuse me, ma'am, can you help us? Our car is out of gas. Could you put some gas in our tank? It's right over there." I became excited at the prospect of participating in the Kingdom.

"I would love to put gas in your car. Let me put the cart back." The girl was so afraid I was going to drive away, she stood out in the cold beside my vehicle. I assured her I would drive right over and instructed her to go back to the warmth of her car. I got into my car and as I started it, a friend of mine walked up to my window. I lowered it. Eyeing the girl suspiciously he asked, "Everything okay?"

"I am about to coax her into the Kingdom. I am so excited."

"Do you think that's safe?"

"Oh, this happens to me all the time. It is all very exciting."

"Okay, but please be careful!"

Dubiously he walked back to his truck to wait for his wife to return from the store.

I drove over to the gas station and parked my car. I pulled out my card and shoved it into the slot, made the purchase and started filling the tank of the dilapidated vehicle. It was a depressing sight, banged up and in dire need of new upholstery. I walked to the driver's side window and motioned the girl to lower it. There was another woman in the car as well and we made introductions. Both women looked weary and used up. The younger one appeared old beyond her years, with haggard features and chipped nail polish. The older one had a dejected expression as if she had given up on life long ago; her only comfort the cigarette that she was smoking.

"You girls are an answer to my prayers. I was longing for a Christmas moment and you two came into my life. Thank you." They both looked at me a little confused and nervous, unsure of me, a crazy lady sticking her head in the car and babbling. But I had a captive audience, so I plunged on.

"Now, it's Christmas, and there are 21 miracles surrounding the Christmas story in the Bible. I counted them. Consequently, wonderful things tend to happen out of the blue this time of year. Do you know Jesus?"

They nodded their heads and told me they were Christians.

"Wonderful, what can I pray for you today?"

The women both looked at me as if I were insane, then looked at each other. The woman in the passenger seat finally spoke.

"I would ask that you pray for my husband and I to quit fighting. We fight all the time, and I just hate it."

"Does he drink a lot?" I questioned

"You know, no more than I do."

I did not pursue that. The miracle had to come from above today, not from a lecture from me.

The younger girl looked up at me and said, "I need a job."

"Okay, what is your skillset?"

"Fast food, convenience stores."

I leaned my head and shoulders into the car window further and instructed the women to hold hands with each other and me. The older woman put out the cigarette and bowed her head. The younger followed suit. For a tiny moment, I drank in the view of bowed heads and tender expressions and reveled in the split second of the sacred in their dismal world. I would never forget that sight. I began to pray to the Father for a Christmas miracle for their circumstances, reminding Him of all the wonderful assurances He gave us in the Bible, all the gifts of hope He dropped like diamonds to be found in the pages of this extraordinary book.

Right there at a gas station standing in the cold, we opened gift after gift of His pledges to us. The women both began to weep, and I could physically feel the hopelessness and hardship leave the two. Holy Spirit came into the car and we each were filled with joy. What seemed impossible a few minutes ago was now so very possible to all of us. I can't describe the sense of elation and wonder we felt. Continuing to weep, they both got out of the car and hugged me. We were having a Christmas moment. I gave them my card in case they needed help.

They drove off and I sat in my car, still feeling the elation and the Holy Spirit. I raised my hands and wept for joy at God's gift to me. I could not stop praising Him. The two women had unwittingly changed everything for me that day.

Suddenly, I had a thought. What if they were not two women down on their luck, but two angels on assignment sent to deliver a Christmas package of their own? With God all things are possible.

Matthew 7:21-23

Matthew 12:46-50

Matthew 7:24-29

Hebrews 13:2

Kingdom Principle: In order to enter the Kingdom, one must know God intimately.

Prayer: "Lord, thank You for Your friendship, Your abiding with me, and our sacred time together. Thank you for the exquisite gems of humanity that You have strewn in my path. Thank You for opening my eyes to their beauty and trusting me to lift them out of the mire. Amen."

Initiation: Create for yourself a sacred space that is reserved for your time with the Lord. In like manner, designate a sacred time that you meet with Him. Make it non-negotiable in your life. Ask if there is anything or anyone to which He wishes to send a package. Listen for His instructions. Then follow them.

What Happened?

_____

_____

_____

DAY 96 – THE LIBRARY – BEVERLY

Over the years, I have studied many Christians' mode of entering the sacred place. Moses went up on the mountain; his quiet time lasted for months. He was also in the habit of going to a tent. Some individuals were so committed to a quiet time, that they did whatever necessary to attain it. One gentleman had to go to such great lengths as to balance on the rim of the tub in the morning in order to stay awake. Another had to move his time to the evening because the Lord told him he was incoherent in the morning hours. One woman, fortunate enough to live by the sea, used snorkeling as her secret space. It was utterly quiet and provided uninterrupted time. Many would simply lie on the floor and "soak" before the Lord. I even heard of a mother of seven children who simply threw the skirt of her apron over her head and exclaimed, "I'm in!"

There have been times in my experience with God, as a young wife and mother, that my sacred place was ironing and praying. The chore was mindless but had to be done. The Lord and I had many delightful visits over that ironing board. In other seasons early in my walk with the Lord, I walked and prayed. I suppose it was something similar to the first couple walking in the cool of the evening with God in the garden. At one time, my sacred place was an elevated walking track around the perimeter of a basketball court at a local gym. Earphones in and praise music on, lap after lap I went, hands lifted in worship. It was a splendid way to meet with God.

Whatever mode of one's sacred space, the platform is a vehicle by which the relationship between God and an individual can grow and become an abiding bond. Out of that bond, disclosure on both sides becomes possible. One might receive instructions for the day, or foreknowledge of what is to happen. Often, the time brings a sense of companionship between two very close friends.

One day as I walked around the track and prayed, I suddenly saw a vision before me. I was in a lovely library with enormous rows of shelves filled with bound books. As far as the eye could see, there stretched rows of bookshelves. A large floor to ceiling diamond paned window gave light to the room. In front of the window, Jesus was seated at a long library table.

"What is this place?" I asked.

"It is the chamber where all the books are housed; these are the archives of all of the acts of the Holy Spirit, from the beginning of time to the end of time."

I stared at all of those volumes and wondered what stories one might find in their pages.

"You are in some of the books," He said simply.

"Me? How am I in the books?"

"Every time you took part in one of Holy Spirit's activities on earth, it was written in the books."

I did not understand what Jesus was saying, and could not think of any wonderous acts I took part in. Reading my mind, He continued.

"Let me give you an example. One rainy day, you were driving to town for groceries when you saw a family stranded on the roadside. They had a flat tire. You stopped, had the man put the tire in your SUV, welcomed the shivering family into your vehicle, and took them to town. The tire was repaired, everyone had hot chocolate and warmed up. You drove them and their repaired tire back to the roadside and dropped them off."

I had completely forgotten that incident. In West Texas that is just what one does. It certainly did not seem significant enough to be written in a book in Heaven. Reading my thoughts again He explained.

"Every act of kindness that has been performed on the earth is recorded in these volumes in Heaven. Any time compassion or charity is shown, it is an act of Holy Spirit."

Suddenly in the vision, the wall to the left of the window split apart and I saw a crowd of men, women, and children in ragged dirty clothing walking toward me, as if pleading for help. A woman was carrying an infant. She came to me and placed it in my arms. I knew I was to take care of these people but had no idea how to do that.

Abruptly the vision ended, and once more I was on the walking track. Disoriented, I walked into the wall. I needed to find a seat and sit down to collect myself. What an extraordinary experience. It was as real as real could be. I had no idea what it all meant, but I sensed it was significant. Years later when I began to work at the Mission, I understood the vision. It was a glimpse into my future. It was a foresight of things to come.

By the same token, a specific incident can also be a foresight, or foretaste of what is to come. It was years ago when one day when I was driving through a carwash. As the vehicle moved past the blowers, a woman walked toward the car with a towel in her hand. She had a striking face and I thought she would make a spectacular portrait for my photography class. I stepped out of the car and approached her.

"Excuse me, I was wondering if I could take a photo of you for my class."

She became suspicious and quite angry, exclaiming, "You diss'n me? You mak'n fun of my face?"

Obviously not my intention, I replied, "Oh no! You have a beautiful face! I think you would be such an interesting portrait. It would only take a minute of your time."

She scowled at me and refused adamantly. She turned to her work of drying the car, muttering under her breath something about stupid white women, and I thought our interview was over. Abruptly, she straightened and looked hard at me.

"You can't take my picture, but do you think you could help me find a better job?"

I was taken aback. It was such an odd request from a stranger. I hadn't the slightest idea how to go about helping her. I told her that I could try to assist her, although this was not an area of expertise for me.

"Here's the thing." She pulled off her cap to reveal her unkempt hair.

I did not know what to say.

"No one will hire me looking this way." I was so confused but asked what could be done to make her more comfortable. She shared with me that we would need to find a specific salon catering to this specific hair type. I made the appointment and picked up my new friend to take her there. As we drove, we got acquainted. Her name was Beverly. She had a son in high school. Judging from her approximate age, she had him at a very early age. She refused to get on welfare. I admired her for that. But she could not make ends meet at her present place of employment, and she had no skill set. Lord, help me, I was beginning to get a glimpse into the plight of the poor. At one point, she turned her head toward me and leaned against the passenger window. Inspecting me closely she asked, "Why you doin' this for me?"

"Because you asked me to help you."

"I'm gay!" she shot back at me.

"I don't care. That's not for me to judge. That is an issue between you and the Lord. I love Jesus, and He loves you. He wants me to help you." She pondered that.

After the hair appointment, I saw the significance of her new look. I suggested we find some new clothes for her job search. That offended her.

"Why I gotta have new clothes? What wrong wit' my clothes?"

"Well, if you want a better job you have to dress for that job, not the one you currently have."

"That matter?"

"Yes, that matters. Come on, it will be fun."

We went to a consignment shop and I pulled slacks and soft blouses for her to try on with shoes to match. She timidly stepped from the dressing room in one of the outfits. I motioned to a mirror. As if facing the gallows, she slowly stepped over to view her reflection. A look of sheer wonderment came over her face. She looked beautiful. A lump formed in my throat, as though I were seeing my daughter in her wedding dress for the first time. She was as delighted as a child on Christmas morning.

Beverly and I became friends. We worked on her resume and filled out applications. I even went to court with her to see the judge about something to do with an expired license plate.

"Hi, Beverly," the female judge said a little sarcastically in her greeting. Then she looked at me and asked suspiciously who I was.

"Just a friend," I replied. She looked over her reading glasses at me with a scowl.

"What kind of friend?"

I immediately thought back to Beverly's comment about being gay. Oh dear! What had I gotten myself into?

"Not that kind of friend," I countered. "I am just trying to help her find a better job. That's all."

She was buying none of it. I began to feel as though at any moment I would be seized by the bailiff and marched off to a cell for some crime to do with aiding and abetting. The judge turned her attention to Beverly again. This was an altogether new understanding of a part of society I knew nothing about. Beverly could not afford to pay her automobile registration all at once, so her license plate on an old beat up van was only good for a month. The amount per month was astronomical compared to paying yearly. Evidently, she had failed to pay last month. Now there was a fine to pay. I came to understand the single mom's dilemma. One flat tire, one hot water heater going out, one too many doctor's appointment, and the whole house of cards comes tumbling down. Finally, the proceedings were over, and it was all I could do not to run out of the courtroom. This was altogether a new experience to me.

Eventually, Beverly did get a better job at a nursing home, with a better salary and with a much better work environment. God reached down and put two very unlikely lambs together in the Kingdom. We both were better for it. It was the first of many astounding encounters for me. I have no idea if that whole affair would be written in the annals of Heaven. It does not really matter. To me, it was an enormous adventure.

Matthew 25:31

Acts 9:10

Acts 10:1-23

Acts 16:9,10

Kingdom Principle: Helping a stranger with no ulterior motive except to be of assistance shatters the barriers between the two domains, and the giver is as touched as the receiver.

Prayer: "Jesus, open my eyes to the difficulties of the people I am unfamiliar with. Show me how to serve them as if I were serving You. Amen."

Initiation: Find a non-profit entity that caters to a people group that tugs at your heart. Volunteer on a weekly basis. Learn the plight of this group and what is needed to help them out of their circumstances. And most importantly, love them as the Father loves them.

How were you changed?

_____

_____

_____

_____

DAY 97 – THE LAME – KIAR

Many who become ill or impaired, or have no hope of medical recovery, become downcast and distressed. In the book of Matthew, there is a poignant verse of Jesus's reaction to the downcast and the distressed.

"And seeing the multitudes, He felt compassion for them, because they were distressed and downcast, like sheep without a shepherd."

He went from village to village teaching in their synagogues and proclaiming the Gospel of the Kingdom and healing every disease and every sickness.

My older sister was born with a defect in her right hand. The fingers never formed, and she was left with only a small palm. My parents were devastated. They were faced with a choice of the plastic surgeon creating a perfect hand that would not function, or a tiny appendage that could function somewhat. My father made the decision to make it function.

Year after painful year, she faced another surgery to create a working finger. Year after year, I watched her hold her bandaged hand up so that it would not throb while reading another book in a long line of thousands of books to pass the time and forget the pain.

In order to make her strong and independent, my parents pushed her to learn early how to tie her shoes, write with her non-dominant hand and to see herself as normal. She was tough and resilient. Yet, one day she posed this question to me.

"How would you feel if every day at school in the lunchroom you had to eat your lunch alone because no one wanted to eat with a one-handed person?" This was in the fifties, and the handicapped were hidden away and ignored. That population were truly the downtrodden.

My sister was much smarter than I, more determined than I, and more dedicated at overcoming every obstacle she faced. She graduated from a private Catholic girl's school with high honors but was barred from her wish to go to nursing school because one of her hands, although functioning, was not like the other hand. She demanded to be tested to see if she could carry out successfully the demands of a nurse, start an IV, or perform a tracheotomy. She could do it all, so the authorities begrudgingly agreed to let her into nursing school.

She became a nurse in the worst emergency room in Dallas, Parkland Hospital. She performed her duties with grace. Later she obtained a couple of master's degrees and became a Professor of Nursing. She was my hero. She had overcome extraordinary odds to live a normal and productive life. She was so heroic and positive, so ready to meet the day and help everyone and anyone.

When I began to learn about signs and wonders, especially creative miracles, I asked her if I could pray for her hand to be made whole. Her response surprised me.

"I like my hand. We have been through a lot together." It caused me to wonder what it might be like to suddenly have an appendage one had never had before. Regardless, I respected her wishes.

Kiar had efficiently and expertly cared for several members of the family in post-surgical recovery. After my surgeries at M.D. Anderson, she nursed me back to health and was able to deal with all my tubes and accessories. The whole family relegated her to sainthood and hoped we would at least be able to serve her coffee in the millennium.

Recently in her retirement years, she developed back problems and needed surgery to ease a pinched nerve. The surgery was a garden variety that would have very little risk. That was not to be the case. The surgery went south, and she woke up with excruciating pain and without the use of her left leg or foot. She was rushed back to surgery but emerged much the same and was devastated she had lost the use of her left leg. Her foot dangled uselessly. She was sent to a rehabilitation hospital for a month to learn to walk again with leg brace and walker, and eventually a cane.

I called to check on her and asked how she was faring. She was distressed and discouraged.

"I need you! Please come at once," she cried. I had never heard her like this. I knew that I had to go to Arizona to her bedside.

The price of an airline ticket could have gotten me to Italy. It was the Christmas holiday and tickets in such short notice were outrageous. I opted to drive. I loaded the car with snacks and audio books as well as music and luggage. The weather report was a little dicey, but I remained undeterred.

The first night was spent in Albuquerque, New Mexico. I checked the weather and was bothered by a snowstorm right in my path of travel the next day. Fearlessly, I loaded up and headed west. Very soon, I hit a blizzard of epic proportion. The highway was snow packed and one could only see the lights of the vehicle in front. We were all going twenty miles per hour. I thought more than once I should turn back. Nevertheless, I was in a large heavy 4-wheel drive and grateful for it. I needed to get to my sister.

As we traveled, we saw terrible accidents along the way. An eighteen-wheeler on its side in the median, a car flipped on its roof and flattened. Wrecks and vehicles stranded in the ditch. Still the snow pummeled us. I was tired and hungry, but I just needed to get to my sister.

"Lord, help me stay on the road, and make it through this." I had never been one to pray for "traveling mercies." What exactly did that even mean? I was quickly becoming a believer.

Finally, I reached Flagstaff and the snow lessened, but the highway was thick with smoke. There was a forest fire around us. The trip was turning into a disaster. I still felt an overwhelming need to get to my sister.

At long last, I reached Prescott after thirteen hours of driving. After checking in to my hotel, I drove to the rehab hospital. It was so good to hug my sister and feel her warmth. Despite her difficulties, she was positive.

The next day, I came to the facility armed with stories of miracle healings. I told story after story of God's grace to the afflicted. Then Kiar's husband and I laid her on her hospital bed and snaked our hands up under her back to the surgical site. As we prayed for healing, the Holy Spirit hit the room. Under my fingers, I felt strands of sinew wiggle. He washed away all of the fatigue of the road and I felt elated. More importantly, she felt elated. As we left the room, she kept saying, "I am floating! I am floating!"

That night, Kiar's husband called the hotel. She had been up and walking without a brace, walker, or cane. The next day they released her from the hospital. God had healed her supernaturally. She was pain free and could walk on her own.

God had healed my sister and made her whole again. Jesus had seen her distress and felt compassion for her. Thank you, Jesus!

Matthew 9:35,36

Isaiah 55:11

Matthew 4:24

Luke 9:1,2

Kingdom Principle: Compassion moves the Holy Spirit to come and brood over a sickness, disease, or botched surgery. The Kingdom door crashes open and the impossible happens.

Prayer: "Jesus, You saw the distressed and downtrodden and felt compassion on them. Teach me this compassion for the people. Amen."

Initiate: Make a point of being aware of those around you, both friends, loved ones, and strangers. Notice their distresses. Ask if you might pray for them.

What did you see?

_____

_____

Compassion moves the Holy Spirit to come and brood over a sickness, disease, or botched surgery. The Kingdom door crashes open and the impossible happens.

DAY 98 – PARALYZED – COOPER

Understanding the ways of the Kingdom of God has been a journey of digging into the Word of God and digging up the principles there. The odd thing is, they are right there in plain sight for any and all to see.

One example would be the story of the Roman centurion, an officer of a ruthless military cohort dominating half the world at the time. Evidently, he was a keen observer and watched the comings and goings and workings of Jesus and His disciples in Capernaum. He approached Jesus on behalf of his servant who was lying paralyzed at home suffering great pain.

Jesus offered to go to the servant but understanding the principles of the Kingdom better than the Jews, the centurion said an astonishing thing.

"Lord, I am not worthy for You to come under my roof, but just say the word and my servant will be healed. For I, too, am a man under authority, with soldiers under me; and I say to this one, 'Go!' and he goes, and to another one, 'Come!' and he comes, and to my slave, 'Do this!' and he does it."

In other words, he understood the hierarchy of authority in the Kingdom just as he understood the hierarchy of the Roman military, the submission of Jesus to His Father and His authority over the natural world. Now when Jesus heard this, he marveled at the officer's faith and told him to go his way. His servant would be healed as the centurion had believed.

Several years ago, our church bought a small house across the street which was named "The Healing Rooms." Administratively, it acted much like a doctor's office. The sick would come and sign in with the receptionist and a file for the patient was created.

Those trained in healing teamed up in threes and were assigned an "examination room." When all was in place, a member of each team would go to the receptionist and receive a file. He would call the patient's name and escort the individual back. After the patient explained his dilemma, the team would lay hands on the person and pray. If they sensed any demonic activity, they would address that.

There were many healed in that little house. It was a glorious time.

Nevertheless, many were not healed. We did not know as much back then, but our hearts were to see people set free from their affliction.

One evening, a young mother brought in her baby boy. While she was pregnant with him, he had a massive stroke in the womb. When he was born, he was paralyzed on his left side and his limbs scissored across his body. The family was devastated.

The doctors had the baby in rehabilitation, but with no results. The teams took turns every week praying for the baby. The mother put up healing Scriptures in her home on every wall. She declared them over her baby all day every day.

Every week, the mom brought the baby. He was always in one brace or another to help with the scissoring. We watched him grow and have a personality. He was adorable, but we saw no results. That mother had the faith to never give up on her child, no matter what the doctors said. And what they said was grim; there was no hope for the child. Still, she stayed strong. I was amazed at her faith.

After about eighteen months of prayer with absolutely no improvement, we just accommodated the mother every week. One evening after prayer, my husband was holding the toddler and teasing him. Suddenly, the child reached up with his left hand and pulled my husband's mustache. Everyone froze. Oh, my goodness! Everyone in the room saw it. The child had been miraculously healed after eighteen months of dogged determination on that mother's part. Everyone rejoiced that night.

A couple of years later at the movie theatre, we saw the child with his family; he looked to be four and was running around like any rambunctious child. No braces, no sign of any impairment at all. Jesus healed the boy in our little healing rooms because of a mother's faith. She did not give up, back down, or accept the doctors' prognosis. Her faith made her son whole.

Matthew 8:5–13

Acts 8:4–8

Acts 9:32–35

Hebrews 10:7

Kingdom Principle: Dogged determination and a "won't back down" attitude about God's wish to heal no matter how long it takes will unzip the Kingdom of God and bring the healing.

Prayer: "Jesus, open my eyes to see the Scriptures about the Kingdom of God and it's principles. Amen."

Suggestion: Look up references in the Gospels to the word "faith." Study its original meaning in the Greek. Meditate on the Kingdom principle of faith.

What did you glean?

_____

_____

_____

_____

Dogged determination and a "won't back down" attitude about God's wish to heal no matter how long it takes will unzip the Kingdom of God and bring the healing.

DAY 99 – KINDNESS – REUNITED

Throughout the Word of God, we are admonished over and over to give to the poor. In every Gospel, Jesus instructs us to give our cloak, our food, a cup of cold water, or our money to the needy. He mentions eternal rewards for doing so. He even says that if we want to be complete (reaching the intended purpose of our lives), we are to sell our possessions and give to charity. Here at the Mission, we take that very seriously. Fortunately, the citizens of our area bring their belongings that they no longer use to the Mission. We in turn give it all away.

There are times at the Mission when the oddest requests are made by our guests off the streets or by the working poor. For them, we are their Walmart, only there is no cost. In the past, requests have been made for such items as Christmas trees, walkers, bedpans, and suitcases. They know the drill. A guest may come to the front desk and fill out a voucher for a certain item. The front desk calls back to the warehouse to see if we have one. If we happen to have it, we are happy to oblige. Of course, there are times we just don't have what they need. It is terribly disappointing.

Sometimes folks will send us a message via our Facebook page. One evening around nine when it was particularly cold and the temperature was to drop into the low twenties, I happened to notice a message. It was a desperate plea from a woman who lived in a travel trailer. She begged for a space heater to keep warm that night. I called the Manager on duty in the main building and asked if he could check the sorting department for me. No, there was no such item.

I knew that there were space heaters in many of our offices, if I could just reach someone who had access to an office. I called the women's dorm and caught the Manager on duty. She had one. I instructed her to delay securing the building until the girl could get there. She was so grateful for our efforts. Was this just a small act of kindness? Not for her.

One day, a man came to the Mission needing a new pair of boots. He had finally landed a job but was required to wear steel toed boots on the job sight. We did not have any steel toed boots in any size, let alone his size. It is a rare and valuable commodity.

Just as the front desk was delivering the discouraging news, a woman drove into the parking lot and came to the front door to deliver some of her late husband's clothing, including a pair of steel toed boots. And yes, they were exactly the right size. The woman cried and said that her husband would have been pleased to know his boots had helped someone keep his new job. Holy Spirit had orchestrated down to the minute this astounding encounter. He truly is partial to the poor. We who work with the poor get to see some astonishing miracles.

Probably the most moving story involved a woman who had emailed the Mission frantically looking for her husband of twenty-six years. They had been staying at another facility that housed men and women separately. Evidently, he had been beaten badly in the men's dorm and had to be sent to the hospital in the night. She was unaware of any of it. When she could not find him, she became frantic. By the time she was made aware that he was sent to the hospital, he was no longer there and apparently on the streets. She emailed the Mission from the public library to see if we had seen him, giving his name as Johnny. We had not. We received a second email from her begging us to look for him.

Across the street from the Mission is an old abandoned building that the regulars lean or sit against while waiting for their next meal. They smoke and chat and wander a bit. Our watchmen keep an eye on things there. Sometimes they will sit in the curb and pass a bottle back and forth as well as cigarettes.

One day our Men's Manager noticed a new face there leaning against a telephone pole. He felt a nudge from Holy Spirit, so he walked over and struck up a conversation with the stranger. Finally, he asked if his name was Johnny. Indeed, it was. Was he looking for his wife? Yes, they had been separated and he could not find her.

Alex informed him that she was frantically looking for him and had contacted the Mission. They walked across the street and Alex called the wife. She and the children raced to the Mission. When Johnny saw his wife, he sank to his knees. She flew into his arms and they cried and cried there on the floor. The children joined in and the scene looked like a pile of arms and legs along with lots of tears.

Holy Spirit had again orchestrated an astonishing miracle, nudging Alex at precisely the right moment, and Alex obeying that nudge.

Luke 12:32-33

Acts 20:35

Luke 6:38

Luke 11:41

Kingdom Principle: Giving is a supernatural act that escorts the giver into the domain of the supernatural.

Prayer: "Jesus, teach me how to have a giving heart. Make me a generous person who lives to give. Amen."

Activation: Make an effort to be a giver in every situation, despite the personal cost.

Record your findings:

DAY 100 – GIFTS – TIFFANY

Jesus, in His time on earth, said a great deal about the poor and how they were to be treated. In the book of Luke, He admonishes His listeners to invite the poor and blind and crippled to their receptions, and they would be blessed since the wretched could not repay them. He went on to say those who did this would be repaid at the resurrection. Indeed, whoever gives one of the little ones even a cup of cold water will not lose his reward.

In his letter to the Ephesians, Paul admonished the church to help the weak, and reminded them of Jesus's own words, that it was more blessed to give than receive.

Kindness is an important commodity in the Kingdom of God. The wisest man in the world declared that, "Happy is he who is gracious to the poor."

At the Mission, we like to have large celebrations for our guests on certain holidays, so they feel special. Jesus commanded us to do so. Each year around July, a very generous woman in our town flies to Las Vegas to make tens of thousands of dollars' worth of purchases at the Dollar Tree Outlet store to be shipped back home. Several of the non-profits in town are contacted to come to the woman's warehouse to pick up mountains of presents for the poor and homeless. Our Benevolence Director then commandeers the Children's Ministry Room to fill the backpacks that she purchased with everything needed to combat the cold weather along with Bibles, candy bars, and bottled water. She is a saint to us and others in town. We could not provide Christmas for our guests without her.

This last Christmas season, we prepared the backpacks along with the turkeys, Paula Dean's sweet potato souffle, green bean casserole, and every conceivable dessert. We decorated the Mission from stem to stern with lights, trees, and an enormous nativity scene.

After the Christmas service, guests would file into the dining room packed with volunteers and sit down to a plate piled high. Christmas carols would break out and everyone would have a wonderful time. As they finished their meal, volunteers would lead them down the back stairs to the Children's Ministry room to be given their gifts, then past my office and up the front stairs loaded down with their many treasures.

On the day of the event, I arrived early to find the line of people already forming. A staff member met me at the car to inform me the news stations were already here for interviews. I raced downstairs to put my things away. Standing by my office door was a woman and a young girl. Behind them was a mountain of cloth knapsacks. On a table stood myriads of festive Christmas stockings filled to the brim with children's toys.

"Hello, what do we have here?" I questioned.

The young girl, about 10 or 11, spoke up.

"These are hygiene packs for the guests. There are 230 packs and the ones with a ribbon tied to them are for women. I made them. And these are stockings I made for the children. There are 50 stockings."

"My goodness! How long did it take you to do all this?"

Solemnly, she replied that she had had the idea at Thanksgiving. She raised the funds to buy all of the supplies and set to work. It took her the entire month to finish her project. Her mother explained it was not a school project; her daughter came up with the plan all by herself and came to her parents for help. Friends and family donated funds for the scheme. She went to Dollar Tree to make her purchases.

"Tell me, what gave you the idea to do such a thing?"

She looked at me earnestly with her big brown eyes and explained, "I just thought that I have a home and a family and lots of stuff; I am loved. I just wanted the homeless to feel loved too."

I wanted to hug the beautiful little girl. She was closer to the Kingdom than any of us. She understood what it meant to extend love to the unlovable. I thought of our philanthropist who did the same with thousands of dollars. I found it ironic that both she and the little girl had gone to Dollar Tree to extend love to the least and the littlest in the Kingdom of God.

I asked the mother if I could take the little girl upstairs with me. I assured her that I worked there. They both came as we made our way to the main hall packed with staff and volunteers dressed in every conceivable Christmas costume. One of the staff members was eight months pregnant and dressed as an elf. It was a hilarious sight. The camera men were already set up and ready to film. I asked the mother of the little girl if the girl could be with me on television. She agreed. I introduced my new friend to the interviewer. On camera I told the child's story. She stood beside me pulling on the sleeves of her Christmas sweater which was embroidered with the words, "Dear Santa, define naughty." The interviewer asked the same question, "What gave you the idea to do this?"

Once again, she explained about the things she was blessed with and how she was loved. That she just wanted them to feel loved too.

All of the staff and volunteers were in tears as they stood by and watched the interview. That girl had an enormous impact on us all.

I wanted viewers to be impacted by this extraordinary act of kindness, to see the Kingdom of God unfold before their eyes. I thought of the Scripture, "And a child will lead them." That prophecy had come to pass.

Luke 14:13

Acts 20:35

Matthew 10:42

Proverbs 14:21

Kingdom Principle: Whether one is a wealthy philanthropist or just a child with an idea, both have the power to boldly step into the Kingdom of God with their generosity.

Prayer: "Papa, teach me this wonderful facet of the Kingdom. Teach me the truth about the power of kindness. Amen."

Activation: Go to the Lord in your sacred place and ask Him for an inspired idea that would help the poor in some way. It might possibly be a project similar to Tiffany's. Plan the fundraising for the project and possibly enlist the help of friends and family.

How did it go?

DAY 101 – THE LEARNING CURVE – WHEELCHAIR

The journey into the Kingdom of God was one of trial and error, discovery, loss, and victory. I have learned that there are very specific doors that access the Kingdom. In like manner, there are behaviors and attitudes that lock the Kingdom up tight.

It almost takes a forensic investigation to find the locks in a patient and then find the antidote for the Kingdom to open. In the previous 100 stories you may have found several ways to open the doors and many ways to unlock the doors that won't budge.

For example, we now know things like fear, bitterness, offense, and practiced secret sin will lock up everything such as healing, multiplication, miracles, and finances.

By the same token, things like repentance, mercy, the seed, the Word, and compassion open wide the heavenly gates.

Studying the Word of God for years has revealed hundreds of ways to open the signs and wonders. Also, studying the Word has revealed as many ways to shut it all down. Don't get me wrong. God is God and can do anything He pleases, but it has been my experience that these remain the same.

While speaking at a conference on Signs and Wonders, I had the opportunity to lay hands on the sick and see them get healed. For some, it was instant. For others, I had to do some serious investigating. Remember, if someone is not healed, the trouble is not at God's end of the table. It is a simple matter of sleuthing the issues in the individual's life that might be blocking a miracle.

Deaf ears were opened, legs grew out, and migraines disappeared. But in each case, some blocks needed to be removed first.

There was a woman at the conference that had been bound to a wheelchair for years. She could not walk and could not stand. She had a disease in her legs called Venice Disease. Her ankles, knees, and hips were all shot, and her back hurt constantly. We began by going down the list of blocks. She was completely open and vulnerable to questions we asked.

She repented of five or so. As she repented, the demons no longer had legal ground to stay, and then we cast those demons out one by one. As the praise and worship kept going up front, we were worshipping as well.

We laid hands on each part of her body and prayed God's glorious Word of healing over her. She reported feeling heat under our hands, as well as tingling. My left hand felt electrical shocks shooting through her.

We told her sometimes the healing does not come until one activates it by trying to do something she could not do before.

We wheeled her to the back of the crowd and into the aisle. We tried to help her out of the wheelchair, but she shooed us away. She stepped out on her right leg, but when she tried to move the left leg, it would not move. She tried over and over to take the step but could not get the left leg to move.

On the fifth try, the left leg moved forward! We all yelped. She moved the right leg again, and this time the left leg followed suit. Up the aisle she walked!

We screamed and cried and jumped and danced. We completely disrupted the service screaming. Right before our eyes she walked! After years trapped in that chair, she was free. The leadership walked back and saw her walking; she reached out and hugged him. We cried and cried.

Above the bedlam she said, "Do you know what is best of all? Just standing! Being out of that chair."

Wow, what a day. What a beautiful day! Thank you, Father!

Romans 12:2

Psalm 107:35

Mark 1:15

Kingdom Principle: Repentance is a key unlocking the door into the Kingdom of Heaven.

Prayer: "Father, when I need to repent, will You whisper in my ear and remind me? Show me my unbelief, my unforgiveness, my fear. Amen."

Process: Ask the Lord to show you the attitudes and resentments that you harbor against those who did you wrong, who betrayed you real or imagined. Write them all down. Now repent of those things that He shows you.

How did it go?

___
___
___
___
___
___
___
___

Repentance is a key that unlocks
the way into the Kingdom of Heaven.

Author's Note

It is my earnest hope that, having read this volume, you were able to be lifted to a new level of understanding and faith concerning the Kingdom of God and its signs and wonders.

My wish for you is that the testimonies of others who were saved, healed, delivered, apprehended, or rescued will build faith in you to believe for your own miracle; and with that faith, you claim those testimonies for yourself concerning your own maladies.

My desire is that you become well versed in the things that might preclude a healing or a miracle and be diligent to remove these from your own lives.

I pray that Holy Spirit inspires you to be more aware of those around you who are ill, hurting, or in desperate need of a miracle, presenting you with an opportunity to reach out to those around you and apply these principles in prayer over them.

Finally, it is my longing that you will make it a habit of becoming someone else's miracle in the marketplace.

With these things in place, I believe the Church will be galvanized into action, and revival will break out across the land.

~ Jena Taylor

JENA RAWLEY TAYLOR

APPENDIX I –
Hinderances to Signs & Wonders

Fear

Jealousy

Offense

Doubt

Identity

Theological Debate

Generational Curses

Depression

Trespasses (Rebellion)

Pride

Focus

Bitterness

Resentment

Unforgiveness

Unbelief

Religious Spirit

Practiced Sin Iniquity

Word Curses

Oppression

Playing the Victim

Ulterior Motive

Jena Rawley Taylor

APPENDIX II –
Entry Points into the Kingdom

Faith	Luke 8:45-48
Tent Time	Exodus 33:9
Wrecking Ball	Acts 9:1-19
Persecution	John 5:10
Testimony	Psalm 78:1-7
Charity	Luke 12:33
The Fast	Isaiah 58:6-12
Poor in Spirit	Matthew 5:3
Destiny	Psalm 139:16
Transformation	Romans 12:2
The Seed	Matthew 13:24
Declaration	Job 22:28
The Word	Isaiah 55:8-11
The Truth	John 3:21
Courage	Joshua 1:9
Face Time	Exodus 34:29
Prophetic Seeing	John 1:45-50

Prophetic Knowing	John 4:16-18
Compassion	Matthew 14:14
Missions	Matthew 10:5-8
Obedience	II Kings 5:1-14
Standard of Measure	Mark 4:24
Childlike Faith	Matthew 19:13-14
Touch	Mark 6:56

About the Author

Jena Taylor earned her bachelor's degree in Fine Arts with a specialization in studio art with a minor in Art History. She went on to receive her Bachelor of Art degree in Art Education. She became a well-known portrait painter in Texas with artist's representatives in every major city and many mid-sized cities in Texas. She had the pleasure of meeting thousands of clients and led many to salvation, as well as the baptism of the Holy Spirit.

One day she was cataclysmically apprehended by Holy Spirit in her studio and was sent by God in opposite directions from the wealthy to the local homeless shelter. Initially she was completely appalled by the grime and filth of the place as well as the stench of unwashed bodies and vacant stares. Jena *fell in love with the people*.

She used her prophetic gifting for the guests off the street but noticed a far more serious need. These dear people were sick, lame, and blind and had no insurance card in their back pocket. They were desperate and had no options.

Jena began to pray for the sick, and shockingly they were being healed. As she became more confident and knowledgeable of the *Kingdom principles of healing*, she saw a marked increase in divine recovery. She became acquainted with hindrances to healing as well. It is her wish to encourage others to believe for their healing, as well as mobilize the church into action.